Frank Sinatra

Sinatra in the 1940s. (Courtesy of Photofest. Used with permission.)

Frank Sinatra

The Man, the Music, the Legend

Edited by
Jeanne Fuchs and Ruth Prigozy

UNIVERSITY OF ROCHESTER PRESS

HOFSTRA
UNIVERSITY™

First published 2007

University of Rochester Press
668 Mt. Hope Avenue, Rochester, NY 14620, USA
www.urpress.com
and Boydell & Brewer Limited
PO Box 9, Woodbridge, Suffolk IP12 3DF, UK
www.boydellandbrewer.com

ISBN-13: 978–1–58046–251–8
ISBN-10: 1–58046–251–0

Library of Congress Cataloging-in-Publication Data

Frank Sinatra : the man, the music, the legend / edited by Jeanne Fuchs
and Ruth Prigozy.
    p. cm.
  Papers originally presented at a conference at Hofstra University.
  Includes discography, bibliographical references, and
index.
  ISBN-13: 978–1–58046–251–8
  ISBN-10: 1–58046–251–0
1. Sinatra, Frank, 1915–1998—Congresses.   I. Fuchs, Jeanne.   II.
Prigozy, Ruth.
  ML420.S56F73   2007
  782.42164092—dc22
  [B]
                              2006039826

A catalogue record for this title is available from the British Library.

This publication is printed on acid-free paper.

Printed in the United States of America.

The compensation of a very early success is a
conviction that life is a romantic matter.
—F. Scott Fitzgerald

Contents

List of Illustrations

Acknowledgments

Although some time has elapsed since the landmark conference devoted to Frank Sinatra at Hofstra University, the excitement that it generated remains palpable in the essays in this collection.

As the brainchild of Professor Emeritus Eric J. Schmertz of Hofstra's School of Law, *Frank Sinatra: The Man, the Music, the Legend* created a new genre of conference activity (along with a previous one on baseball and Babe Ruth—also an inspiration of Professor Schmertz) in that it focused on a preeminent figure from American popular culture. Both Professor Schmertz and his codirector, Natalie Datlof, must be applauded for this innovation and the resounding success of their efforts. We thank them for providing an environment that stimulated three days of intense discussion, entertainment, and activity around a true American icon.

We are privileged to participate in the work of the conference committee and its subsequent editorial board. In particular, we want to thank our colleagues who aided in preparing this volume, Dr. David Lalama and Dr. Stanislao Pugliese.

The entire staff of the Hofstra Cultural Center deserves our thanks for its support and especially Dr. Alexej Ugrinsky, editorial consultant, and Carolyn Patterson for her diligent attention to multiple manuscript revisions.

We would like to thank Suzanne Guiod, editorial director, at the University of Rochester Press for her guidance in this undertaking, as well as Terri Jennings of Jennings Publishing Services for her work on the design and layout of this book.

In addition, we are grateful to George Kalinsky, Martha Swope, and Photofest for the photographs that grace this volume.

Even though our champion was not present for the main event, we along with hundreds of conference participants and, indeed, the rest of the world paid homage to him. The music may have stopped, but we all went on dancing.

Copyright Acknowledgments

The editors of this volume and the contributors would like to thank the following publishers for granting permission to use copyrighted material.

From Alfred Publishing Co., Inc., "Night and Day," words and music by Cole Porter © 1932 (Renewed) Warner Bros. Inc. All rights reserved. Used by permission.

From Alfred Publishing Co., Inc., "I've Got You Under My Skin," words and music by Cole Porter © 1936 (Renewed) Chappell & Co. All rights reserved. Used by permission.

From Alfred Publishing Co., Inc., "Guess I'll Hang My Tears Out to Dry," words by Sammy Cahn, music by Jule Styne. © 1944 (Renewed) Chappell & Co. All rights reserved. Used by permission.

From Hal Leonard Corporation, "All the Way," words by Sammy Cahn, music by James Van Heusen. © 1957 (Renewed) Maraville Music Corp. All rights reserved. Used by permission.

From Glocca Morra Music (ASCAP) Next Decade Entertainment, Inc., "Last Night When We Were Young," words and music by E. Y. "Yip" Harburg and Harold Arlen. All rights reserved. Used by permission.

From Allen Ginsberg, *Collected Poems 1947–1980.* © 1984 by Allen Ginsberg. Reprinted by permission of HarperCollins Publishers. All rights reserved.

From Allen Ginsberg, *Collected Poems 1947–1980.* © 1984, 1995 by Allen Ginsberg. Reprinted by permission of The Wylie Agency (United Kingdom) Ltd. All rights reserved.

From *MAD,* no. 54 © E.C. Publications, Inc. All rights reserved. Used by permission.

Introduction

Jeanne Fuchs and Ruth Prigozy

In the twentieth century, Frank Sinatra became a legend not only in the field of popular music, but also in almost every aspect of American culture. Although he died before the end of the century, two critics dismiss the exact chronology bluntly, "To hell with the calendar. The day Frank Sinatra dies, the twentieth century is over."[1] Looking back on the last century, we find three figures who dominated specific eras: Bing Crosby, Frank Sinatra, and Elvis Presley. Despite early denigration by critics, each acquired devoted fans and eventually each won approval from even the most hardened opponents among the critical cognoscenti. Crosby achieved popularity in the thirties, peaked in the war years, and faded in the fifties when Elvis Presley made his unforgettable public debut before hordes of shrieking fans. Crosby, charming and affable, served as a symbol of enduring American values when our security was threatened by a dangerous enemy. Elvis Presley, the post–World War II phenomenon, opened our eyes to no less than a new generation's repressed sexuality.

Sinatra, who started as a singer in the forties, was somehow able to express perfectly the loss, loneliness, and romantic yearning that those years inspired. Unlike any other figure of the century, Sinatra was able to reach new audiences with each passing decade; the new Sinatra of the fifties was unlike the thin, soulful but sometimes comic figure of the war years. He became the tough yet vulnerable leading man—singer and actor—with a new kind of voice and musical delivery that startled listeners and made millions of new fans after the bobby-soxers of his youth had moved on to families and suburban life. Remarkably, he was able—with new management, new friends, new music, and new film roles (and selected television appearances) along with (and not despite) accounts of notorious associations and personal peccadilloes—to become an integral part of our culture. The name Sinatra would become known to everyone—and by the end of the century, Frank Sinatra had become an icon—a symbol of the best and worst in our society, with the best so good that the worst would always be forgiven.

Mark Twain and F. Scott Fitzgerald, among other writers, recognized that something in our culture loved the "bad boy" in each of us—not just in Huckleberry Finn and Jay Gatsby. Perhaps that affection for the imperfect child in the American male can be traced to the history of the settlement of the United States, as have been so many peculiarly American traits.[2] There is no doubt that Sinatra embodied the duality of our culture as did no other figure of our time, and that is what makes him a true American icon. Sinatra continues to fascinate the public years after his death in 1998. There have been almost a dozen books published about him since 2000, many of them biographies that try to discover the man that existed beneath the façade of the celebrity.

In this volume, we will look not only at Sinatra as the consummate singer, but also as the versatile performer, whether as actor, dancer, or comedian. In every case, we cannot help but be aware of Sinatra as a cultural influence: on the Beat Generation of the fifties—indeed, on Jack Kerouac himself; on the would-be "cool" swingers emulating the Vegas antics of Sinatra and his Rat Pack friends; and even on the rock 'n' roll generation. Sinatra came to be the embodiment of our achievements and our desires, our successes and our failures. His associations with political life and virtually every major figure in public life and the arts made him ubiquitous in the pages of newspapers and magazines. If we had to select one image that the whole world came to recognize as that of the quintessential American, it would be Sinatra's. Thus, the portrait that this book will draw is that of a genuine American icon—a performer who became so important to our culture that the history of the era cannot be complete without a serious examination of his achievement and his influence.

Part 1 of this volume is devoted to Sinatra and his music. Whatever one may say about him, Sinatra cannot be faulted for his music, for that is where his true genius lay: music remains his most enduring legacy. In some ways, the music stopped with his passing, but in others, in both the figurative and literal senses, the music will never stop. Pete Hamill stresses the importance of music in Sinatra's career when he focuses on some of the good movies after the comeback and adds perceptively, "He also made some junk. But he simply didn't take acting seriously enough to become a great actor."[3] He continues, "Too often he settled for the first, most superficial take, avoiding the effort that would force him to stretch his talent, acting as if he were double parked. Too often, in too many movies, he cheated the audience and cheated himself. He never cheated in the music."[4]

Sinatra never treated a song as if he were double-parked. As with all great art, the work involved in producing a seamless, apparently effortless piece is concealed from the audience. The singer made it look and sound easy. From his days with Tommy Dorsey, he learned a discipline and professionalism that would persist throughout his career. He became a stickler for detail. He himself once said,

"Whatever else has been said about me personally is unimportant. When I sing, I believe, I'm honest. . . ."[5]

In many respects, Sinatra was a romantic in spite of himself. His choice of songs, as Hamill notes, comes down to one basic subject: loneliness. "His ballads are all strategies for dealing with it. His up-tempo songs are expressions of release from loneliness."[6] Solitude and isolation form major themes in romantic literature.

The contributors to this section analyze and discuss Sinatra's technique and its development: his breathing exercises, his legendary phrasing, his intelligent use of the microphone (his "real" instrument, he said), and the intimate tone and mood he established because of it. Nonetheless, the feelings expressed and his ability to communicate them came from within. Loneliness and solitude, the feelings of the outsider, coupled with his sense of rebellion informed his entire persona, which was a romantic one. The dark sensual side, the longing for a lost love, the flirting with danger, the possibility of physical violence (many commentators, critics, and even friends, use the analogy of the prizefighter when talking about Sinatra's life and career) all contribute to the personal brand of lyricism that Sinatra exuded and communicated so headily to the audience. That audience could be in a saloon, a theater, at home, on a beach, in a car, or anywhere in the world. Sinatra's message transcended place. He was the sum of his experiences both personal and professional. He was a complex individual. He was someone others, both men and women, could identify with in the low as well as high moods. Everyone has had ups and downs, but few can communicate the depth of emotion, the longing, and the passion that one has experienced in so precise and poignant a manner as the master. Sinatra the balladeer suffered, but was not self-pitying even though the pain was palpable. He became the "Tender Tough Guy."[7] Unlike Crosby, Sinatra's "singing revealed more than it concealed."[8]

Despite the tough guy attitude (a sort of John Garfield of music), Sinatra could and did reveal a tenderness and vulnerability that struck a universal chord. Regardless of the many triumphs and the close associations with those in "high positions" (he literally made it to the moon), the singer from Hoboken did not forget the struggle he had experienced to succeed. He never shed his sense of injustice and his championing of the underdog, even though he became, in his later years, a close friend and supporter of Ronald Reagan. These qualities set him apart from many performers and underscored his deeply romantic streak. In the essays devoted to Sinatra's music, we are able to study that artistry and the versatility that characterizes his musical performances.

In "The Musical Skills of Frank Sinatra," David Finck pinpoints the musical characteristics that made Sinatra a consistently fine performer throughout his career. By examining specific songs from the hundreds recorded by Sinatra, Finck illustrates the singer's development from crooner to swinger to unique stylist. He links Sinatra's mastery of both spoken and musical language to his attention to the way instrumentalists approached music.

Samuel L. Chell, in "Frank Sinatra's Artistry and the Question of Phrasing," centers his remarks on the singer's legendary phrasing. Chell achieves his goal through a close analysis of the elements that constitute phrasing. These include Sinatra's understanding of the connection between composer and interpreter, his role as a master storyteller, and his ability to think both vertically and horizontally.

Joseph Fioravanti stresses the side of the Sinatra persona that is the "herald of alienation and loss" in his essay, "Hanging on a String of Dreams: Delirium and Discontent in Sinatra's Love Songs." The central focus is on songs of sexual longing, tormented dreamscapes, and disillusion. In his poignant analysis of songs of fleeting and even doomed love such as "Guess I'll Hang My Tears Out to Dry," "Last Night When We Were Young," and "I've Got You under My Skin," Fioravanti likens Sinatra to an "alchemist."

In "Jazzin' Sinatra: Three 'Understated' Arrangers: George Siravo, Johnny Mandel, and Quincy Jones," Arnold Jay Smith traces how arrangers "were born" in the big band and swing era. He then segues into an interpretation of these three subtle arrangers who made it seem as though Sinatra was pulling the band with him and not the other way around.

David Wild, in "They Can't Take That Away from Me: Frank Sinatra and His Curious but Close Relationship with the Rock 'n' Roll Generation," explores the love-hate relationship between Sinatra and the Rockers: Love or at least admiration on their part and hate on Sinatra's part. Sinatra had "swagger and attitude" and was always a rebel—the Rockers craved and appreciated this. Finally, Sinatra's attitude softened toward them into a kind of father-son relationship.

Ruth Prigozy, in a meditation on celebrity, discusses the affinities and differences between Frank Sinatra and one of his most popular rival singers in her essay, "Dick Haymes: Sinatra Stand-In or the Real Thing?" Prigozy traces how the two band singers, similar on so many counts, ended their careers on very different notes. There was no "second act" for Haymes, whereas Sinatra never saw the curtain come down on his career.

Part 2 looks more closely at Sinatra's interaction with and influence on popular forms of entertainment, such as television, movies, and more indirectly modern dance, and the writers of the Beat generation. This section traces the creation of Sinatra, the legend, from the shy, awkward, skinny boy with the bow tie (gently ridiculed in numerous comic strips); to the "hip" swinging leader of the pack; to the aging, lonely figure who expresses his angst not only in his music (*Only the Lonely* album), but also in several screen roles that depict a hardened man of the world trying to make it through the night. Sinatra's life illustrated the American propensity to reject even the idea of failure, the determination to succeed at all costs, and indeed to demonstrate the antithesis of F. Scott Fitzgerald's rueful notation that there are no second acts in American lives. Most of the world was familiar with Sinatra's biography even as he lived it: the kid from Hoboken; the big band singer who attracted screaming bobby-soxers to the Paramount theater in New York City; the budding movie actor whose awkwardness was always outshone by his smooth delivery of a song; the young democrat who popularized *The House I Live In* and helped African Americans find their rightful places on the bandstand; the passionate lover and husband of Ava Gardner—a liaison that would leave him permanently scarred after their breakup; the Las Vegas swinger and cohort of gangsters; the benefactor and enemy of countless show business colleagues; the friend of the Kennedys, ultimately rejected by them because of his "unseemly" associations; and finally, the touring showman who refused to stop performing even after he had "retired," even after he could no longer deliver the lyrics with even a shred of the old voice, until even his memory of those lyrics began to fade. Perhaps it is Sinatra's sheer tenacity that has made him live on as an American legend; for perhaps no other figure in the entertainment world has appealed to the imaginations of so many generations and so many nations. The essays in this section span not only Sinatra's career, but they indicate as well his influence on the culture of his and later generations.

Roger Gilbert, in "Singing in the Moment: Sinatra and the Culture of the Fifties," assesses Sinatra's role in the decade following his debut as a popular vocalist. By comparing Sinatra's shifting public image with such familiar figures of the era as Marlon Brando and other method actors, artist Jackson Pollock, and poets Allen Ginsberg and Robert Lowell, Gilbert illuminates both Sinatra's impact on his era and at the same time sheds new light on that troubled decade.

In a similar vein, Blaine Allen, in "Frank Sinatra Meets the Beats," extends Sinatra's influence to include the leaders of the Beat generation, Ginsberg again, in an analysis of Sinatra's place in his poetry, and then Jack Kerouac for whom Sinatra's performances were models for his own literary work. The author concludes by including cartoons that show Sinatra as a beatnik who is transformed into a man-in-the-gray-flannel-suit—suggesting perhaps the price Sinatra had to pay for his resurgent popularity.

Philip Furia, in "Sinatra in (Lyrical) Drag," discusses many of Sinatra's major recordings, which were originally sung by female performers on the Broadway stage years earlier. Furia's analysis demonstrates Sinatra's ability to transform each song and to create a new singing persona in the process. His discussion is conclusive evidence of Sinatra's role—along with that of lyricist Sammy Cahn—in the development of the romantic music that would forever be associated with him.

In a study of Sinatra's television career, "Sinatra Meets Television: A Search for Identity in Fifties America," Ron Simon focuses on the different Sinatra personalities offered to the viewers and the conflict between those personalities and the contemporary taste for the "average man" as exemplified by Garry Moore and quintessentially, Perry Como. Simon's essay offers a detailed history of Sinatra and the new medium that would soon become, as Simon notes, "America's favorite pastime."

James F. Smith discusses the cultural phenomenon known as "the teenager," in his essay, "Frank Sinatra and Elvis Presley: The Taming of Teen Idols and the *Timex Show*." Smith compares Sinatra and Elvis Presley, noting how both were able to transcend the youth culture in the first decade of their careers. He pays special attention to the *Timex Show* special episode of May 1960 and to the images of both singers that would survive into the next century.

Anyone familiar with the American film musical will forever cherish the exuberant dancing duets performed by Gene Kelly and Frank Sinatra. Jeanne Fuchs, in "Frank Sinatra: Dancer," presents Sinatra's dancing, a frequently overlooked aspect of his artistry. This chapter focuses on Sinatra's dancing in three films with Kelly and establishes how they helped Sinatra make the transition from band singer to movie star. The analysis of Sinatra as dancer adds a new dimension to his image as a musical performer.

Lisa Jo Sagolla's essay, "Dancing to Sinatra: The Partnership of Music and Movement in Twyla Tharp's *Sinatra Suite,*" also treats dancing, but here we learn of Sinatra's influence on noted choreographer Twyla Tharp and on the famous ballet star Mikhail Baryshnikov. In her discussion of Tharp's *Sinatra Suite,* Sagolla demonstrates how Sinatra's vocal performances guided both choreographer and dancer.

Anyone scrutinizing Sinatra's image after the 1940s cannot help but see the transformations in his image that have been described previously in this introduction. Walter Raubicheck, in his essay, "From Sam Spade to Tony Rome: Bogart's Influence on Sinatra's Film Career," offers an analysis of the influence of another American legend on Sinatra: Humphrey Bogart. Raubicheck demonstrates that Sinatra's appeal is like Bogart's in its admission that "toughness does not preclude feeling, that a sense of irony does not preclude a sense of beauty."

Patric M. Verrone's essay, "Sinatra Satire: Fifty Years of Punch Lines," provides a concluding perspective to this collection, showing that because he had become a genuine American icon, the varying images Sinatra cultivated throughout his life came to serve as the subjects of satire. He was seen in a wide variety of cartoons, from the early forties through the decades-later controversial depictions in Garry Trudeau's *Doonesbury* strip, along the way satirized in *MAD* magazine and *National Lampoon.* Among the most memorable and widely seen comedy routines satirizing Sinatra's iconographic images were those performed by Joe Piscopo and Phil Hartman on *Saturday Night Live* on the singer's later years. Certainly by those years, Sinatra was known throughout America and the world; his image—through these satirical renditions—was recognizable to every generation.

We all know that Frank Sinatra did not relish the controversy and condemnation he frequently stirred, but we also know that his image would not have been so powerfully alive today had he not been so complex. The essays in this volume deal with Frank Sinatra, a complex and intriguing figure who came to be a genuine legend in American culture throughout the twentieth century, surviving, as we shall demonstrate in the following pages, into and perhaps beyond the twenty-first century.

Notes

1. Roy Hemming and David Hajdu, *Discovering the Great Singers of Classic American Pop* (New York: Newmarket Press, 1991), 117.

2. Leslie Fiedler, *Love and Death in the American Novel* (New York: Criterion Books, 1960); D. H. Lawrence, *Studies in Classic American Literature* (New York: T. Seltzer, 1923); Harry Levin, *The Power of Blackness* (New York: A.A. Knopf, 1970).

3. Pete Hamill, *Why Sinatra Matters* (New York: Little, Brown and Company, 1998), 178.

4. Hamill, *Why Sinatra Matters,* 178.

5. Steven Petkov and Leonard Mustazza, eds., *The Frank Sinatra Reader* (New York: Oxford University Press, 1995), 6.

6. Hamill, *Why Sinatra Matters*, 69.

7. Hamill, *Why Sinatra Matters*, 96.

8. Hamill, *Why Sinatra Matters,* 130.

Part 1

SINATRA AND HIS MUSIC

1

The Musical Skills of Frank Sinatra

David Finck

Preface

As close as the ties may be between music and mathematics (rhythm, scales, and chords are structured numerically), music is a discipline that is fraught with subjectivity, enveloped by ideas about what is artistically good and bad. Experts are often called upon to disassemble and analyze the written and recorded material of composers and performers in an effort to explain the intentions of these artists and why their work is important or beautiful. Of course, individuals each have differing ideas about value and beauty.

The analysis of musical interpretation is even more complex. No two performances are ever the same, resulting in a greater diversity of opinion. Perceptions about rhythm, phrasing, *vibrato,* and sound production all depend on the listener's personal musical experience and emotional response. There is no right and wrong in the discussion of interpretation. However, ideas can be expressed about what is believed to be admirable about an individual's musical interpretation.

Musical *admirableness* is a somewhat less subjective topic because it depends on more than just opinion. It requires an understanding of the fundamentals of music, knowledge of the structure of a particular composition, and an awareness of an artist's musical skills and limitations. Undoubtedly, the admirableness of someone's musical interpretation is more easily determined when the artist, as in the case of Frank Sinatra, is a consistent performer. Consistent performances are crucial to the analysis of an artist's musical development because they offer the listener assurance that the performer is in control of his or her skills and the quality of the performances is not purely accidental. This permits us to identify and analyze confidently the sonic devices employed by an artist as he or she interprets music.

Listeners have their favorite Frank Sinatra performances and are attracted to them for different reasons—the swing, phrasing, sound, and so forth. Of the hundreds of recordings made by Sinatra, a few examples will be cited in an effort to illuminate some of the admirable qualities found in his musical contributions.

The Musical Skills of Frank Sinatra

Frank Sinatra was perhaps one of the first vocalists of the twentieth century to develop the ability to communicate American popular songs to listeners in their most complete form—the music and lyrics presented simultaneously—without ever sacrificing the importance of one for the other. He integrated and balanced swing, tone color, phrasing, diction, and intonation in a way that created unequaled performances. Some of the more memorable recorded performances were made in the late 1950s and 1960s, a period during which he released recordings for both Capitol Records and his own label, Reprise. It is at this time that Sinatra seemed to have cultivated and refined the skills that created the sound and style that defined him.

Sinatra's early recordings for the Victor and Columbia labels (1939 to 1952) offer pleasant renditions of American popular songs. He sang in tune and with a beautiful sound but clearly lacked the swing feel that would later become one of his trademarks. In the early 1940s recordings with the Tommy Dorsey Band (1940 to 1942), discerning listeners will notice Sinatra's use of *sostenuto* and *vibrato*. In *sostenuto*, each note is carried to the one that follows leaving very little space between them. This, in combination with his rapid *vibrato,* creates for the listener an awareness of the act of singing. It is common for singers to become overly focused on the sound of their own voices. They listen to themselves sing instead of concerning themselves with the delivery of the composition. The resulting performances are usually less than admirable because the singers tend to deliver a performance in which they make themselves more important than the song they are singing. The young Sinatra is guilty of this; there is a vocal self-consciousness that is detectable in his early recordings. Stylistically he was more of a crooner during that period, a style that could be described as "corny"-sounding when compared with his later approach. It is important to recognize that the feeling generated by the Dorsey rhythm section (piano, bass, drums, and guitar), usually a two-beat feeling (a rhythm in which beats one and three are emphasized within an existing four-beat pulse), as well as the style of the orchestrations (distribution of notes of an arrangement to specific instruments or voices in an ensemble), required that Sinatra approach the vocal line as he did. In these early recordings, we hear evidence of what will later become one of Frank Sinatra's most important musical attributes and a fundamental element found in successful performances: He maintained a strong musical connection with his accompaniment. Sinatra's ability to maintain this relationship so consistently is one of the skills that sets him apart dramatically from just about every other singer of his genre. Attack, delay, diction, phrasing, and *vibrato* are among the tools he used to fuse with his musical surroundings. However, it was undoubtedly his sense of rhythm that proved to be his most powerful tool.

The time spent with the Tommy Dorsey Band allowed Sinatra to obtain and begin to refine much of the technical and musical material that would later be included in his stylistic vocabulary. His later vocal performances are saturated with big band swing rhythms and jazz articulation and phrasing. This kind of information can only be acquired by observing instrumentalists. Saxophonist Jerry Dodgion, who played with Sinatra in 1959 and 1960, confirms, "Frank used to always tell us that he learned a great deal while he was on the Dorsey Band—especially about breathing. In those days the singers always sat up on the stage with the band during the instrumental numbers. Frank said that he used to sit there and watch the way Dorsey's back would fill up with air between phrases."[1] This is an early indication that, unlike most vocalists, Sinatra's early musical education involved observing instrumentalists as opposed to simply imitating other singers. This big band experience would prove invaluable as he developed his approach to the interpretation of music.

In 1957, Frank Sinatra released *A Swingin' Affair!* for Capitol Records.[2] From this point forward, listeners become aware of a stylistic change. The sound of Sinatra's voice is deeper, richer, more resonant, and he seems to have abandoned his crooning style. His approach is more direct, uses less *vibrato,* and the notes have less *sostenuto.* By the mid-1960s, a new Frank Sinatra has completely emerged and the quality most identified with his style of singing has become evident: his ability to groove.

A musical groove is the rhythmic feeling that is created by the relationship between pulse and sound. The proper placement of the sound against the pulse (whether that pulse is audible or implied) gives the sound rhythm. Words such as *swing, funk, samba,* and *reggae* are all used to identify types of grooves associated with specific rhythms (these rhythms are often derived from dance). Successful playing, singing, or dancing within a groove is the result of the proper execution of those rhythms within the framework of a pulse. The word *swinging* is used to identify well-executed rhythm against a pulse. This defining characteristic, grooving (or swinging), is a big part of what distinguishes Frank Sinatra from just about every other singer. Somewhere between the late 1950s and early 1960s, he abandoned his crooning style and realized that for vocalists, the key to swinging is more dependent upon where the singer stops notes than where the notes are started.

One of Sinatra's tools for discontinuing sound was his use of diction, especially his use of consonant sounds. When a word ends in a consonant sound, the note that accompanies it can be easily stopped. A sound that has a clearly defined ending when placed against an existing pulse can be used to function rhythmically and can therefore be incorporated into the groove of a song (in Sinatra's case this is usually a swing feel). Many singers do not groove because they sustain notes for so long that they sabotage the rhythmic relationship between the vocal line and the pulse of the music.[3]

Critics who are opposed to altering the original written lyric of a song may object to Sinatra occasionally replacing the word *the* with the word *that* when performing a song. Taking this liberty must not be dismissed as irreverence; there is musical intention in doing so. Sinatra knew that the word *that* grooves more than the word *the* because the sound of the end of the word *the* can be somewhat unclear while the sound of the end of the word *that* has a very clearly defined ending. Because it ends in a consonant sound, Sinatra was able to use the word *that* to make a contribution to the swing groove. Additionally, since the word *that* is essentially a word with a short sound, it can be punctuated and accented in ways that the word *the* cannot. Mixing long and short sounds also allowed Sinatra to give lyrical emphasis to certain words. A sustained word and its accompanying note can be made to have greater meaning when the surrounding words are not sustained. Like Sinatra, skilled instrumentalists often incorporate this technique in performance.

Sinatra combines his ability to groove with his sensibilities about his accompaniment to create ideal renditions of songs. An example of this may be heard by listening to the George and Ira Gershwin composition "A Foggy Day" from Sinatra's 1961 Reprise recording, *Ring-A-Ding-Ding!*.[4] The accompaniment in the first statement of the song (commonly referred to as the first chorus) is played in a broken-two feeling in the rhythm section. The sound of the voice is cushioned by strings and saxophones, which are playing sustained sounds. Sinatra sings fluidly and with a *legato* approach. In the second chorus, the bass and drums change from the two-beat feeling to a four-beat feeling. Strings are replaced with the brass and the long sustained sounds are substituted with shorter ones. Here Sinatra shortens his notes and adjusts his rhythmic placement, fully participating in the newly established swinging feeling. The rhythms that he chooses are generally traditional big band swing figures, material that he no doubt acquired during his time spent with the Tommy Dorsey Band. These rhythms are always calculatedly and confidently positioned within the structure of the accompaniment.

The groove of Frank Sinatra is beautifully captured on the Reprise recordings on which he is featured with the Count Basie Band. Sinatra sang rhythmic figures in very much the same way the band played them. Interestingly, the Sinatra swing style works as well with the Count Basie Band as does the style of Joe Williams, who also made numerous recordings with Basie, though stylistically they are quite different. The Williams style is clearly rooted in the blues tradition while Sinatra's essentially is not. Sinatra shaped his approach around the orchestrations and the way in which the band played them. Sinatra and the Count Basie Band had a similar feel for time; the rhythmic figures were executed in the same way with the resulting grooves powerful and the phrasing masterful.

Without question, phrasing is one of the most challenging aspects of vocal performance. Everyone phrases when speaking. Spoken language has starting and stopping points, long and short sounds, antecedents and consequences, inflection, cadences, and natural places to breathe. These components also exist in music. Songs are constructed by combining musical language (a series of organized sounds) with spoken language (a series of organized words). The key to Sinatra's masterful phrasing is that he had a command of both languages and could speak them simultaneously. This is not a simple task and can prove to be especially challenging when the words and music were written at different times or have different authors. In actuality, few vocalists have been able to do it, but Frank Sinatra was capable of fluently expressing both musical and lyrical ideas with tremendous regard for the intentions of both composer and lyricist.

Frank Sinatra's bilingual abilities are demonstrated exquisitely on the 1963 Reprise release, *The Concert Sinatra*.[5] A collection of eight compositions featuring flawless orchestrations by Nelson Riddle, these recordings are extraordinary examples of Sinatra's mastery of maintaining the delicate balance between words and music. They also illustrate how, more than any other singer, he understood their relationship with each other.

The bulk of the recorded work of Frank Sinatra is a catalog of unsurpassed renditions of songs. His talent and cultivated skills are worthy of the highest admiration. In his lifetime, Sinatra created a unique approach to the interpretation of songs. It is a style that is uniquely his and uniquely American. It is born of an instinctive and profound understanding of American language and American music and the ways in which the two can be combined.

At a Carnegie Hall performance in the early 1980s, Mickey Wiessman, who at the time was part of Sinatra's management team, encountered legendary jazz trumpeter Miles Davis in the cafe in the lobby of the theater. "He was there with Cicely (Tyson). We spoke for a while and I remember he told me that he got much of his phrasing from listening to Frank's records. He said that he learned from Sinatra."[6] This statement from Miles Davis, who probably influenced more jazz musicians than anyone, is the greatest compliment that a musician could receive.

In music, as in any art form, the exchange of ideas is fundamental to the learning process. The contribution that Frank Sinatra made to the education of musicians is more than substantial. His performances overflow with information that has educated generations of musicians, especially jazz musicians. He offered a wealth of information from which future artists may draw.

Notes

1. Jerry Dodgion, in discussion with the author, David Finck.

2. Frank Sinatra, *A Swingin' Affair,* Capitol, CDP 7 94518, © 1956. Reissued on CD, Capitol, CN 96088, © 1998.

3. Consider the following: N is a note, S is maximum sustain, and G is groove. Assuming that there is an existing pulse, as N approaches S, G approaches zero. As the *sostenuto* of notes increases, the amount of groove decreases.

4. Frank Sinatra, *Ring-A-Ding-Ding,* Reprise, R/R9–1001, © 1961. Reissued on CD, Reprise CN 46933, © 1998.

5. Frank Sinatra, *The Concert Sinatra,* Reprise, R/R9–1009, © 1963. Reissued on CD, Reprise/WEA, CN 47244, © 1999.

6. Mickey Weissman, telephone interview with the author, April 1991.

2

Frank Sinatra's Artistry and the Question of Phrasing

Samuel L. Chell

Everyone who listens to Sinatra talks about his phrasing, whether or not they know anything about music.

—Harry Connick, Jr.

Of all the frequently cited explanations for Sinatra's supremacy among interpreters of American popular song, none is more commonplace—with musicians, critics, and fans alike—than the quality referred to as his "phrasing." Yet when pinned down, those who invoke the term are invariably hard-pressed to define, let alone demonstrate, precisely what is meant by a word virtually inseparable from any discussion of Sinatra as a singer. Certainly, matters of breathing, articulation, and rhythmic sense—a musician's unique way of fitting matter to meter—must be considered in the analysis of phrasing. Equally important, though, are questions about the artist's understanding of the relation between composer and interpreter, performer and creator, person and persona. In other words, an interpreter viewed by many as "the master storyteller" must necessarily have a complete if innate grasp of his text and its presentation as well as acting theory. It is a combination of these elements—musical, theatrical, psychological—that constitutes Sinatra's phrasing, the meaning of which can best be understood through close analysis of selective, representative examples from the recordings themselves.

Especially useful as a touchstone to Sinatra's artistry is "Night and Day," a song which, as Will Friedwald has carefully documented,[1] he performed and revised throughout his career. In fact, six versions recorded between 1942 and 1962—including orchestral arrangements by Stordahl, Riddle, and Costa as well as spare accompaniments by Red Norvo's quintet and Al Viola's solo guitar—provide an index to the defining and developing qualities of Sinatra's phrasing.

The 1942 version, a ballad with scaled-down orchestration by Axel Stordahl,[2] features a fresh and flawless voice executing a style Sinatra himself dubbed as "bel canto."[3] The sustained vocal lines and uninterrupted stream of breath lend credibility to the singer's claim that studying the breathing techniques of Tommy Dorsey led to a "revelation."[4] Whereas Fred Astaire, for whom the song was written in 1932, treats the lyric as a series of one- and two-bar units, the four-bar phrase is the basis of Sinatra's interpretation. Moreover, by breathing two bars ahead of the bridge, or C section, in this forty-eight–bar ABABCB song, he fuses these otherwise discrete sections of the song ("I think of you [breath] night and day, day and night . . ."). The effect is the promotion of an illusion in which obsession by love is nonstop, unpunctuated by the diurnal caesuras separating night from day.

Although the 1947 recording, with expanded orchestration by Stordahl,[5] is approximately the same tempo as the earlier version, Sinatra's increased freedom with rhythm, melody, pitch, and articulation slows down the feel of the song, directing attention away from the underlying dance tempo to its contained internal drama. This time he lingers slightly longer on "you" in "you are the one," immediately heightening the personal message of the song by emphasizing the human subject of the singer's longings. Through a similar borrowing of time, he speeds up "the roaring traffic's boom," thus setting up a marked contrast with the "lonely room" as a place not merely of silence but also of boredom. Although the breathing markers of the Dorsey-inspired 1942 version remain in place, Sinatra allows himself more latitude within those parameters, bending the pitch and altering the melody not just in the repeat of the bridge but in the song's opening chorus. His self-acknowledged indebtedness to Billie Holiday is becoming evident in this later recording. From Dorsey, he learned the technique of breathing; from Holiday, as Gene Lees has observed, he learned how to make a sophisticated craft sound as "natural" as an intimate conversation or personal confession.[6]

Following these two ballad versions of the song are two up-tempo recordings from the 1950s. In both, Sinatra exhibits the unfaltering sense of time that alone would separate him from all other singers. Sonny Payne, the legendary drummer with the Count Basie Band, once said Sinatra was the only vocalist who could make him swing.[7] Perhaps it is no exaggeration to claim that Sinatra can make any orchestra—regardless of its size and instrumentation—swing. First, there is his ability to remain always on the back part of the beat, never disturbing the pulse by lunging out of the "pocket" established by the rhythm section. Second, Sinatra's close attention to phonetics—including the full value of consonant and diphthong sounds—is analogous to the articulations that are part of a great jazz saxophonist's rhythmic vocabulary. Third, like certain jazz masters such as tenor saxophonist Coleman Hawkins (with whom Sinatra recorded on a Metronome jazz all-star session), Sinatra thinks vertically as well as horizontally. His mind is on rhythm as much as on melody, and the responsibility for making the melodic statement swing is as much on him as on the bassist, guitarist, and drummer.

The 1956 Nelson Riddle arrangement of "Night and Day"[8] announces rhythm as its theme from the introduction's opening three quarter notes, played by brass just slightly behind the beat. Sinatra comes in immediately, replicating the articulation of the brass in his enunciation of the song's title. The remainder of the song becomes a call-response exchange, with Sinatra in the first chorus initiating instrumental riffs and, in the second, imitating them. The hornlike character of the voice, its coequal status with the instruments in this spirited session, is emphasized by Sinatra's dropping final consonants—the "g"s in "yearning" and "burning"—as well as entire words ("silence" replaces "in the silence"). Like a carefully conceived jazz solo, the vocal evolves from playful riffs to sustained *legato* lines, leading to a triumphant cadence. Instead of the written minor seventh, Sinatra sings the final "night and day" on an exuberant tonic note, underscoring this version's preoccupation less with longing than with the joy of loving—and of making music.

This same arrangement is practically grafted onto a live 1959 recording in which the band is silent while Sinatra and the Red Norvo Quintet ad-lib the first half of the performance.[9] Perhaps nowhere else in the recorded repertoire does Sinatra swing harder, employing a rhythmic vocabulary that virtually erases the distinction between jazz singer and jazz instrumentalist. In this case, the singer clearly subordinates lyric meaning to propulsive swing. In the opening phrases of the tune—"night and day . . . only you beneath the moon," he spaces the words equally, placing each on the back part of the quarter notes comprising the walking bass line. In the interplay with Norvo's vibes, the singer seems to have the best of it, which may explain the momentary but unmistakable audible smile in Sinatra's voice. Moreover, in the game of tension and release, the voice definitely has an advantage over the percussive vibraphone. It sustains the "Why" in "Why is it so?" for six beats, maintaining interest by varying the pitch, before riding the beat for the last three words—"is it so." Sinatra may be matching chops with Red Norvo but the combination of drama and playfulness, of adventurousness and total self-assuredness, seems more likely to invite comparison with Louis Armstrong's trumpet.

Even more than musical technique, Sinatra's special relationship with his material is what sets him apart from his peers. Many of the assessments of Sinatra's artistry after his death have brought to light the paradox of a performer equally renowned for his fidelity to the composer's intentions and for his ability to stamp his personal identity on any piece of music. Sinatra's is an art of interpretation; the encounter between a strong reader and a strong text.[10] When addressing the complex relationship between the singer and the American popular song, it is as misleading to credit the singer for submerging his own ego to the composer's intent as to regard the song as a mere vehicle for the attributes of the singer. Rather, the singer is like a screen actor, less concerned with adapting himself to the role in the song as making the song expressive of his own image.[11] He creates a believable persona that, in the narrative-dramatic context of the song, is capable of convincing the listener of the song's emotional truth. On the one hand, every note Sinatra sings demonstrates Stanislavsky's credo that an actor must live the part every moment he is playing it; on the other hand, Sinatra's interpretations beginning in the

1950s are enriched by audiences' awareness of the drama of the singer's life and career. As a resurrected star, he has become a signifying entity, a survivor with whom the listener feels an immediate and deep sense of identification. In this respect, Sinatra's phrasing goes beyond questions of interpretation to the rhetoric of character itself. To admire his phrasing is to be drawn to the force of personality behind the songs.

Sinatra's 1961 recording of "Night and Day" features a large studio orchestra playing an overblown, movie-score arrangement by Don Costa.[12] Most singers would be simply overwhelmed by the enhanced sonic effects or relegated to the role of one more melodic voice within the texture of the *Gesamtkunstwerk*. Sinatra, however, uses the ballad tempo to reinvent the performance of his first recording of the tune. This time he includes the verse with its repeated notes marking the passage of time. Moreover, without taking a breath, he segues into the chorus by holding "day" for a full seven counts, as if to remind us that the years have lessened neither his passion for loving nor his love of singing. No singer gets more mileage, more dramatic expression out of a vowel sound than Sinatra does. The diphthong /ay/—a succession of two vowel sounds, the back vowel /a/ and the front semi-vowel /y/—receives its full phonetic value in Sinatra's articulation of "night." But the other vowel sounds—"day," "moon," "un" in "under"—operate exactly like diphthongs in Sinatra's treatment of them. He closes off the vowel sound quickly, moving the top of the tongue forward to completion of the succeeding consonant sound. Whereas lesser vocalists hang on to the vowel and avoid the unmusical consonant sound, Sinatra senses the dynamic connection between the two sounds. A pretty but static tone is neither as interesting nor personal as one that has movement and life.

Even Sinatra cannot rise above the bombastic ending of the 1961 arrangement, which crescendos in a single measure to the tonic note and then explodes into an orchestral thunderstorm. Less than a year later, Sinatra would repossess the song in a live performance accompanied only by guitarist Al Viola.[13] After introducing "one of the best songs written in the last hundred years," Sinatra proceeds to give a wistful, meditative interpretation unconstrained by a regular tempo. Instead of emphasizing connected phrases, Sinatra here employs extended pauses after each "night and day," as though extemporaneously searching for the next idea. The singer's well-documented indebtedness to Mabel Mercer—who could transform vocal roughness into high dramatic art—is perhaps nowhere more in evidence than in the final B section of this performance. At the mention of the word "torment," the voice takes on a burr, which it manages to dislodge by the final recitation of the song's title. The singer's use of the minor seventh instead of the tonic at this juncture not only restores the composer's intention but retains the melancholic mood that has been so carefully constructed up to this point. Of all versions of the song, this one contains the quietest "lonely room" because it is exclusively Sinatra's to inhabit.

Our appreciation of Sinatra's phrasing is conditioned by our underlying awareness of its rarity—along with its inseparability from a "golden age" of songwriting that is unlikely to be repeated soon. In today's hit-driven market in which "occasional" has replaced repertory music, in which the emphasis is solely on the performance and production rather than the interpretation of music, the question of phrasing no longer has relevance to the makers of popular music. (Imagine the inappropriateness, if not absurdity, of discussing the phrasing of Elton John or Michael Bolton, of Janet Jackson or Madonna.) As John McDonough has observed, "There's no interpretative art if one is interpreting only one's self."[14] The praise of Sinatra's phrasing is an acknowledgment of his place as the last vital interpreter of a rich tradition to a mass audience. Others will sing the same songs to small groups of discriminating listeners, but none will link us simultaneously to a body of great musical literature as well as to each other as Sinatra did. More than the greatest singer or entertainer of the twentieth century, he remains the most recognizable symbol of a commonly shared culture.

Notes

1. Will Friedwald, *Sinatra! The Song Is You: A Singer's Art* (New York: Scribner's, 1995), 42–54.

2. Frank Sinatra, "Night and Day," Bluebird, RCA CD 2269-2, © 1942.

3. Petkov and Mustazza, *The Frank Sinatra Reader*, 16.

4. Howard Reich, "The Virtuoso," *Downbeat,* August 1998, 13.

5. Frank Sinatra, "Night and Day," Columbia CD C2K 65244, © 1947.

6. Gene Lees, *Singers and the Song* (New York: Oxford University Press, 1987), 106.

7. Ed O'Brien and Robert Wilson, *Sinatra 101: The 101 Best Recordings and Songs Behind Them* (New York: Boulevard Books, 1996), 128.

8. Frank Sinatra, *A Swingin' Affair,* Capitol CD 7-94518, © 1956.

9. Frank Sinatra, *Frank Sinatra with the Red Norvo Quintet Live in Australia*, Blue Note CD 37513, © 1959.

10. Harold Bloom, *The Anxiety of Influence* (New York: Oxford University Press, 1973). [The author is referring to one of the main premises that runs throughout Bloom's book that of the "encounter" of a "strong reader" (Sinatra) with a "strong text" (the song).—Ed.]

11. Richard Dyer, *Heavenly Bodies: Film Stars and Society* (London: Macmillan, British Film Institute Cinema Series, 1986), 11.

12. Frank Sinatra, *Sinatra and Strings,* Reprise CD 9-27020, © 1961.

13. Frank Sinatra, *Sinatra in Paris,* Reprise CD 9-4587-2, © 1962.

14. John McDonough, "The Music," *Downbeat,* August 1998, 19.

3

Hanging on a String of Dreams: Delirium and Discontent in Sinatra's Love Songs

Joseph Fioravanti

Sinatra played many roles in his lifetime. As a performing artist, he could be the roustabout, the joker in black tie, the ingratiating host, the leader of the Rat Pack, the roué, the scamp, and the aging lion in early autumn, but here, in this chapter, we'll focus on his most enduring persona: the knight of the woeful countenance who grieves over past promises and lost possibilities. This is the dominating theme of his best work, captured on disk in the mid-fifties. In his middle years, the prince of Hoboken became the herald of alienation and loss.

Always at his best when he explores the forbidden zones of desire, he delves into the contradictions at the heart of the human condition. It has been said that he "searched unflaggingly for the perfect love," and when he did not find it, he explored "the bowels of abandon and heartbreak with equally unflagging diligence."[1]

Love's Poisoned Apple

While baby boomers were bopping to the beat of electrified guitars, Sinatra educated the rest of us concerning the vagaries of courtship and sexual union: the good, the bad, the hurt of it. In our cluttered, private sanctuaries, we dated and we mated. We danced and romanced to his songs. Even as we clung to each other with other couples weaving over a dance floor, Sinatra was our muse. He "lit the corners of dark rooms for those who had to keep searching."[2]

The first song we will examine is by Harold Arlen and Yip Harburg and bears the fetching title, "Last Night When We Were Young." It was recorded by Sinatra and Nelson Riddle on March 4, 1954. It is from Sinatra's first major album on the

Capitol label, *In the Wee Small Hours.* All sixteen songs are meditations on sexual longing, tormented dreamscapes, and disillusion.

Harburg's sixteen-line lyric is a masterpiece of compression. While the central event here is a brief sexual encounter alluded to rather than recounted, a sense of desolation permeates each line. Shattered love is merely the catalyst. It is a brilliant exercise on some of life's most perplexing mysteries: time, desire, and the futility of memory.

In each of the song's three choruses, in three successive opening lines, the theme of temporality is introduced with the initial words: "last night," "today," and "now." Time is a seamless web with no clear distinction between the past and present. This idea is further reinforced by the repetition of the closing line, "Ages ago—last night." Like Poe's celebrated raven echoing the lone word *nevermore,* this phrase gains by repetition a mocking finality. Time is like the fading mantle of snow that covers Charles Foster Kane's last visible link to his cherished past. Yesterday's love, however beatific, can never be relived nor revisited except with a residue of pain.

The sweet sadness that accompanies spring's first greening stirs desire and awakens memory and, in some instances, brings to mind remembrances of an April love that died on the wing. An echo of this annual complaint occurs in the opening line of the song's bridge, "To think that spring had depended on merely this . . . ," consigning the act of love to a mechanical deed, removed from consequence. Yet, within the lyrical context, the deed seems momentous as well as momentary. Even the heart has its seasons. What promised to be an auspicious start, when seen in flashback, evaporates with the dew on the rose.

Memory is a poor substitute for the rush of desire and unrestrained pleasure in the consummation of the act of love. Once the moment passes, it cannot be sniffed nor savored like Napoleon brandy. It dies aborning like the May fly that hatches, mates, and dies within the compass of a scant few fugitive hours.

The reiterated phrase "ages ago" reminds us that time has no starting point and no conclusion. All is flux. Lovers come and go, acting out the same rituals, vowing the same vows. Even in constancy, there is change. Since nothing endures long without changing, the axiom holds true. In all of Sinatra's recorded music, this song comes close to being a death rattle.

Yet despite its mordant message, we are deeply moved by Sinatra's haunting performance. His voice is dominantly lower register accompanied by suggestive and plucked strings and whispering reeds. By utilizing diminished strings and low woodwinds with an occasional oboe passage and harp, the music keeps its distance, filling in the pauses, never getting in the way of Sinatra's rich and resonant voice. His phrasing is masterful. On the vowels of key words, he holds the beat and stretches the note as if clutching to hold on to the feeling. Consider the recurring mantra, "ages ago." Ordinarily it takes but four short syllables. In the word *ages,* Sinatra holds the long *a* for three beats, caressing the sound as his mellifluous voice gives subliminal shadings that quiver and throb.

In the concluding lines of the bridge:

> To think that something so splendid
> Could slip away in one little daybreak

he attacks *daybreak* by dividing it into halves: *day* and *break*. By stretching the word *day* for two extra beats, he introduces dramatic ambiguity. Not the soft surrogate "sunrise" but day/break. Day not only marks the cessation of warm, enveloping darkness and sleep, it also creates a fissure that cleanly dissects time-*was* from time-*now*.

The first two choruses of this song carry the burden of world pain and weariness with fairly conventional imagery, but the bridge rings with indecision, signaling a dramatic shift:

> To think that spring had depended on
> Merely this—a look, a kiss;
> To think that something so splendid
> Could slip away in one little daybreak

The speaker, having internalized the cosmos, discovers that love looks not with the eyes, but with the mind.[3] The incantatory phrase *to think* is both a summons and a storm warning. Memory, the least trusted of the muses, will not go quietly and can never retrieve what is lost and precious.

The mind may entertain the folly of its ways, but the heart is loath to cast aside its hoarded shards of broken memories. To convey this sense of impasse, Riddle's instruments fade in and out, giving Sinatra the stage as he goes from *mezzo piano* to *più forte* in delivering the periphrastic phrase (*to think*). His utterance pierces the silence and then quivering strings respond as wind sighing in some remote savanna. The next time, Sinatra gives a sudden burst of *fortissimo* when he repeats the phrase *to think* while, in closer proximity, Riddle's agitated horns growl like massing thunderheads.

The closing line, "When we were young last night" ends with an astonishing *diminuendo* with both singer and orchestra retreating, passion spent, in a swift downward spiral to a fading whimper.

A Fever in the Blood

Pop music is rife with bondage titles. "Body and Soul," "Prisoner of Love," and "Let Me Go, Lover!" immediately come to mind. Of all the knock-me-down and punish-me-some-more songs, Cole Porter's "I've Got You under My Skin" deserves some special mention.

It describes a one-sided love that is doomed from the start. What gives this song its special cachet is its simple understated elegance and sophisticated structure. Written in beguine tempo, the song is fifty-six measures long, with repeated notes and eight measures of triplets.[4] It seems to gather itself and thrust outward in a series of convoluted turns. It is a musical cocktail that pours smoothly despite the urgency of its message.

The subject is not love but obsession. The result is not satisfaction but futility. Like Keats's pining lover in hot pursuit of the girl on the Grecian urn (forever close but always out of reach), there is no turning back.

As the title implies, this song is all about an unsatisfied sexual craving. In the dialectic between body and mind, "Under My Skin" speaks directly to the subcutaneous itch, a fever in the blood, a soul on fire. Nothing less than total submission to and immersion with the deified object could possibly yield relief: a consummation impossible to fulfill. More fiendish than the legendary Iron Maiden (whose fatal embrace was swift and certain), Cole Porter's sardonic wit implies that love in these modern times is a slow and agonizing death from a hundred thousand tiny cuts.

When Sinatra and Riddle recorded this song in 1956, the intent was to orchestrate a series of prolonged and accelerating bolero passages.[5] Sinatra demanded a long crescendo after an easy, swinging lope for the first four verses. The opening verse is cued to a piano punctuating short phrases with audible plink-plinks, providing a Basie-like pulse against a background of whispering reeds, soft trombones, and muted horns. Sinatra's calculated "let's take it nice'n'easy" initial approach is the calm before the tempest that moves the song from smirky insouciance to frenzied lament.

The instrument bridge that follows Sinatra's opening run kicks in with a souped-up Latin beat that overlays a brilliant twelve-bar trombone solo by Milt Bernhart that builds to a peak with Sinatra leaping on board to reprise the last two verses. Both Sinatra and erupting brass straddle the beat like two lovers approaching orgasm. Once the song peaks, Sinatra and musicians, dog-tired, fade to a drowsy swoon.

While Sinatra leaps nimbly from line to line, he stretches key notes and words as a means of deepening perception. Most conspicuous is his stylistic use of the pronoun *you* (a word that recurs fifteen times in a twenty-four line song). In the repeated phrases, "I've got you under my skin," he sustains the onomatopoeic "ooo" sound for nearly two beats. (The suggestion here is that pain and pleasure are grafted to the same twig: the pining lover is denied possession but prodded by overwhelming desire.) On two occasions, both early and late, Sinatra splits the word *you* into two syllables, giving us "you-woo." (An echo of the fragmented self? The stuttering schoolboy confusion of one untutored in sexual intrigue?) When we finally get to the concluding verse, Sinatra, spilling over with emotion, neatly underscores the heart-over-head dichotomy when he momentarily slows down to punch out each of the four syllables in the word *men-tal-i-ty*. It prolongs the rhythm of a series of short phrases, extends the line, and sustains the thematic unity of Porter's intent.

Will Friedwald endorses the sexual message that animates the song. He notes the "atavistic off-the-chord energy" of Bernhart's trombone solo that heats up the bridge, creating the necessary frenzy to ignite Sinatra who "rams the lyric home with nothing short of orgiastic fury."[6]

A closer listen to Sinatra's phrasing in the last two verses (specifically the last nine lines of the song) shows the performer taking a few liberties with the original piece without compromising the message. Sinatra, shaking himself free from time-worn idioms that have fallen on deaf ears, gathers his impassioned self into a final assault on the citadel of love. In the line "And repeats in my ear," he interjects the phrase "How it yells!" after the word *repeats*. In the concluding verse, with trumpeting brass at high tide, sweeping away any vestiges of impotence, Sinatra gives full expression to his stifled desire. He elevates the pitch on the first word in "*don't* you know, little fool" and then holds the note for close to three beats. He repeats the process midway through the final verse on the opening word in the line "*but* each time I do. . . ."

Again, with a view toward defining a streetwise directness, Sinatra lapses into his native Hoboken idiom. The ongoing refrain "got you under my skin" is translated as "ga—*chu* under my skin." Sinatra also throws in a line-stretching "step up!" by way of introducing the line "Wake up to reality." With these touches, Sinatra claims the song as his own.

In a poll conducted by Solters and Roskin in 1980, music fans were asked to list their favorite twenty-five Sinatra recordings. "I've Got You under My Skin" topped the entire survey. Friedwald calls this recording the "coup de grace of Sinatra's uptempo masterpieces."[7]

The Hermit's Lament

Sammy Cahn and Jule Styne collaborated on the score of *Glad To See You,* an obscure show that never made it to Broadway and closed in Philadelphia on November 13, 1944. In 1945, the Harry James Orchestra recorded "Guess I'll Hang My Tears Out to Dry," a song from the show, with a Kitty Kallen vocal. The recording scarcely made a ripple until Sinatra recorded the song the following year on the same Columbia label. It was Sinatra, a close friend and working partner of the Cahn-Styne team for RKO and MGM, who resurrected this song from the limbo of forgotten show tunes. Sinatra's second recording of this song on his Grammy-winning album *Only the Lonely* raised this song to the status of an American classic.

Cahn's sophisticated lyrics and Styne's tightly wound melody with problematic octave leaps posed difficulties for any untrained singer. It took the combined wizardry of Sinatra and Nelson Riddle to mount the song in a 24-carat setting.

This song (as with the other eleven songs in *Only the Lonely*) addresses the aftershock of a doomed love affair. The introductory verse, just seven bars long, establishes a brooding presence and sets the tone:

> The torch I carry is handsome,
> It's worth its heartache in ransom,
> And, when the twilight steals,
> I know how the lady in the harbor feels

Evoking the image of Bartholdi's colossus at the gateway to New York's storied harbor seems forced at first glance, for it requires a leap of faith to equate the torch of freedom with a quixotic quest for the shining beacon of love's dominion. Yet strained allegorical references abound in lyric poetry and music. As darkness spreads its mantle over the city, the situation seems ripe for Diogenes to swing his lamp, peering into shadows for the likeness of a kindred soul.

The message of the ballad is found in three stanzas and a chorus that tells us all we need to know. The first of the three stanzas becomes much more specific than the opening verse, conveying the inner climate of the troubled singer in concrete images:

> When I want rain,
> I get sunny weather,
> I'm just as blue as the sky;
> Since love is gone,
> Can't pull myself together:
> Guess I'll hang my tears out to dry

Since nature in its Olympian disdain for human folly is impervious to personal appeals, what are we to make of the tag line, "Guess I'll hang my tears out to dry"? There are moments of perversity in everyone's life when that which we seek runs counter to the grain. One must cope with disappointment. Still, the tag line raises the possibility that more must be involved. As a metaphor, it is far-fetched. Is it a weak stab at humor? Is it the kind of hyperbole that passes for mindless conversation in polite social circles? The second stanza isolates the speaker from the rest of the human race:

> Friends ask me out,
> I tell them I'm busy,
> I must get a new alibi;
> I stay at home and ask myself
> Who is he?

The speaker stands accused by his own testimony. He is reduced to turning inward from the fray of erotic entanglements, underscoring his craven retreat. When the tag line follows the question, in responding to the query, it becomes as banal a response as "crying over spilt milk" and as feckless as hanging out the wash.

The chorus or bridge of the song that follows the second stanza alters the voice (hence the persona of the speaker) just enough to raise significant doubt about his resiliency:

> Dry little tear drops,
> My little tear drops,
> Hanging on a string of dreams;
> Fly little mem'ries,
> My little mem'ries,
> Remind her of our crazy schemes

The sing-song pattern of repetition, alliteration, broken syntax, and elided syllables betray a stiffening resistance to threatening reality and possibly a headlong retreat to the cozier confines of the nursery. Thus, twelve lines into the song proper, the speaker has regressed from adult to child. Just maybe that string of dreams adorned with little teardrops could very well be a distant rainbow.

Memory is the umbilical cord that tethers us to an ambivalent past filled with mingled joy and pain. We would be free of the poisoned mixture, but at what cost? The past directs and shapes our thoughts and colors our fantasies. The rainbow beckons and promises redemption, but only if we take leave of our senses.

Doggerel phrases (fly little mem'ries/my little mem'ries) recall days of ever-green innocence. The five-year-old releases the captive ladybug and urges a home-ward journey. Except in this song, the message is "*remind* her of our crazy schemes."

"Crazy," no doubt, but is not the medley of love a crazy quilt of confusion and desire coming together for a few fleeting seconds of stolen bliss before the next obstacle? The singer has gone to the well once too often and now finds it dry.

In the last stanza, the mundane becomes momentous. Alienation is no longer a temporary condition. Soliciting bad advice and then following through with a desperate plan of action, he is no closer to his heart's desire.

> Somebody said just forget about her,
> So I gave that treatment a try,
> Strangely enough I got along without her,
> Then one day she passed me right by . . .

The final tag line becomes a stifled sob, a silent scream. All he can manage is a show of nonchalance, the final refuge of malcontents: Oh, well, I guess I'll hang my tears out to dry.

New Wine in Old Bottles

As Sinatra aged, his voice filled out and deepened. While he was still a big band vocalist in the early forties, his voice was a clarinet pitched to a higher key. He was more of a sweet tenor than a baritone. On occasion, he displayed his facility in the falsetto range. It did not yet have the heavy gravity and resonance of a true baritone.

Over time, his vocal cords thickened. The voice acquired a huskier *vibrato*. His lower intonations had more breath and texture. When you compare his earlier Victor recordings done with the Tommy Dorsey Band with Sinatra's later Columbia releases, it is evident that his more comfortable register deepened from middle C to B flat. In his recording of Kurt Weill's "September Song" for Columbia Records in New York City on July 30, 1946, Sinatra is just as strong below the stave in low B as he is an octave higher. During his reign at Capitol Records (1953 to 1963), Sinatra possessed a natural *tessitura* with tonal colorations up and down the scale. His heavier *vibrato* lends buoyancy and ensures a *legato* vocal line, reflects emotion, infuses the voice quality with harmonic richness, centering the pitch, and promoting a seemingly effortless glide in sudden key shifts.[8] In Peter Welding's felicitous description, "The voice had deepened to a warm, resonant cello-like baritone . . . giving his singing much greater emotional weight."[9]

"Guess I'll Hang My Tears Out to Dry" requires a supple voice that dominantly hovers in a lower range, from low F (bass territory), G, A, and E. Yet, at the same time, there are three strategically positioned octave jumps that erupt like cloudbursts. Sinatra's mature voice is the perfect medium to express the contained tensions and explosive release in the music.

From the dirgelike opening verse with its phobic distaste for sunny weather in hushed and woeful measure to the first stanza, where a full octave leap propels the melody into the middle range, from major to minor key, a dynamic is established between brooding stillness and sudden manic outcries. This pattern holds for the next two stanzas, from a diminished key in the closing line to *agitato* in the opening few beats of the succeeding stanza. The music has an ebb and flow mimicking the peaks and valleys of a roller coaster ride.

Sinatra masterfully delivers the verse and tag line ("guess I'll hang my tears out to dry") in a muted *mezzo piano* that creaks and breathes like pilings at a ferry stop, swaying in sucking water. Then, on cue, his voice soars in all its burnished and well-honed muscularity, a thing of wonder, a falcon breaking free of its restraining ligature, pitch perfect. In the song's closing refrain:

> Oh, well, I
> Guess I'll hang my tears out to dry

he executes a beautifully wrought *fermata,* holding the note on the word *well,* for four and a half seconds; he follows this with a seamless *legato* glide: "well-1 -1 -1 . . . I . . ." going from full voice to *fortepiano* in the concluding tag line. Nelson Riddle adds a tinkling celesta on the fadeout that harks back to the earlier bridge with its doggerel verse, evoking the fading final notes of "Twinkle, Twinkle, Little Star."

Sinatra and Nelson Riddle collaborated on more than fifteen albums for Capitol. Riddle was a classicist, paring here and there, creating a clean line. He knew when to mute his brass and woodwinds so as not to clog a lyrical passage. He knew how to insert agitated strings and the loonlike cry of a disturbed French horn or oboe to add a dash of color to an articulated nuance. His command of the whole canvas of instrumentation was unquestioned. "Guess I'll Hang My Tears Out to Dry" is but one of the dozen songs recorded in the Capitol album, *Only the Lonely.*

In his study of Sinatra's reliance on Riddle's scoring, Charles Granata encapsulates Riddle's approach to the dominant songs in this album: ". . . against a somber background of understated strings speak judicious traces of instruments like French horn, oboe, flute, clarinet, bassoon, and trombone, and the barest wisp of a rhythm section. Semi-classical in feel, each four minute tune is a short story of gloom and despair transformed into a cry for sympathy."[10] A brilliant seven-bar solo by Al Viola in the prefatory verse is the only accompaniment for Sinatra's opening plaint. It never intrudes or distracts from the voiced words. It fills in the pauses and held silence in a fetching feminine yield against Sinatra's sinewy feints and caresses.

As Donald Clarke accurately observed, when Sinatra came along in the early forties, the songs he helped to popularize "are about sexual desire in disguise, a modern misconception of romantic love."[11] Sinatra himself has volunteered the secret of his singing success: "Music to me is sex—it's all tied up somehow, and the rhythm of sex is the heartbeat. I always have some woman in mind for each song I arrange; it could be a reminiscence of some past romantic experience or just a dream scene I build in my imagination."[12]

Sinatra's most loyal fans in the fifties were light-years removed from an earlier generation that doted on shallow pop songs of concocted sweetness, syrupy clichés, and primly manicured declamations of love triumphant. In the mid-to-late fifties, Sinatra graduated from crooner to celebrity artist, a magician and poet, an alchemist of torn and twisted emotions, who elevated pop music by using it to explore those hidden swamps where we hibernate while waiting to be liberated from ourselves.

For all of his excesses and controversies, in Sinatra, the jokester and the mournful loser fertilize and feed off each other. The yin and yang of existence frequently pull Sinatra the artist in opposite directions. For this, his fans are eternally grateful and richly rewarded.

Notes

1. John Floyd, *All Music Guide* (San Francisco: Miller Freeman, 1972), 325.

2. Donald Clarke, *All or Nothing at All* (New York: Fromm International, 1997), 264.

3. William Shakespeare, *A Midsummer Night's Dream,* ed. William Higley Durham (New Haven and London: Yale University Press, 1918), act 1, scene 1, line 234.

4. Alec Wilder, *American Popular Song: 1900–1950* (New York: Oxford University Press, 1972), 243.

5. Will Friedwald, *Sinatra! The Song Is You: The Singer's Art* (New York: Scribner's, 1995), 233.

6. Friedwald, *Sinatra! The Song Is You,* 234.

7. Friedwald, *Sinatra! The Song Is You,* 233.

8. Cornelius L. Reid, *A Dictionary of Vocal Terminology* (New York: Joseph Patelson Music House, 1983).

9. Peter Welding, liner notes to *Where Are You?* Capitol Records, © 1957.

10. Charles L. Granata, *Sessions with Sinatra: Frank Sinatra and the Art of Recording* (Chicago: A Capella/Chicago Review Press, 1999), 139.

11. Donald Clarke, *All or Nothing at All,* 79.

12. Ray Coleman, *Sinatra: A Portrait of the Artist* (Atlanta: Turner Publishing, 1995), 121.

Sinatra at Madison Square Garden, "The Main Event," 1973. (From the lens of George Kalinsky. Used with permission.)

4

Jazzin' Sinatra:
Three "Understated" Arrangers—
George Siravo, Johnny Mandel, and
Quincy Jones

Arnold Jay Smith

Jazz Singing

The debate continues: Was he or was he not a "jazz singer"? Frank Sinatra would never refer to himself as anything other than a saloon singer. Even though Bing Crosby suggested that anyone could sing as he himself did, especially in the shower, Crosby was truly a jazz singer in his phrasing and general approach to a song: smooth and laid back.

So what does "jazz singer" mean? If you put a dozen jazz experts in a room, you would get thirteen definitions, and probably all would be correct. In Sinatra's case, his arrangers helped in no small measure in making him a hard-driving, swinging singer, a musician among musicians. He could not read music well, yet he conducted and sometimes arranged for Dean Martin, Sylvia Syms, and a critically acclaimed collection of Alec Wilder set pieces. Sinatra hummed and pointed and the musicians in the orchestras understood perfectly. His vocal forte was improvising around the melody, more to the point, around the lyrics. His arrangers did the rest: writing for him, if not always around him, leading him.

Arrangers

We are all familiar with Nelson Riddle's subtle punchy smoothness and Billy May's powerhouse swing charts. However, do we remember George Siravo's prescience, let alone how important to Sinatra were his charts? What about how Johnny Mandel really put the jazz imprimatur on the Reprise era with the album *Ring-A-Ding-Ding?* How influential a figure was Quincy Jones in the repertoire of latter-day Sinatra? These three arrangers gave listeners the impression that Sinatra was taking the band with him. Utilizing musical understatement, rather than being pushed from underneath, Sinatra was having them along for a joyous ride.

Arranging in and of itself was not important to anyone but other musicians and was rarely spoken of until local or territory bands presaged the swing era in the early 1930s. The arrangers came from within the ranks of the aggregations themselves, a saxophone player, a trumpeter, often the leader, or most often, the pianist. He (in the case of pioneer Mary Lou Williams, she) was rarely mentioned on 78 rpm record labels or on the air. It was radio hookups that propelled those territory bands into national prominence.

To draw the natural conclusion, those same live broadcasts helped create the swing era. For all of its less-than-a-decade popularity, the late 1930s to early 1940s was the last time jazz and popular music coincided. Swing seems to have had the most lasting effect on music in general and jazz in particular, save perhaps, bebop. However, it was not until the territory bands got swamped by their nationally broadcast successors, or coprogenitors, that the arrangers strode to the front ranks. Benny Goodman hired Fletcher Henderson, he himself leader of one of the best and most complex dance bands. Tommy Dorsey hired Sy Oliver after the latter helped make Jimmie Lunceford's band such a swinging orchestra. They began to assume not only a prominent role, but also eventually a dominant one as the bands competed with each other for dancers and listeners as they gathered at the bandstand. The "sound" of the band became the sales ticket. In the case of Glenn Miller, it got the better of the musicianship and the sound began to wag the dog with the soloists becoming little more than window dressing between themes.

Band Singers

Every band had vocalists. Some were mannequins used as props to sway and clap during the instrumental portions of the tunes. Others had style, something that turned audiences on. Some bandleaders resented that. In 1976, while we were sitting in the kitchen at New York's Village Vanguard cobandleader Thad Jones asked me rhetorically, "Why should I give attention to a singer who's going to leave me when she feels she's achieved 'stardom'?" Others knew they were onto something; it was a way to make a difference in the band business. They tried to hold onto their singers. The near mythic Dorsey-Sinatra contract stands high among those examples. While the singers remained with the bands, arrangers were called upon to write for them. Axel Stordahl, who was to become Sinatra's personal conductor/arranger at Columbia, came from the Dorsey organization.

You can imagine the concern when the singers went solo as an indirect result of a union-imposed recording ban in the 1940s. New kinds of arrangements needed to be written. There were no band signatures that needed to be adhered to. Ballads became the rage and strings rather than brass and reeds were accented. When Sinatra sang in that style, crowds would scream and sigh. Led by shills in the audience, the "bobby-soxers," as they were called, swooned and fainted on cue. Because Sinatra had already created that kind of atmosphere with Dorsey, his star rapidly ascended as though also on cue. As all gathered [at the Sinatra conference] well know, as if by decree, he was, indeed, different. He appeared vulnerable, a naïf in need. In short, he took his audiences out of themselves and into his own realm. Sinatra was singing, as the listeners were vicariously experiencing his feelings.

Sinatra Sets the Mood

Again, it was the arranger who led the way. Some A & R (artists and repertoire) man probably reasoned, "Hey, there is mood-setting music for the movies, why not for crooners?" Lush strings, swelling emotionally, pulling Sinatra along with them, actually pushing up from the rear, as it were, saying, "Okay, Frank; give 'em a tug; make 'em scream, emote."

There was that other side of Sinatra, the lightly swinging, slightly off-the-beat Sinatra that showed itself on arrangements that, until recently, were never properly credited. Richard Rodgers's favorite waltz, "Lover," comes immediately to mind. (Rodgers himself disliked the use of jazz interpretations and decried the taking of his 3/4 time, almost-sacred masterpiece and converting it to a swinging profane 4/4.) The label copy reads, "conducted by Axel Stordahl." To the conditioned listener, it sounded like the orchestra and the singer were not in the same studio, although that could not have been true at that time in recording technology . . . or could it?[1] Interestingly, "Lover" initially appeared on *The Voice,* Sinatra's and Columbia's first long-playing (LP) compilation of 78s.[2] Almost as an afterthought, it was the only swinger on a collection of ballads.

We now know that chart had been written by George Siravo, a name very few remember from that period. (Siravo told me that the other so-called "Sinatra swingers" were squelched by Columbia in favor of the more marketable ballads.) In later years, Siravo, who was essentially Sinatra's "live" conductor in clubs, would write and arrange under his own name. However, his work with Sinatra remains an example of how Frank could experimentally rework lyrics, a pattern that would become a staple of his style. On those recordings, he whistled or shouted expostulations. I am describing here one relaxed and happy man, not one who was described as embarrassing and at the end of his career. As a young Sinatraphile, I was amazed that the man could sing more than soppy ballads: he could swing! If the pundits at Columbia had shown some spunk, Sinatra might have gone to that next level sooner than he did.

You rarely saw Siravo's name on Columbia Record labels because Stordahl was the conductor of record and for the most part the arranger of all those ballads. However, it was Siravo who did those first swing-oriented charts such as "Lover," "American Beauty Rose," "Five Minutes More," "Saturday Night (Is the Loneliest Night of the Week)," "All of Me," and so many more (1950). These early finger-poppers set the tone for what would become Sinatra's patented approach to a song. Some of those selections formed the nucleus of Sinatra's first Columbia LP, *Swing and Dance with Frank Sinatra.*[3] The tunes became a permanent part of his repertoire both live and in renewed recordings with new arrangers on Capitol as well as Reprise. The charts left *obligato* and solo space for artists such as cornetist Bobby Hackett ("I've Got a Crush on You"), tenor saxophonist Babe Russin

("Should I"), baritone saxophonist Ernie Caceres ("You Do Something to Me"), trumpeter Billy Butterfield ("The Continental," "Nevertheless") as well as space for a reunion with his former boss and bandleader Harry James ("Farewell, Farewell to Love").

At Last, Real Jazz Charts

Fast forward and the Sinatra-Riddle-May combinations have standardized those swinging charts to which Sinatra has added the concept album, which featured the subtle lushness via Riddle or the sometimes string overkill of Gordon Jenkins. Sinatra left Columbia and Capitol behind to be captain of his fate with the formation of his own Reprise Records. Right out of the box, by instinct and taste, he chose a jazz bass trumpeter/arranger who had recently scored, in revolutionary fashion, the movie *I Want To Live* because the soundtrack utilized jazz musicians on screen and off.[4]

Johnny Mandel had done some fine arranging for Count Basie, Mel Tormé, and others, but he refined his musical penmanship with *Ring-A-Ding-Ding*. Like Siravo, Mandel wrote around Sinatra, allowing him room not only to swing, but also to rewrite some lyrics. "The Coffee Song," for example, a long-lost Siravo-Columbia chart, shows up loose and natural. Mandel mutes the brass and allows the reed section to hum along.[5]

The May trademarks, bright brass and sensuous reeds, all served their purpose. However, this was a new Sinatra, the hipper, laid-back model, the guy who takes the band with him rather than the other way around. The title track created a new expression for the devil-may-care swinger, "Ring-A-Ding-Ding." We are treated from the get-go to a Sinatra who does not seem to need the background. The band needs him to round out the arrangements, to add a top, a melody, or another note of harmony. On "Let's Fall in Love," there is a moment of tension created by nothing, no note, no music, no instrumentation of any kind. It comes after the verse, which, by the way, follows the bridge-as-introduction gambit. There is a full bar pause and then "LET'S(!) Fall In Love."[6]

It is with *Ring-A-Ding-Ding* that Sinatra lets us know that there are no sacred cows in his barn. While he had been re-recording his RCA and Columbia hits for Capitol, with *Ring-A-Ding-Ding* he begins the same for Reprise. He now flies to yet another plane on the wings of Mandel, one of the premier jazz arrangers of our time. Only this time it is a true collaboration as Sinatra appears to be pulling the band with *him*. For example, his punchy and already jazz-oriented "A Foggy Day" with a small group on Capitol[7] becomes a full blast band on Reprise (*Ring-A-Ding-Ding*), and it is clear that he is after an entirely new approach. The LP was an all-too-short teaser of what was to come: a Sinatra that was going to swing us into good health.

Bringing It All Home

It all culminates with Quincy Delight Jones. Prior to his branching out into the many fields of endeavor that have made him rich and famous, Jones was a trumpet player and later an arranger whose freshness and rhythmic punctuation were his trademarks. He formed a big band filled with major jazz stars and a book filled with his own music and took it around the world. After touring and recording, Jones became a jazz A & R director for a number of record companies. His charts even begot jazz hits; but most of all, he developed a sound that was identifiably and undeniably his own. His arrangements for Count Basie remain among the best that band played and are instantly recognizable. The Quincy Jones–produced arrangements (they are not always from his pen) for the second Basie-Sinatra studio recording was so well received and felt so good that Sinatra took him and the Basie Band on the road. William B. Williams, the late deejay on the late WNEW, asked Sinatra why he and Jones did certain things differently on that LP. Sinatra replied that they did not want to give anything away before it was time, the element of surprise, as it were. (What could be more "jazz" than that?) For example, on "I Wish You Love," he sings the verse *rubato* with strings only,[8] as though leading to the ballad with which we have grown familiar from versions by Gloria Lynne and Eydie Gorme. Without warning, Sinatra breaks into a rhythmic refrain, thereby putting his own personal stamp on it and forever changing the way the world would hear the tune.

The Jones-Sinatra collaboration resulted in the first, and for a long time the only official, live Sinatra recording, *Sinatra-Basie at the Sands.*[9] (Recently, the formerly bootlegged Australia tour was granted legal status.) What the Jones productions really accomplished was to make all other arrangers for Sinatra obsolete. Many believe his were the heartiest, most satisfyingly comfortable charts Sinatra had ever worked with. Even when he revisited the Riddle, May, and Don Costa arrangements, there was now a looser suave, bravura feeling that suited the elder statesman Sinatra. Thanks to the Jones arrangements, Sinatra could play around more with the lyrics, punctuate with vocal rhythmic interpolations, and elongate musical phrases crossing bar lines. As musical director, Jones understood the familiarity Sinatra had with the tunes and their lyrics. He designed around him, integrating the voice into the charts. Some of the arrangements on *It Might as Well Be Swing,* the Sinatra-Basie-Jones second collaboration, were originally written for a previous Basie collection. Jones adeptly omitted melody lines so that Sinatra could put in his own.

The Glory of Understatement

These three arrangers—George Siravo, Johnny Mandel, and Quincy Jones—never really needed vocal material to flesh out their work. Their subtle, understated instrumental arrangements stand on their own as demonstrations of the drama and tension by which jazz, and indeed all music, is defined. It is almost phenomenological. Their writing becomes a function of the nonevident interfacing with what exists. Only in someone of the instinctive musical stature that was Sinatra's could the symbiosis of the two musical disciplines be brought to fruition. In addition, the arrangers loved that Sinatra always "gave the band some" during the instrumental interlude on virtually every selection.

Sinatra's work with small groups on his early radio shows and on tours showed him the way to utilize space and time as only a jazz singer could. Most of his contemporaries never quite grasped this notion. Siravo, Mandel, and Jones just expanded the terrain.

Notes

1. When Siravo was interviewed by phone for this chapter, he replied, to a question about tracking, "Read it in my book!" Siravo never got to publish his tome. He died in early March 2000. What he did tell me was that he was asked by Sinatra to "lay down" (record) four "charts" (arrangements at the Columbia Studios on East 30th Street, New York City (also known as "The Church") and that he (Sinatra) would return at a later date, presumably to overlay his vocals. We know now that to be the case.

2. Frank Sinatra, *The Voice,* Columbia, LP CL743, © 1955 [78s recorded 1945].

3. Frank Sinatra, *Swing and Dance with Frank Sinatra,* Columbia, CD CK 64852, © 1950.

4. Johnny Mandel, *I Want to Live* (soundtrack), United Artists, LP UA-LA-271G, © 1958.

5. Frank Sinatra, *Ring-A-Ding-Ding,* Reprise, CD 27017-2, © 1960.

6. Frank Sinatra, *Ring-A-Ding-Ding.*

7. Frank Sinatra, *Songs for Young Lovers and Swing Easy,* Capitol, CD CDP748470-2, © 1954.

8. Frank Sinatra, *It Might As Well Be Swing,* Reprise, CD FS 1012-2, © 1963.

9. Frank Sinatra and Count Basie, *Sinatra-Basie at the Sands,* Reprise, CD FS1019-2, © 1966.

5

They Can't Take That Away from Me: Frank Sinatra and His Curious but Close Relationship with the Rock 'n' Roll Generation

David Wild

Rock and roll smells phony and false. It is sung, played, and written for the most part by cretinous goons and by means of its almost imbecilic reiteration, and sly, lewd, in plain fact, dirty lyrics . . . it manages to be the martial music of every sideburned delinquent on the face of the earth . . . [It] is the most brutal, ugly, desperate, vicious form of expression it has been my misfortune to hear.

—Frank Sinatra (1957)

Frank never did like rock 'n' roll. And he's not crazy about guys wearing earrings either, but hey, he doesn't hold it against me and anyway, the feeling's not mutual. Rock 'n' roll people love Frank Sinatra because Frank Sinatra has got what we want: swagger and attitude. He's big on attitude, serious attitude. Bad attitude. Frank's The Chairman of The Bad. Rock 'n' roll plays at being tough, but this guy's . . . well, he's the Boss, the Boss of Bosses, the Man, Big Daddy. The Big Bang of Pop. I'm not going to mess with him—are you?

—Bono, lead singer of the rock band U2,
introducing Frank Sinatra before his acceptance of the
Legend Award for Lifetime Achievement at the Grammy Awards (1994)

The relationship between Frank Sinatra and rock 'n' roll cannot be said to have started particularly smoothly. Indeed, we are speaking of a relationship that never exactly blossomed into a full-blown love affair. Sinatra never popped up with Jimi Hendrix and wowed the crowds at Woodstock with a guitar-heavy, acid-tinged version of "Come Rain or Come Shine," he did not jam with the Grateful Dead at the Fillmore or collaborate with The Who on a full-blown rock opera entitled *Sammy.* To date there are no Sinatra album releases titled *Songs for Swingin' Rockers* or *Only the Punky.* Thankfully, Sinatra never got truly desperate and tried to form a brand new spandex-clad Ratt Pack with members of that 1980s metal group Ratt.

On the other hand, by 1960—only three years after making his "cretinous goons" comment—Sinatra was both gracious or market-savvy enough to publicly welcome Elvis Presley, almost certainly the hip-shaking leader of those cretins, back from the Army on his ABC-TV "Frank Sinatra Timex Special." The unlikely but historic duo traded songs: Elvis crooned "Witchcraft" and Frank sang "Love Me Tender." Eventually Sinatra would not only cut Beatles songs—he hailed the George Harrison–penned "Something" as "one of the greatest songs of the last twenty years" despite occasionally crediting it wrongly to the team of Lennon and McCartney. It should go without saying—but will not here—that Sinatra sang the hell out of the song.

Though few of Sinatra's rock-related recordings would end up atop the pantheon of his prime recordings, Sinatra would cut numerous songs by singer-songwriters with assorted rock ties, including Paul Anka, Neil Diamond, Jimmy Webb, Billy Joel, Stevie Wonder, Sonny Bono, Joni Mitchell, Paul Simon, Jim Croce, and Neil Sedaka. He would record a few duets with his daughter Nancy, something of a minor rock deity in her own right since the days of "These Boots Are Made for Walkin'" and "How Does that Grab You, Darlin'?"

By the time of his successful *Duets* collections of 1993 and 1994, Sinatra could be heard vocalizing along with top rockers like Chrissie Hynde of the Pretenders and, most notably, Bono, with whom Sinatra made beautiful if controversial music on "I've Got You under My Skin." Together they even filmed an MTV-ready video clip for the song. Sinatra and Bono would develop something of a mutual admiration society, though Bono's introduction at the Grammys suggests they still agreed to disagree on at least one piercing matter. This suggests that some things never change; legend has it that Sinatra had future rock star Leon Russell removed from the piano at one 1960s recording date because of his famously long hair.

In one of his last public appearances, Sinatra was saluted on his eightieth birthday with a TELEVISION special taped at the Shrine Auditorium. He was honored by rock notables including Bob Dylan, Bruce Springsteen (a fellow New Jersey homeboy who sang a pretty convincing "Angel Eyes"), and, unlikely as it might seem, Hootie and the Blowfish.

Yes, the man being honored that night once attacked rock 'n' roll as "a rancid-smelling aphrodisiac," but over the years, Sinatra apparently grew at least somewhat accustomed to rock 'n' roll's stony stench if not its unkempt face. Like some begrudging, hot-and-cold, father-son relationship, the Chairman and the rockers gradually came to a separate peace as time went by. Indeed, in his book *Sinatra: The Artist and the Man,* John Lahr reports on a fascinating get-together that occurred a few months before that eightieth birthday gala, which involved a dinner and sing-along at Sinatra's Beverly Hills home with Springsteen, his wife Patti

Scialfa, and Bob Dylan breaking bread alongside Steve Lawrence and Eydie Gorme.[1] Apparently, Springsteen and his fellow rock royalty were savvy and respectful enough to understand who the real boss was and which twentieth century artist had truly proved himself to be tougher than the rest. This same quality may explain why Sinatra and rapper L. L. Cool J hit it off quite nicely during a meeting brought about by mutual friend Quincy Jones. True cool—at whatever age, in whatever genre—apparently recognizes true cool when it sees it and hears it.

Back in the 1980s, Sinatra even seemed for a time to become an unlikely armchair rock critic of sorts, penning letters to the editor and taking characteristically assertive public stands against a few younger musicians who rubbed him the wrong way. When he quite rightly perceived 1980s pop hero George Michael bellyaching about the trials of stardom, he wrote the *Los Angeles Times* to tell Georgie Boy to "fly to the moon on gossamer wings." When Irish gadfly rock diva Sinead O'Connor refused to perform after the National Anthem while on tour in America, Sinatra, the famously proud patriot, stood tall against her stance.

If Frank Sinatra never came all the way to rock 'n' roll, rock 'n' roll would eventually demonstrate the good taste to come much of the way toward the Chairman of the Board. And why not? Well before rock 'n' roll changed the dress code of show business, Sinatra became a sort of early prototype for the modern rock star in terms of his complex persona and his intense impact on his audience. Beyond being one of the greatest vocal stylists ever, Sinatra can be seen as the missing link between crooners and rockers. What was the Rat Pack, really, but the very first supergroup? In the cult of personality that popular music increasingly became, Sinatra broke ground by defining a new sort of postmodern cool. Sinatra was a red-hot sex symbol, the original swinger, an edgy rebel, and an unparalleled singer of songs with the heart of a poet and the dogged temperament of a prizefighter. That sounds a lot like rock 'n' roll.

Along with his lighter touch and unparalleled phrasing, Sinatra gradually brought a newfound darkness and nerviness to popular culture—a brutal honesty that separated him from the likes of Bing Crosby and all that came before him. Give a listen to one of Sinatra's least sophisticated, more rhythm-and blues-inflected tracks like the 1952 "Bim Bam Baby"—one of his last recordings for Columbia—and it is clear Sinatra was rocking and rolling even in the prerock era. Well before Elvis shook up his platinum pelvis, Frank Sinatra had enough earthy rock 'n' roll star power to kick off a cultural revolution without really trying.

Before Beatlemania, there was "Swoonatra." More than twenty years before the Beatles invaded, Sinatra was bringing a predominantly female audience to screaming frenzy with his historic shows at New York's Paramount Theater starting in 1942. As reported in Nancy Sinatra's *Frank Sinatra: An American Legend,* the hysteria was compared to the Children's Crusade of Europe's Dark Ages.[2] In his unauthorized biography, *Sinatra,* Earl Wilson recalled:

I was caught in these "swooning" panics, or riots, as they came to be, in my reportorial duties and can attest that Frank generated as much sexual excitement among those bobby-soxers as the Beatles or Elvis Presley ever did. Moreover, I think the teen-age girls were more in love with their Frankie. The Sinatratics, however, did not throw their panties or bras at Frank. They were too young for it.[3]

Over the years, I have spoken with assorted rock-related figures who had associations with Sinatra, including his rocker daughter Nancy Sinatra, Paul Anka, Neil Diamond, Sonny Bono, and Jimmy Webb, as well as a few other collaborators, such as Phil Ramone, Quincy Jones, and Bob Gaudio. They provide insights into the curious, somewhat tortured, but very real connection of Frank Sinatra and rock 'n' roll.

Nancy Sinatra—certainly Frank Sinatra's most direct connection to the rock 'n' roll world—recently told me that she felt her father had moved well beyond thinking of rock as one big goon squad of cretins. She said of her father's famed antirock diatribe:

If we could ask him if he would take that back, he would say "Yes," based on my own personal knowledge and awareness of him. He learned a lot and I think he was probably talking about whatever was happening at the time that was very noisy, where you couldn't understand any of the words, which still happens today, actually. But he also understood the Beatles, Bob Dylan, and Bruce Springsteen, and guys like that he felt he had something in common with. Who knows, but I think he would take it back because he never would intend to stop young people from experimenting with their music, because he's got a granddaughter who is a punk rocker, you know. And he was very supportive of her. I think it's one line out of context.[4]

Paul Anka—whose "My Way" is still perhaps the song most closely associated with Sinatra—points out that Sinatra was not particularly out of line in his initial perception of rock as some passing fad. Indeed, Anka, who began his career as one of the early teen idols of rock, admits that rock 'n' roll music was perceived as being quite likely a passing fad even by many of those who were making those early rock recordings. "They all thought Frank was cool," says Anka. "Maybe later some of the British bands and artists were putting down Sinatra and Tony Bennett, but you never heard it from the Americans." Anka recalls an old Dick Clark tour on which Sinatra was a regular topic of admiring, even worshipful talk. "We'd have like the Top 20 literally on a bus and we always talked about Sinatra and his Pack, the way they dressed and how cool they were. It seemed all the more cool because all we had was this teenybopper existence and the future was an enigma to most of us."[5]

Jimmy Webb—who had the honor of having the Chairman cover his pop standards "MacArthur Park" and "Didn't We"—told me this year that he finds Sinatra's remarks about rock being made by "cretinous goons" to be "quite an adept turn of phrase." As Webb says, "I don't think there can be any minimizing his initial disgust with the whole business. I think a lot of his apathy toward rock 'n' roll was because he loved lyrics. He's a Johnny Mercer man. But he also had a sense of what *Sgt. Pepper Lonely Heart's Club Band* was about as a recording, what was in the grooves, so to speak. They had kind of legitimized the Beatles' act and put out a different kind of recording. Well, he was acutely aware of that and wanted to do something like that."[6]

Neil Diamond—who, growing up young and Jewish, found himself deeply moved by Sinatra's plea for tolerance in the 1945 short film *The House I Live In*—was thrilled many years later to have Sinatra cover "Sweet Caroline," "Song Sung Blue," and "Stargazer" as well as to record "The House I Live In" with Sinatra on *Duets II*. When asked why rock fans eventually learned to love Sinatra, Diamond said, "The fact that he will probably end up being the greatest singer of popular music in our century probably has something to do with it. People ultimately will recognize quality and uniqueness that goes beyond today's fad or tomorrow's new guy on the block."[7] In other words, whoever was the new kid on the block, there was little doubt who ultimately was the adult who owned the whole neighborhood.

Bob Gaudio—who is better known for his work with Frankie Valli and the Four Seasons than for collaborating on one of Sinatra's commercial flops, the intriguing 1969 song cycle *Watertown*—told me the following regarding Sinatra's attempts to find a new sound in the *Age of Aquarius*. "I don't know if Sinatra ever really embraced rock 'n' roll," says Gaudio. "What Sinatra always embraced to me were songs. I think Sinatra had more respect for songwriters than songwriters have for themselves. That's what I observed of my relationship with him. If he found a song that knocked his socks off, and it turned out it was a 1950s doo-wop song, I think he would probably do it. I think at some point he realized, hey, it's rock 'n' roll, you know, but there are some songs here."[8]

"He really was the first rock star," Sonny Bono told me only a few weeks before his untimely death. Bono—who penned the Sonny and Cher hit "Bang Bang (My Baby Shot Me Down)," which Nancy Sinatra recorded and which Frank Sinatra later reworked for his masterful 1982 album *She Shot Me Down*—noted that "Sinatra did to the teenagers and the young women in his age group what the Beatles did to their group and what so many young acts do now. He just turns them on, you know? It's the same thing Mick Jagger has but in a different way. It's a magical thing and they are just turned on. That's a rarity."[9] This elusive but palpable quality was so magical it was undeniable whether you happened to be a Bono or a Bono.

Phil Ramone—who produced Billy Joel and Paul Simon and other rock figures as well as being chairman of the boards for Sinatra's *Duets* albums—feels similarly about Sinatra's raging, genre-crossing charisma:

I truly believe that he was the first rock star in the sense of popularity, the explosion of people. I think a lot of people in the beginning might have thought that rock 'n' roll had banal changes and a lot of simplicity that didn't really compare with the standards of the Cole Porters and the Rodgers and Harts and those people. I don't think it was until the 1960s that he started seeing that "Bridge Over Troubled Waters" is a good song. I'm convinced that at the right time the guy would have done Dylan and many of the songs of Simon and Garfunkel. Probably he would have had a good time with a Rolling Stones tune. Later rock people like Bono find that their parents played that music and look and realize, "This has got validity, it swings." It's not like people are sitting around and listening to Crosby and Perry Como records now. The Sinatra swagger is the ideal thing.[10]

My contention here is that Sinatra rejected rock in no uncertain terms initially because:

1. Rock 'n' roll represented a direct threat to his own commercial status. John Lahr reports that, one night in the 1960s, while waiting to take the stage, Sinatra looked at his audience and said to Jimmy Van Heusen, "Look at that. Why won't they buy the records?"[11] Certainly some fans were buying the records even then, but the truth is that there were fewer hit records. The chief reason in Sinatra's mind was likely rock 'n' roll and its increasing stranglehold on radio and retail sales. Sinatra had been through huge ups and downs in his career before rock 'n' roll, and reasonably he was in no mood to embrace another genre that could bring him down at all. Smart, proud, and—lest we forget—monumentally gifted, Sinatra quite reasonably did not want anybody or anything hastening the arrival of the September of his years, much less the October, November, and December.

2. Rock 'n' roll was a musical genre he reasonably found to be, relatively speaking, an unsophisticated musical form. Frank Sinatra had endured a bad brush with novelty records while working with the heavy-handed Mitch Miller during his days with Columbia—the horror that is "Mama Will Bark" comes to mind here. It is likely that the lyrical slightness of much of early rock 'n' roll, as opposed to the depth and more refined wit of the standards Sinatra made his own, left him unimpressed. Rock presented a whole new rule book. What Sinatra may not have realized at the time of his denunciation was that, only a couple of decades later, in some punkish corners of rock, his words "brutal, ugly, desperate, vicious" would sound like the highest sort of praise. Just take a listen to the Sid Vicious version of "My Way."

3. Rock music soon became a point of division in youth culture that threatened to make virtually anything of an earlier vintage seem passé. Rock made it more difficult—but not impossible—for Sinatra to stay on top of the pop charts. A few of his covers of rock-era songs would be released as singles—including a 1969 cover of Little Anthony and The Imperials' "Goin' out of My Head" and a 1974 take on Jim Croce's "Bad, Bad Leroy Brown"—but they would fail to climb into the Billboard Top 40, which had long been his natural habitat.

When rock 'n' roll became defined as what was "cool" and "happening," a constellation of prerock music stars were wiped out or hobbled professionally, but Sinatra was ultimately far too towering a figure in American music to be put out to pasture just yet. Still, a performer as vital as Sinatra must have been rightly, righteously, outraged that anyone would possibly see him as old and in the way. Consider, then, where Mia Farrow went soon after her marital split with Sinatra—to meditate with the Beatles and the Maharishi. At the same time, consider the fact that Farrow once complained of Sinatra's Rat Pack pals, "All they know how to do is tell dirty stories, break furniture, pinch waitresses' asses and bet on horses." Skip the part about horses, and you have a solid profile of your standard issue rock 'n' roll lifestyle.

Time healed most, if not all, wounds between Sinatra and rock. From the start, rock 'n' roll stars would mix their harder-edged material up with ballads—musical territory that to this day is almost impossible to cover without borrowing at least a little something from Sinatra. In the early 1980s, Linda Ronstadt would enjoy considerable success with a series of albums that found her teaming up with long-time

Sinatra associate Nelson Riddle and singing standards—a long way from her rocky days throwing down "Tumbling Dice." In the 1980s, Harry Connick, Jr.—though dismissed by many critics as a second-rate Sinatra sound-alike—performed a genuine public service by helping to reintroduce old standards and the very archetype of the romantic crooner to the MTV-age audience with his *When Harry Met Sally* soundtrack.

I tend to think that many music lovers in their mid-forties (roughly my age) assumed in their teen-age years that there had to be something wrong, something uncool, about Frank Sinatra. First and foremost, because their parents like him so damn much—yet another example of guilt by generational association. I believe the change came for most when they actually bothered to take the time to listen to Sinatra. Mine was the generation that arrogantly assumed Keith Richards had invented the very concept of cool. To hear Sinatra sing a song—almost any song really—was to understand otherwise and give props to our past.

As the twentieth century—Sinatra's century—progressed, old musical battle lines blurred and common ground emerged. Reviewing a Sinatra–Dean Martin concert at the Westchester Premier Theater for the *New York Times* back in 1977, the late critic Robert Palmer noted, "Rock and the older mainstream, once mutually hostile and mutually exclusive, seem to be converging slowly but inexorably." Over the years, rockers of all sorts—including John Lennon, Randy Newman, and Bono—wrote songs for Sinatra that sadly went unrecorded by him.

Most recently, long-standing Sinatra fan Elvis Costello—the son of a big band singer—recorded an album with Burt Bacharach titled *Painted by Memory* that seems in part a nod to *Only the Lonely* and some of the Sinatra's other haunted song cycles. On tour with Bob Dylan and Joni Mitchell at the time of Sinatra's death, Van Morrison offered an inspired tip of the hat by covering "That's Life." Even the town of Las Vegas itself has today become a rock 'n' roll capital, with Rat Pack–style cross-fertilizing with every sort of contemporary hard rock sound. One of the few pleasant chart surprises of 1998 was the massive success of a proud musical son of Long Island, former Stray Cat Brian Setzer, who, with his wonderfully retro Brian Setzer Orchestra, proved there remains a huge market for truly swingin' big band rock 'n' roll.

Whatever his politics were over the years, Frank Sinatra was always a rebel, and, to his credit, he was one before rock music made it acceptable and utterly conventional to define oneself as such. Whether he liked it or not, Frank Sinatra rocked, and in the end that was something even a cretinous goon could come to understand.

Notes

1. John Lahr, *Sinatra: The Artist and the Man* (New York: Random House, 1997), 83.
2. Nancy Sinatra, *Frank Sinatra: An American Legend* (Santa Monica: General Publishing Group, 1995), 64.
3. Earl Wilson, *Sinatra: An Unauthorized Biography* (New York: Macmillan, 1976), 40.
4. Nancy Sinatra, interview with author, March 19, 1998.
5. Paul Anka, interview with author, May 4, 1998.
6. Jimmy Webb, interview with author, March 31, 1998.

7. Neil Diamond, interview with author, June 11, 1998.

8. Bob Gaudio, interview with author, April 13, 1998.

9. Sonny Bono, interview with author, January 2, 1998.

10. Phil Ramone, interview with author, March 16, 1998.

11. Lahr, *Sinatra: The Artist and the Man,* 79.

6

Dick Haymes:
Sinatra Stand-In or the Real Thing?

Ruth Prigozy

The title of this chapter is, clearly, facetious. I would not have spent the hours working on these remarks had I not known, from the outset, that Dick Haymes *is* the real thing. Today, however, he is probably the most neglected great American ballad singer from the golden age of the 1940s and the most deserving of a celebration at a conference devoted to Frank Sinatra. For, make no mistake, this chapter represents not only a celebration of Dick Haymes, but a disinterment as well. As proof, when I mentioned to a former student I had taught many years ago that I was working on a study of Dick Haymes, she replied that she had never heard of him. For me, that was proof that, for a generation now in their late forties, Haymes never existed. What happened to this singer whose "glorious deep baritone had warmed the American 1940s"?[1] As Gene Lees says, "A star is someone who was one when you were young; no one ever achieves that status with you after you pass your middle twenties,"[2] and Gary Giddins remarks on his first perception of Sinatra, who "suggested the quintessence of adulthood, an altered state I deeply coveted."[3] For me, then, Dick Haymes was a star of my own childhood, but the tragedy is—and it is a quintessential American tragedy—his radiance lives on primarily for a small but dedicated group of aficionados in the Dick Haymes Society. They have helped me immeasurably in my effort to resuscitate the glory of that voice, the integrity of the diction, the dedication to the lyrics of the finest music of our century.

Many admirers of American popular music of the swing era are unaware that Haymes's records often outsold Sinatra's; in 1944, the powerful gossip columnist, Louella Parsons, praised "the famous young singer who is now taking his place with Bing Crosby and Frank Sinatra . . . the only other Hollywood crooner who can be placed in that category."[4] The problem was that Sinatra cast a shadow over

Haymes from the beginning. Helen Forrest, the noted band singer with Harry James, said that he always seemed to be filling in for Frank. Actually, although Haymes did join the James Band after Sinatra left, did sing with Tommy Dorsey after Sinatra decided to make it on his own, and also left Dorsey to try to make his career in the same way Sinatra had (the two were actually on the same bill for one week after Sinatra had given notice to Dorsey—Sinatra even introduced Haymes on stage), the path to the top was clear. A band singer had to try it on his own, for it became evident early on that the era of the big bands was rapidly ending. Haymes, to his credit, always spoke well of Sinatra, reportedly saying that as long as Frank was around, "there'll be work for the rest of us." Nevertheless, Sinatra was always one step ahead of him.[5]

Other similarities in the two singers' careers include their marriages to the most beautiful movie stars, Sinatra's to Ava Gardner, Haymes's to Rita Hayworth; public scandals and notoriety; their movie contracts, Sinatra's with MGM, Haymes's with Twentieth Century-Fox; and, most striking, their sudden and crushing loss of popularity by 1953. F. Scott Fitzgerald said that there are no second acts in American lives,[6] but Frank Sinatra proves him wrong. Sinatra had the greatest second act in show business history, but Haymes, despite years of comeback attempts, failed. Why? Perhaps that is the real subject of this chapter, for it involves some meditation on celebrity, specifically on success and failure in the public eye, familiar to anyone exploring American cultural history in the twentieth century.

Dick Haymes's biography reveals how unusual his background was for a 1940s band singer. He was born in Buenos Aires, Argentina, in 1918, to a Scottish-English cattle rancher and his wife, a musical comedy singer. When his father's ranch was wiped out by a drought, his parents separated, and Marguerite Haymes opened a dress shop in Rio, but soon moved to Paris, where she and her two sons, Dick and his half-brother, Bob, later a songwriter, were educated in Swiss and French schools. In 1936, the family returned to the United States and lived in Connecticut. Dick attended schools in Tarrytown, Peekskill, and Montreal. Years later, after his singing successes, Marguerite opened a vocal school in New York. Dick always resented her many public claims that she had taught him to sing.

Like Sinatra, Haymes first sang in public in New Jersey, and then joined the Johnny Johnson and Bunny Berigan bands at $25 a week. He went to Hollywood, where he started writing songs while trying to enter the movies. (He had a bit role in 1938.) He even formed his own band, the Katzenjammers, while at the same time working as a radio announcer. His break came when he returned to New York and tried to sell his own songs to Harry James, who rejected the songs but hired Dick as a band singer. His first number one hit, "I'll Get By" (1941), was made with the James Band. Now married to actress Joanne Dru (his second marriage), he tried California again, worked briefly in the movies, and sang for a short period for Benny Goodman and then for Tommy Dorsey, replacing Sinatra. Like Sinatra, Haymes credited Dorsey for teaching him how to breathe properly while vocalizing, and Harry James for teaching him to sing every single song "with all my heart." He would never sing a song he himself did not like or believe in and perhaps that explains why, among the hundreds of songs he recorded, there are very few inferior selections. After his first nightclub appearance in 1942, he was signed by Decca Records and became one of their top-selling singers. He was given his own radio show, *Here's to Romance,* and on the strength of his hit records (at least six top-selling records in about six years), he was signed to a seven-year movie contract with Twentieth Century-Fox. The songs he recorded in these years have justly come to be known as classics; indeed, his recording of "You'll Never Know" (1943) was the number one version, with Sinatra's in second place. Other hit recordings included "The More I See You" (1945), "It Might as Well Be Spring" from his film *State Fair* (1945), and the 2.25 million-selling "Little White Lies" (1947).

On screen, he was less successful (but remember Sinatra in *The Kissing Bandit* [1948], or *Take Me Out to the Ball Game* [1949]?). Although he was always attractive and exciting while singing (think of him dancing with Vivian Blaine and singing "It's a Grand Night for Singing" in *State Fair*), he came across as the boy next door. Yet Fox named him one of its top box office stars for 1945, along with Betty Grable. Only one other film is in any way remarkable, notably for how well he and Grable were paired: Billy Rose's *Diamond Horseshoe* (1945). He was handsome, in a clean—even antiseptic way—and his turned-up nose and sandy hair precluded him from playing the heroes whose looks and demeanor suggested danger, much like Dana Andrews in *State Fair*—a type Sinatra was to embody later in his film career. By the late 1940s, Haymes's film career was at a virtual standstill (after Twentieth Century Fox, he made a few films, even appearing in a supporting role in *One Touch of Venus* [1948] with Ava Gardner and Robert Walker), but his records sold heavily, often outselling those of Crosby, Sinatra, and Como. His radio work continued.

During these halcyon years, Haymes had managed to marry four times (he would marry twice more[7]), each breakup leaving him with financial obligations to ex-wives and children. His fourth marriage, and the cause of the scandals that were forever to be associated with his name, was to Rita Hayworth. The Motion Picture Academy in Los Angeles has many Haymes files filled with newspaper clippings about his bankruptcy, marriage, drinking, bouts with Hayworth in public places, and efforts by the U.S. government to deport him. The government, aided undoubtedly by Harry Cohn, head of Columbia Pictures, who resented Haymes's marriage and influence on his star, tried to deport Haymes under the McCarren Act. It is a sorry affair—an unmitigated disaster for the singer, and a source of the negative stories by scandal sheets like *Confidential*—that plagued him to the end of his life. I might add that Haymes never gave his side of the story except in a statement printed by *Modern Screen* magazine (October 1953) and brief remarks to interviewers, both of which have been overlooked by journalists interested only in scandal. His life was turned into a sordid soap opera by Rita Hayworth's biographers; most notably by the one-sided account by Barbara Leaming, who never interviewed anyone a reader might have considered remotely sympathetic to Haymes.

His career foundering, his debts insurmountable, he was hospitalized several times for hypertension. His work in films was almost over, as was his recording career, in an era that had no use for the love songs he sang with so much feeling, and his drinking was out of control. A reporter in the *New York Daily News* (August 28,

1960) remarked, introducing a 1960 interview with Haymes, "What happened to him? One year his records outsold all competition. . . . He was the boy next door." Haymes replied, "I'll tell you what happened to me. *State Fair* happened to me. Sweetness and light clobbered me." That image is ironic, for he was an international sophisticate of aristocratic taste.[8]

After his breakup with Rita Hayworth, he left the United States for England and ultimately became an Irish citizen. The rest of his life consisted of efforts to make a comeback. His singing never faltered. A reviewer in the *New York Journal-American* in 1954 praised a nightclub appearance: "He stands up straight and sings out straight—and it's fine." That was his way—he sang the words as Sinatra did in his best efforts, with complete integrity to the lyrics and melody. After another brief marriage to singer Fran Jeffries, with whom he shared nightclub appearances, he returned to England, married again (he now had six children), and tried a series of comebacks in the 1970s which were remarkably well received. In 1970, *Variety* wrote, "The ravages of time had taken very little from what was always conceded to be the best voice of his pop era." His return to the Cocoanut Grove in 1972 drew praise from reviewers complimenting his "caressing voice . . . still deep and rich."[9] Haymes had matured, publicly taking responsibility for his personal and career problems. "The heavy drinking started when I was feeling sorry for myself, which is absolutely no excuse."[10] In the early 1970s, he admitted: "I wouldn't be presumptuous and say that I have now grown up, but perhaps I've finally scratched the surface of adulthood. . . . In retrospect I feel that at the height of my career, I was living on the fringe of life. It's a trap that's easy to fall into because everything is so laid out for you in this business. But maybe I've started having humility, with manhood mixed in."[11]

He was in the middle of another comeback, hoping to succeed as a screenwriter, and had cut two fine albums in the late 1970s, when he contracted lung cancer and died in 1980. His obituary in *Billboard* italicized the failure but celebrated his vocal achievement:

Haymes had sold seven million records in one year—[1948]—but no one in the 1970s gave a damn. He earned more royalties that year than any other recording artist, including Sinatra, Crosby, Como—and the hell of it was that Dick still sang beautifully despite the alcohol and constant smoking. Dick had one thing going for him that some of us will never forget. His low notes were the fattest, the most musical, the best in the business. Of all the twentieth-century singers, Crosby, Sinatra, Como, Presley—no one could touch him down in the low, ballsy register.[12]

Those who knew Dick Haymes and those who know popular music of the period are unanimous in their admiration. Bobby Scott, his arranger and accompanist in later years, called him:

. . . a monument to musical good taste. . . . He was a *completed* person early in his career. . . . His sole intent was to sing beautiful songs beautifully and reflect correctly the strength and genius of the songwriter's design. . . . His voice had a liquid quality, a fluidness that was as mesmerizing as the murmur of a mountain rill. That wonderful attribute coupled with impeccable enunciation made his 1940s recordings the hallmark of those years. I still hear his voice singing certain songs even if someone else is performing them, "Little White Lies," "It Might as Well be Spring." . . . Only Sinatra and Billie Holiday and a very few others have had this ability to put their mark on songs by the singularity of their performance.[13]

Will Friedwald agrees: "When we talk about Dick Haymes . . . we're talking about a genuinely superior artist and easily the best of the post-Bing generation (outside of Billy Eckstine)."[14] Friedwald notes that you can listen to Haymes's ballads for hours without tiring of them.[15] I agree that Haymes's mostly ignored recordings of 1957 are his best though least commercial. "Haymes's *Moondreams* matches Sinatra's *Close to You* for unsettling introspection. On the hit-making Deccas, Haymes came off as assured and even-tempered; here he's just a little bit trembly and messed up, exactly the mood that Ian Bernard's offbeat stylized scores require."[16] These albums are testimony to Helen Forrest's appraisal, "He caressed the lyrics of a love song better than anyone. . . . In my mind, no one ever sang a love song better than Dick. Not Sinatra, not anyone."[17] Singer Frankie Laine says, "I always sensed a promise of great things to come when I heard him sing. His voice was rich and warm, a great baritone with a great intonation and projections of warmth."[18] For Margaret Whiting, "Dick had learned a certain way of breath control that produced a distinctive masculine sound. He was a charmer, beautifully articulate and well-educated . . . women just fainted."[19]

How could such a great singer be relegated to such obscurity? The answer lies not only in Dick Haymes's life and trials, but in the era as well. Certainly, the 1950s had lost interest in the romantic love songs of the 1940s, but why did no one play Haymes's later albums—as moving in their loneliness and sense of an ending as anything Sinatra recorded? Perhaps a look at the two singers in the context of a peculiarly American attraction to failure will shed some light on the tragic neglect of Dick Haymes and the loss to our musical heritage.

Most of us are familiar with the desperation of Sinatra's bleak early 1950s efforts to revive his stalled career, and it has become part of our folklore that *From Here to Eternity* (1953) put him on his feet. Musically, his connections with Billy May and Nelson Riddle, along with a brand new persona for a swinging era, put him back on the hit charts. For Haymes, the movie career had faded and, handsome as he was, he never had the edge that Sinatra cultivated. Sinatra's most important forbear in films was John Garfield, who introduced into the bland *Four Daughters* as early as 1938 a type of hero who appealed to audiences drawn to his dark, even dangerous, and sexually provocative image. (Sinatra's role in *Young at Heart* [1954], however, is a pallid imitation of Garfield in the original film.) Sinatra's background and new contacts enabled him to exploit the public's desire for heroes that threatened the conformity of 1950s culture—James Dean and Marlon Brando come to mind immediately—but the type was always there, and it appealed to women. Ironically, although in real life Dick Haymes was as much a ladies' man as Sinatra was, in films he projected only clean-cut decency. In an age that had turned to rock 'n' roll, there was little room for his voice and dedicated singing.

Furthermore, Sinatra's promoters were tougher and more knowledgeable about the music business than Haymes's managers and Haymes were. He was forced to spend the remainder of his life trying to keep his head above water financially, while Sinatra became an entertainment behemoth. Gary Giddins remarks, perceptively, that when Sinatra remade himself, "he remade his generation in the process." As Margo Jefferson recently noted, "Not only did Sinatra have unparalleled power in the music industry, he got to act out a lavish drama of masculinity that thrilled the entire culture,"[20] and this is in contrast to his early persona which has been described as androgynous. Haymes tried to come back through his marriage to Rita Hayworth, but the personal troubles were insurmountable, and he never restarted his film career. Ironically, the role he always wanted to play, in *A Tree Grows in Brooklyn* (1945), won an Academy Award for James Dunn. As Bobby Scott noted, Haymes "was a dinosaur who had lived through the ice age to emerge in a wide-eyed misunderstanding." Nevertheless, he was a courageous man, and he never even tried to join the new wave of singers, remaining true to his art for the last twenty-five years of his life. He was hurt and bitter about the stories that filled the newspaper whenever he opened them, and sometimes those feelings undermined his performances, but it is a tribute to his immense artistic integrity that he carried on in the face of defeat and humiliation. Always a gentleman, he never spoke harshly of any of his contemporaries.

When Haymes opened triumphantly at the Cocoanut Grove in 1972, he was described as "virtually untouched by time and adversity."[21] Although his last albums were made with small backup groups, of the final one produced by the Dick Haymes Society, *Stereo Review* praised the remarkable level of performance, adding that Sinatra recently backed out of a scheduled recording session, perhaps facing "what everyone has known for some time, that his voice has become a very worn and ragged instrument. Yet his diehard fans are probably not even aware that Dick Haymes *is* recording, and recording superbly much of the repertoire that Sinatra is no longer able to handle."[22]

I have already suggested some of the reasons why Sinatra enjoyed a second life, while Haymes faded into obscurity—Sinatra's new charismatic persona, on screen and off, his new swinging 1950s style and his Rat Pack notoriety in the 1960s, and, above all, the sheer output of his recordings. Haymes, with a great voice, warmth, sophistication, sex appeal—in person, if not on screen—spent twenty-five years trying to reclaim some of his early success. Perhaps one of the reasons is that he became more attractive in his self-destructive behavior than he had ever been in his best years. Bobby Scott said that he gave the press and the public all the ammunition they fired at him. His rich baritone voice affirmed a masculinity that made his trials into fodder for scandalmongers seeking weakness and vulnerability. Perhaps also the very public attempts to scale the mountain of success doomed those very efforts. Perhaps the specter of his determination, crushed by intervals of cruel neglect, appealed to a public entranced with celebrities who fall from great heights. If, as Leslie Fiedler put it, in America nothing succeeds like failure, then Dick Haymes, in those terms, reached the pinnacle—oblivion. "Even his own fans held it against him that he wasn't as famous as Frank Sinatra."[23]

But he could have had a better screen career—his role in a minor film, *St. Benny the Dip* (1951) for Edgar G. Ulmer, now a cult film noir director, suggests that under the right direction—which Sinatra had—he could have widened his range of roles. He was not a bad actor; he was simply typed, and he had no one to guide him. Similarly, he could have had more success in the 1950s with up-tempo recording (listen to his marvelous "Between the Devil and the Deep Blue Sea" [1956] or "Slow Boat to China" [1958] if there is any doubt), but no one pushed his greatest recordings and made it possible for him to reach new audiences. Admittedly, he was his own worst enemy, but that is not the only answer.

There have been many examples of artists resurrected years after their deaths. Fitzgerald, too, was forgotten when he died in 1940; his old friend Ernest Hemingway, like Sinatra, was at the height of his success with more honors awaiting him than Fitzgerald ever received. In the late 1930s, when both were at a party celebrating Hemingway's Spanish Civil War film, Fitzgerald was repelled by Hemingway's self-absorption as he rode the crest of success. Fitzgerald said that he and Hemingway could never be in the same room again. Fitzgerald was the quintessence of failure to his generation—as Mike Romanoff said, he was even a failure at failure. Nevertheless, look at what the years have done: a few years ago, some critics listed the best books published in English in the twentieth century, and after *Ulysses* (which few actually read), there is *The Great Gatsby*. Hemingway is much farther down on that list. I do not like lists, nor do I think they mean much in measuring artistry. However, it is instructive that Fitzgerald has been resurrected so wholly that we cannot talk about the greatest American writers without citing Fitzgerald and Hemingway. Why is that not the case with Haymes and Sinatra?

One reason is that a singer has to be *heard* to be appreciated. In New York, there is not one major outlet for classic popular music; the last, WQEW, which was bought by Disney for teen music in 1998, played some Dick Haymes, but not nearly as much as Michael Feinstein, Jack Jones, Harry Connick Jr., and others of current popularity. Another list is instructive: WQEW did a "listeners' countdown" of the best 156 songs of the year. In 1997, Haymes had four songs on the list, the first at number 42. In 1998, he had only two, numbers 118 and 145. Obviously not all of the station's listeners remembered Haymes. Younger listeners simply are not given the opportunity to hear him. Also, he died too soon, so he cannot refashion himself for the MTV generation as Tony Bennett has done. However, Dick Haymes probably would not have done that anyway. (Ironically, there are few radio stations today anywhere in the United States that play Sinatra or the great Bing Crosby.)

The Great Gatsby is in every bookstore, and teachers routinely assign it to students. In popular music, there is no equivalent. If you want to purchase Dick Haymes CDs, you had better use your Internet connection to Amazon.com, which carries the largest selection. Recently, Border's had only two—and that is the norm in music stores in New York City. What can the availability be throughout the United States? A few years ago, after the successful Sinatra television miniseries, the *Hollywood Reporter* announced a miniseries to explore "the Life of Dick Haymes."[24] It never materialized. Even Gene Lees, who wrote one of the most moving accounts of Haymes in his last years, cut the chapter on Dick Haymes out of an updated edition of his book.

So, at the huge homage to Frank Sinatra in 1998, I paid tribute to a man who admitted late in life, "Whatever happened in my life, either good or bad. . . . I find myself directly responsible for. What's past is past; it's a different era. And very possibly I am a different man. There is such a thing as rebirth."[25] Those words are inexpressibly moving, coming as they do from a man who had been a genuine star, respected and admired by other singers. For a better understanding of why I have undertaken this resurrection, search out the magnificent 1950s recordings originally released as *Rain or Shine* (1956) and *Moondreams* (1957), collected in the CD, *Dick Haymes: The Best of the Capitol Years* (1990), and re-released in 2006. The voice is not the full-throated baritone of the 1940s, but, as Friedwald notes, *Moondreams* matches Sinatra's *Close to You* for "unsettling introspection."[26]

Haymes's purity of style, a voice that never lost its depth, and above all, an uncanny ability to extract latent meaning from even the most familiar and even banal lyrics mark him as one of the greatest popular singers of the century. Sadly, the story of his life is all too familiar to students of the culture of celebrity in twentieth-century America.

Notes

1. Lees, *Singers and the Song*, 133.
2. Lees, *Singers and the Song,* 127.
3. Gary Giddins, *Visions of Jazz* (New York: Oxford University Press, 1998), 220.
4. Louella Parsons, *L.A. Examiner,* April 4, 1944.
5. Richard Grudens, *The Music Men* (Stony Brook, NY: Celebrity Profiles Publishing, 1998), 112.
6. F. Scott Fitzgerald, *The Notebooks of F. Scott Fitzgerald,* edited by Matthew J. Bruccoli (New York: Harcourt Brace Janovich/Bruccoli Clark, 1978), 58, n. 428.
7. His wives were Edythe Harper, Joanne Dru, Nora Eddington, Rita Hayworth, Fran Jeffries, and Wendy Smith.
8. Lees, *Singers and the Song,* 129.
9. *L.A. Herald Examiner,* April 28, 1972.
10. *New York Times,* obituary, March 29, 1980.
11. *Los Angeles Times,* October 10, 1971.
12. Dave Dexter, *Billboard,* April 12, 1980.
13. Lees, *Singers and the Song,* 128–29.
14. Will Friedwald, *Jazz Singing* (New York: Da Capo Press, 1996), 194.
15. Friedwald, *Jazz Singing,* 194.
16. Friedwald, *Jazz Singing,* 196.
17. Friedwald, *Jazz Singing,* 196.
18. Grudens, *The Music Men,* 25.
19. Grudens, *The Music Men,* 24.
20. Margo Jefferson, *New York Times,* June 1, 1998.
21. *Hollywood Reporter,* May 1, 1972.
22. Peter Reilly, "Dick Haymes: As Time Goes By," *Stereo Review,* May 1979. (Reprinted in *Dick Haymes Society Newsletter* 39, 1996), 62–64.
23. Bobby Scott, "The Dick Haymes Enigma," in *Gene Lees Jazzletter,* August 1984. (Reprinted in *Friends of Dick Haymes Newsletter* 22, 1985), 6.
24. *Hollywood Reporter,* November 17, 1992.
25. Lees, *Singers and the Song,* 132.
26. Friedwald, *Jazz Singing,* 196.

Part 2

SINATRA AND POPULAR CULTURE

Oscars for *From Here to Eternity*, Donna Reed and Frank Sinatra, 1953. (Courtesy of Photofest. Used with permission.)

7

Singing in the Moment:
Sinatra and the Culture of the Fifties

Roger Gilbert

In a wonderful autobiographical essay Barbara Grizzuti Harrison pays tribute to Frank Sinatra, J. D. Salinger, Albert Camus, and Marlon Brando as a group she calls the "Gods of the Fifties," and reminisces about the spell these figures held over her and others her age in Bohemian New York.[1] Her inclusion of Sinatra in the company of these ostensibly more serious artists suggests that hip young people at the time saw no significant gap between a ballad from *Only the Lonely* and an existentialist manifesto. In effect, Harrison constructs an alternative Rat Pack, one that may never have gathered at Jilly's to drink and schmooze until dawn, but that more accurately reflects the spirit and significance both of Sinatra's best work and of the fifties as a whole. In this essay, I'd like to offer a series of brief comparisons between Sinatra and various key figures and works of fifties culture in support of my view that he is one of the premier artists of that unjustly maligned decade, an artist whose work embodies the same essential themes and qualities that can be found in virtually all the best work of the period. In making these comparisons, my aim is not to reduce Sinatra's stature but to magnify it, by suggesting that he deserves to be assessed alongside his not only obvious peers, fellow singers and entertainers like Dean Martin and Bing Crosby, but among the very finest artists of the period in every major medium.

The 1950s was an extraordinary moment in American culture, richer perhaps in its totality than any other decade of this century besides the twenties. Such a claim runs counter to our received notion of the period as one of deadening gray-flannel-suited conformity and father-knows-best complacency. Critics and historians tend to locate real aesthetic renewal in the sixties, with the emergence of folk-rock, pop art, and other countercultural forms that present explicit social and political programs. Yet I would argue that precisely because the culture of the fifties for the most part avoids direct political speech, it more fully embodies the tensions and fears of its moment. Unlike much sixties art, the best art of the fifties is not didactic but dramatic. That is, it expresses the point of view not of someone who knows all the answers and is generously sharing them with us, but of someone struggling to find order, coherence, and value; who is plagued by contradiction and ambivalence; and who is improvising temporary solutions without any faith that they will work for long. Underlying the best work of the fifties is a profound anxiety about such problems as the place of the individual in the world, the rift between private feeling and public duty, the fragility and instability of the self. Masculinity in particular becomes fraught with tension in the fifties. Manhood is no longer a known quality to be tested on the battlefield; rather it is a much vaguer and more ambiguous commodity that seems to cost as much in psychological pain as it pays out in material pleasure.[2]

Why place Sinatra in the fifties? His first great success, after all, came in the forties, and indeed, he may never have equaled the heights of popularity he enjoyed in his early bobby-soxer phase. However, while Sinatra's work in the forties is technically innovative in many respects and deeply satisfying on its own terms, it lacks the total commitment, complexity, and seriousness of purpose that we find in the work of the next decade. That is why I'm insisting Sinatra's proper historical setting is the fifties, the period in which he fully emerges as a great artist. We are all familiar with the story of Sinatra's early fifties near-death and resurrection, and I will not dwell on the personal and professional circumstances contributing to that transformation; but let me briefly characterize its effects on his work. In the fifties, the emotional chiaroscuro that was only hinted at in Sinatra's forties work is focused, sharpened, intensified. The upbeat songs become faster, louder, harder, more driving, at times almost frenetic, with a latent violence that often explodes in their second-chorus crescendi. (The greater dynamic range of the LP and hi-fi must have facilitated this shift, but surely, it was much more than technological.) At the same time, the ballads become slower, darker, deeper, with an edge of bitterness cutting the sweetness that had defined the young Sinatra's voice. Most importantly, Sinatra discovered that he was something more than a singer or an entertainer: he was an actor. An Academy Award for the role of Maggio provided dramatic confirmation of this insight, but it was in his music that the change became most palpable.

The great innovation in American acting of this period was the technique popularly known as "the method," developed in Russia by Konstantin Stanislavsky and disseminated in the United States by Lee Strasberg.[3] Sinatra played alongside the two most prominent American method actors of the fifties—Montgomery Clift and Marlon Brando. His best dramatic film performances clearly show the influence of the method style (though he apparently lacked the patience to shape and hone his roles that some of his method-trained colleagues possessed—stories abound of his exasperation with Brando's insistence on repeated takes in *Guys and Dolls*). However, if Sinatra was not a full-blown method actor, he was surely a method *singer,* if "method" is understood to mean a commitment to principles of honesty, authenticity, presence, and total absorption in the moment. Sinatra's ability to lose himself in a melody, to bring his own experience to bear on a lyric, to inhabit each song as fully as an actor inhabits a role, is legendary. The sense of live immediacy he conveys in his best recordings, of genuine rather than simulated emotion, is precisely equivalent to the method actor's rejection of theatrical sham and polish in favor of raw expression.

More specific analogies between Sinatra's musical techniques and those of method acting also suggest themselves. Method actors like Brando and Clift were notorious for their halting, inarticulate speech; Sinatra derisively referred to Brando as "Mumbles." By allowing themselves to risk inaudibility, method actors were deliberately stripping away the convention of perfectly enunciated stage delivery, creating a mode of expression that felt closer to the inward self with its hesitations and uncertainties, its reluctance to enter the light of speech. As a singer, Sinatra prided himself on his clear diction, yet it could be said that he developed close musical equivalents of the Brando mumble. His slurring *portamenti* and *glissandi,* his tendency to stay behind the beat, his willingness to let hints of raspiness enter his voice, his sudden shifts of dynamic and timbre, all these become part of an expressive vocabulary that does with musical notes what a method actor does with words. We do not listen to Sinatra to hear a melody sung exactly as written, just as we do not watch Brando to hear lines uttered crisply and precisely. A certain blurring and roughening of edges is part of the way both artists infuse their performances with feeling. Perhaps what is most crucial to both, and indeed to fifties art in general, is the powerful sense of *the involuntary* that they convey, of sounds and gestures welling up from the self of their own accord. Tics, twitches, spasms, winces, groans: these and their aesthetic correlatives are key ingredients in much fifties art, marking the place where the conscious ego loses control of the means of expression, whether voice, paint, language, or body.

One result of this willingness to let involuntary forces enter and shape the artist's work is a heightened sense of vulnerability that pulls against the prevailing norms of masculine self-possession. For all his muscle and bravado, Brando is perhaps most moving when he displays a nearly androgynous fragility, whether howling for his wife in despair or nervously slipping on a woman's glove. Sinatra's work in the fifties shows a similar split between aggressive masculinity and wounded introversion. Much of the dramatic power of his singing lies in his ability to move from confident swagger to helpless withdrawal, often in the course of a single song. As an interpreter of lyrics, Sinatra always had a special genius for locating the precise moments where a brittle facade cracks and underlying pain or doubt is inadvertently exposed. Such moments are by no means confined to mournful ballads; the greatest of all his swinging records climaxes with the anguished line "Don't you know little fool / You never can win." Like Brando, Clift, and James Dean, Sinatra enormously expanded the emotional palette of his art, incorporating shades of self-pity, longing, rage, bitterness, panic, and despair that no popular singer had previously touched.

The young practitioners of the method were not the only film actors doing important work in the fifties. A number of established stars whose careers stretch back to the thirties began to play darker, more volatile roles that sacrificed heroic charm for psychological complexity. Gary Cooper, Henry Fonda, James Stewart, even John Wayne, all gained with middle age a striking capacity for showing weakness, pain, and fury, exposing fault lines in the idealized male images propagated by their early talkies. Of these, Stewart went furthest in exploring the underside of the masculine ego, especially in Westerns directed by Anthony Mann and thrillers directed by Alfred Hitchcock. Stewart's finest performance undoubtedly came in Hitchcock's *Vertigo,* perhaps the greatest film of the fifties and a work that invites direct comparison with Sinatra's brooding ballad albums. Stewart's character Scotty, obsessive, passionate, tortured, paralyzed by fear and uncertainty, furious at the discovery that he is in love with an illusion, is the very embodiment of Sinatra's voice on songs like "I'm a Fool to Want You" or "Angel Eyes."

At this point, I should like to make a specific and perhaps perversely technical comparison between *Vertigo* and Sinatra's singing. Anyone who has seen Hitchcock's film will recall the stunning shot in which Scotty gazes down a long stairwell in terror as it seems to lengthen and recede before his eyes—a brilliant visual expression of the condition that gives the film its title. Hitchcock explained in an interview that he achieved this effect by simultaneously tracking back and zooming in, thus maintaining the size of the image while altering its perspective. The result is a radically subjective view that pulls us deeper into Scotty's tormented psyche. I suggest that Sinatra achieves a very similar effect through a comparable manipulation of his two primary instruments, voice and microphone. When his voice softens in moments of vulnerability, he moves closer to the microphone; when his voice strengthens, he moves away. Thus while the objective volume of Sinatra's singing remains relatively constant, the degree of interiority he projects varies dramatically, creating moments of identification in which the inner space of the self opens up and we feel ourselves drawn vertiginously into its depths. Like Hitchcock's camera, Sinatra's microphone measures the shifting landscape of the psyche, adjusting to its peaks and hollows with uncanny precision.

The rendering of a purely interior space is also a major feature of the most significant painting of the fifties. Unlike the many celebrity painters who produce conventionally pictorial canvases, Sinatra in his own painting chose to emulate the severe and essentially unpopular style of the Abstract Expressionists—a style requiring a large measure of daring and great confidence in the value of one's own vision. Major retrospectives were recently on display in Manhattan featuring the work of two of the most important abstract expressionists, Jackson Pollock and Mark Rothko, and it is tempting to see in these two painters the emotional poles that govern Sinatra's work of the fifties. Pollock's famous drip paintings, with their jittery, hyperactive energy, their tangled spatters, and clashing colors, surely have something in common with the great up-tempo albums and their almost maniacal elation faintly tinged by panic. (Think of Nelson Riddle's arrangements as musical Pollocks, full of restless polyrhythms, layers of instrumental color, and an endless supply of "smears.") In addition, Rothko's contemplative canvases, with their blocks of delicately modulated color, share the introspective ache of the ballad albums, their womblike immersion in erotic pain.

Such analogies may seem fanciful, but it can be argued that Sinatra shares more basic aesthetic principles with Pollock and his colleagues as well. The abstract expressionists were sometimes known by the catchier name "Action Painters," a term meant to convey their belief that a painting is best understood as the record of an act or process, the trace of the artist's physical movement over the face of the canvas. I suggested earlier that Sinatra might be called a method singer; I now propose that he be considered an action vocalist. Sinatra's best recordings, like his concert performances, always have the quality of live events, of actions rather than mere recitations. Just as we are continually aware of Pollock's choices, his split-second swerves, hesitations, and thrusts as he wields the brush, so in listening to a Sinatra track we can hear the impulsive gestures of his voice as it carves its own path through a song. Improvising, ad-libbing, bending, or embellishing a melody and condensing or stretching out a lyric, Sinatra is constantly making choices as he sings, and surely, that is where much of the excitement of his music lies. There is a tangible riskiness in his best performances, a willingness to leap without knowing exactly where he will land. As a result, his records contain occasional clinkers, clams, sour notes, and failed effects; but these stand as evidence of Sinatra's total commitment to the moment in all its unpredictable power.

All of which quite naturally leads us to jazz. In his recent book, Daniel Belgrad explores the connections between action painting, jazz, and other areas of fifties culture, suggesting that they share a fundamental emphasis on the value of spontaneity, improvisation, and free expression.[4] Belgrad never mentions Sinatra, nor indeed does he touch on other aspects of popular culture; for him the spontaneous arts of the decade were all created in opposition to mainstream American culture and its values of conformity and regimentation. However, as Harrison's memoir suggests, people at the time simply did not see the yawning gap between intellectual and popular culture that we now do. Jazz, literature, painting, movies, even television, all were capable of generating real aesthetic excitement, an excitement intimately connected with a sense of spontaneity. (This was the golden age of live television, after all.)

Jazz is of course the most spontaneous of all the arts in its essential dependence on improvisation. Setting aside the irresolvable question of whether Sinatra should himself be considered a jazz singer, it is well documented that he and jazz musicians shared a profound respect for one another, rooted in their recognition that spontaneity was the essence of their respective arts. Miles Davis, arguably the most influential jazz player of the fifties, often cited Sinatra as a key influence on his own phrasing and repertoire, and his most famous LP, *Kind of Blue,* is clearly indebted to concept albums like *Only the Lonely.* (This record was one of the first forays into modal jazz, a style that opened a freer field for improvisation and a darker emotional palette than swing and bebop; as a result, it offers something like the immersion in pure mood that Sinatra's ballad albums achieve.) As a performer, Davis shared much of Sinatra's edgy allure, together with his ability to bring audiences into himself, to create a powerful sense of solitude even in the midst of a crowded nightclub. One of the more notorious ways in which Davis achieved this effect was by turning his back on the audience while he played, a more ostentatious version of Sinatra's tendency to close his eyes when singing. Both these gestures seem to exclude the spectator while subtly inviting them deeper into the performer's inner self. The two men briefly discussed working together, but as Davis explained in his autobiography, he was not willing to play backup for any singer, even Sinatra. Indeed, it is hard to imagine two artists of such forceful subjectivity sharing any stage or groove; each instantly dominated whatever setting he was in, and together their magnetic fields would surely have clashed.

Jazz had a major influence on much of the literature of the fifties, especially the work of the beat writers. Insofar as the Beats anticipate the sixties rock 'n' roll culture that dismissed Sinatra and his generation as "squares," one might expect them to have little in common with the singer. Again, however, that assumption ignores the basic continuity of fifties culture, the lack of sharp divisions between high and low, popular and avant-garde, mainstream and margin. Indeed, to the Beats as to other young hipsters, Sinatra was the very embodiment of beatness, and his voice resonates throughout many of their seminal works. Jack Kerouac's novel about Buddhist enlightenment and the San Francisco poetry scene, *The Dharma Bums,* quotes no fewer than three Sinatra songs, "Learnin' the Blues," "We'll Be Together Again," and "Wee Small Hours," seamlessly and not ironically integrating them into its meditations on Eastern religion.[5] Kerouac's close friend Allen Ginsberg also drops allusions to Sinatra freely and follows his music well into the sixties. His 1971 volume, *The Fall of America,* which records his travels around the country, tracks Sinatra's evolving style in the mid-sixties, noting the elegiac melancholy of *September of My Years,* as well as the flirtation with Black vocal styles in *That's Life.*[6] The Beat writers may not have had Sinatra's income and glamour, but clearly they shared many of his values: a love of street slang; a penchant for nocturnal peregrinations; a restless need to keep moving; an attraction to emotional intensity and extremity; an enormous appetite for sex, booze, and talk; and above all the conviction that a good work of art must embody the spontaneous energies that went into it.

The fifties writer whose work and career most closely parallel Sinatra's is not a Beat, however, but the poet Robert Lowell, often associated with the confessional school of poetry. Confessional poetry is so called because it tends to focus on painful or sordid aspects of the poet's private life—mental instability, family traumas, unhappy marriages, and love affairs. The candor with which Lowell made his personal travails the subject matter of his poems in the fifties struck many critics at the time as unseemly or shocking; poets were expected to maintain a graceful distance from us, not to expose their psychic wounds before our eyes. Having already labeled Sinatra a method singer and an action vocalist, I will round out the list by pronouncing him a confessional crooner. Sinatra did not of course sing songs explicitly alluding to his broken marriage, his misery with Ava Gardner, his professional setbacks, his bouts of suicidal depression, but in a sense he did not need to; his audience already knew the facts and could easily fit them to the emotions in the song. No one listening to Sinatra's ballads can doubt that he is singing about his life; the emotional honesty in his voice is its own overwhelming evidence.

Lowell's career and Sinatra's parallel one another in interesting ways. Both men enjoyed great early success in the forties doing work notable for its virtuoso technique; both went through periods of neglect, frustration, and artistic struggle; both eventually broke out of their slumps to achieve even greater success, producing works in the fifties that sacrificed polish for directness and expressive power. Lowell was clinically bipolar and had to be hospitalized several times; Sinatra was a self-described manic-depressive. Both men became involved in presidential politics, Sinatra as a supporter of John Kennedy, Lowell of Bobby Kennedy. However, the best indication of their affinities can be had from the work itself. Lowell's poem "The Drinker," from his 1964 volume, *For the Union Dead,* would be right at home on *Only the Lonely* or *No One Cares,* with its wrenching portrait of a boozehound tortured by reminders of his departed lover. If only Sinatra had chosen Lowell instead of Rod McKuen as a collaborator—what an album they could have made.

In conjoining and collating these various specimens of fifties culture, I hope I have not seemed to imply that they are all exactly the same. Each of these artists has a very specific and distinct genius that cannot be confused with anyone else's, Sinatra included. I am convinced, however, that when one looks at the best, most compelling and exciting work of the period, a certain shared sensibility begins to emerge. Whether in painting, film, jazz, poetry, or popular song, the art of the fifties tends to explore interior spaces with an honesty and urgency that obeys no fixed program but responds only to the impulses of the moment. Sinatra's voice is a major expression of an aesthetic that insists on the primacy of the isolated self battling its own doubts and fears, discovering its own powers and pleasures, singing its own song.

Notes

1. Barbara Grizzati Harrison, "Oh How We Worshipped the Gods of the Fifties," in *Legend: Frank Sinatra and the American Dream,* edited by Ethlie Ann Vare (New York: Boulevard Books, 1995), 121–28.

2. See my essay "The Swinger and the Loser: Sinatra, Masculinity and Fifties Culture," in *Frank Sinatra and Popular Culture: Essays on an American Icon,* ed. Leonard Mustazza (Westport, CT: Praeger, 1998), 38–49.

3. For an excellent discussion of method acting in relation to fifties culture see Leo Braudy, "'No Body's Perfect'": Method Acting in 50s Culture." *Michigan Quarterly Review* 35 (Winter 1996), 191–215.

4. Daniel Belgrad, *The Culture of Spontaneity: Improvisation and the Arts in Postwar America* (Chicago: University of Chicago Press, 1998).

5. Jack Kerouac, *The Dharma Bums* (New York: Viking Press, 1958).

6. Allen Ginsberg, "Bayonne Turnpike to Tuscarora," *Collected Poems 1947–1980* (New York: Harper and Row, 1984), 468.

8

Frank Sinatra Meets the Beats

Blaine Allan

No evidence indicates that Frank Sinatra and any of the principals of the Beat Generation ever actually met. Instead, their paths crossed in the topography of post–World War II culture, located in sectors dedicated to music, poetry, youth, masculinity, and popular appeal and significance. As Roy Carr, Brian Case, and Fred Dellar indicate in their Beat Generation scrapbook, they could be found in the terrain of "the hip," suggesting one facet of such a subcultural process by affirming its forces of both inclusion and exclusion: "The hipster always assumes that the membership is filled, even when—particularly when—he is the only cat on the case."[1] When Carr, Case, and Dellar compress Sinatra with the Beat Generation, they do so within the districts of style, performance, appeal, and influence, affirming the potency of his talents and image, and endorsing his overall impact in the 1940s and 1950s, in particular. For their purposes, the significance of Sinatra, in relation to the Beat Generation and the moment of hip, was that he "sang on behalf of Young America."[2] Such a suggestion, and the elusiveness of the rest of their discussion, indicates Sinatra's capacity to serve as a point of identification, as a slate onto which space values can be written in order to gain access to cultural capital of a kind Sinatra himself undeniably possessed.

Three examples, from the realms of literature, biography, and parody, suggest ways that Sinatra has been portrayed in writing in relation to his near-contemporaries in defining youth culture in the United States, the Beat Generation. In one, Allen Ginsberg writes Sinatra into the contemporary United States that he conveys in his poetry; in another, Jack Kerouac writes Sinatra onto himself; and finally *MAD* magazine writes Sinatra into the mass-culture rendition of the Beat Generation.

An emblem of the contemporary United States from the 1940s on, Sinatra found his way into the writing of Allen Ginsberg, a poet "of these states," intimately concerned with the conditions that surrounded him during the same period. Sinatra appears by name, however, only four times in Ginsberg's *Collected Poems 1947–1980*—more occasions than Charlie Chaplin, Bob Hope, John Wayne, Elvis Presley, Thelonious Monk, or Sammy Davis, Jr., but fewer than Albert Einstein, Franklin Roosevelt, Nelson Rockefeller, Bob Dylan, or William Blake.

Sinatra formed part of the soundtrack, as Ginsberg peripatetically explored ideas of his contemporary United States. In autumn 1965, the year of *September of My Years,* in "Beginning of a Poem of these States," contemporary tunes from generations that Ginsberg embraced rise from the car radio as he approaches Nevada:

> Mud plate of Black Rock Desert passing, Frank Sinatra
> lamenting distant years, old sad voic'd September'd recordings,
> and Beatles crying Help! their voices woodling for tenderness.[3]

Later in *The Fall of America*—a book-length poem documenting Ginsberg's travels during the years 1965 to 1971—Sinatra reappears in "Bayonne Turnpike to Tuscarora," singing his then-recent hit, "That's Life" (with an additional, brief allusion to Nancy Sinatra, also Top 40 at the time) as part of the 1967 radioscape that is underscored with the escalating Vietnam war:

> Evergreens in Snow
> Laundry hanging from the blue bungalow
> Mansfield and U Thant ask halt Bombing North Vietnam
> State Department says "Tit For Tat."
>
> Frank Sinatra with negro voice
> enters a new phase—
> Flat on his face 50 years "I've been a beggar & a clown
> a poet & a star, roll myself in July
> up into a ball and die."
>
> Radio pumping
> artificial rock & roll, Beach Boys
> & Sinatra's daughter overdubbed microphone
> antennae'd car dashboard vibrating
> False emotions broadcast thru the Land
> Natural voices made synthetic,
> phlegm obliterated
> Smart ones work with electronics—
> What are the popular songs on the Hiway?
> *"Home I'm Comin Home I am a Soldier—"*
> *   "The girl I left behind . . .*
> *I did the best job I could*
> *   Helping to keep our land free*
> *I am a soldier"*
>
> Lulled into War
> thus commercial jabber Rock & Roll Announcers

False False False
"Enjoy this meat—"
Weak A&P SuperRight ground round
Factories building, airwaves pushing . . .[4]

In 1979, over a decade later, Ginsberg raised the image of Sinatra, alluding to his mob connections and the 1963 Kennedy assassination, but also to the failures to recognize the anomalies of nature and culture represented by a desert development as insistently urban as Las Vegas:

> Aztec sandstone waterholes known by Moapa've
> dried out under the baccarat pits
> of M.G.M.'s Grand Hotel
>
> If Robert Maheu knew
> who killed Kennedy
> would he tell Santos Trafficante?
>
> If Frank Sinatra had to grow his own
> food, would he learn
> how to grind piñon nuts?
>
> If Sammy Davis had to find original water
> would he lead a million old ladies laughing
> round Mt. Charleston to the Sheepshead Mountains
> in migratory cycle?[5]

Ginsberg's first allusion to Sinatra apparently arose in the 1958 "Laughing Gas" poem that originated in dental work and Ginsberg's first experience with nitrous oxide. His first mention of music in "Laughing Gas" refers to "the nostalgic / piano Muzak in the wall . . . where've I heard that/ asshole jazz before?" but at some point, while the dentist is working Ginsberg hears Sinatra singing:

> I take my pen in hand
> The same old way sings Sinatra
> I'm writing to You give me understanding
> I pray sings Sinatra
> Can I never glimpse the round we have made?
> Write me as soon as able sings Sinatra
> O Lord burn me out of existence
>
> You've got a long body sings Sinatra
> I refuse to breathe and return to form
> I've seen every moment in advance before
> I've turned my neck a million times
> & written this note
> & been greeted with fire and cheers I refuse to stop
> —thinking—
> What Perfection has escaped me?[6]

As a poet who drew on sensations of the moment, Ginsberg understandably included Sinatra. Sinatra images appear because his music occasionally turned up in Ginsberg's aural sphere. However, Sinatra also represented distinctive forces for Ginsberg. The Sinatra of these four poetic moments is individualized, and—as in so many commentaries—identified with the protagonists he created in his performances. He is a singer with particular vocal traits, but he also constitutes a product of modern mass culture, separated from nature and history.

While Ginsberg's relations to Sinatra can be found principally in his poetry, Jack Kerouac's are located more in his biography. Parallels in the lives of Sinatra and Kerouac exist, and it would be possible to tease out meaning in two boys born in the working-class Northeast of immigrant parents in the first half of the century; two sons of forceful, domineering mothers who commanded loyalty of their boys; two men, multiply married and reportedly promiscuous, both of whom also sought the company of men to create peer groups in which they took or were widely seen to have roles as leaders; both alcohol-dependent and reportedly prone to depression; both with early careers that seemed to promise a social and political progressivism that later evolved into more evidently traditionally conservative positions; both defining figures for their youth and popular music of their own generation, but ill-at-ease with the music and youth cultures of their later lives; and both jazz-inspired artists who combined current, popular music with the creative capacity of the English language. Such relations are the stock-in-trade of a form of comparative analysis, in which historical figures are treated as fictional characters who might occupy the world of a story in parallel, without ever being aware of each other. Sinatra likely knew about Kerouac, but Kerouac clearly occupied a world different from Sinatra's and their actual paths would have little reason to cross. Kerouac, however, was a Sinatra fan.

In 1961 or thereabouts, Jack Kerouac created an artifact that did bring Sinatra and him together and that has circulated unofficially and gained tantalizing significance. Kerouac had proposed writing as a spontaneous, automatic, and uncensored activity, and operated with the oral and musical properties of language strongly in his mind as part of his creative method. For him, linguistic lines and musical lines had equivalence. In his essay "Essentials of Spontaneous Prose," Kerouac repeatedly refers to writing as "blowing," as if typing could be compared to playing a horn, or, like Ginsberg, as if language itself were based on breath and principally had meaning when spoken. Perhaps then it is not surprising to learn that one of the tools of Kerouac's trade was the tape recorder, on which he was able to spin out original prose and poetry, or afterward to read back his own work. Kerouac performed publicly, like many poets delivering unaccompanied readings, but also with musicians: in person with David Amram, and on a couple of albums on which he was accompanied by Steve Allen, Zoot Sims, and Al Cohn. Kerouac and Amram also collaborated on the soundtrack of Alfred Leslie and Robert Frank's film *Pull My Daisy,* for which Kerouac recorded semi-impromptu commentary and spoke dialogue for all the characters. According to Leslie, the decision to have Kerouac speak the words in the film was made after he and Sinatra heard a recording that Kerouac had made of the original script on which Symphony Sid Torin's radio show played in the background.[7]

This tape may not survive, but another tape Kerouac made of himself reading while he listened to music does. Interleaving passages from the novel *Doctor Sax* and the stream-of-consciousness *Old Angel Midnight,* Kerouac spins two Sinatra albums: the 1959 release *No One Cares* and the 1955 *In the Wee Small Hours.* According to biographer Gerald Nicosia, Kerouac had been a fan of Sinatra as a teenager in Lowell, Massachusetts, in the late 1930s (as he had also enjoyed the Eberle Brothers, Helen O'Connell, and Cab Calloway). When he moved to New York City to go to the Horace Mann School and later Columbia, his tastes broadened to embrace jazz—an association for which he and the Beats would be known—and the big bands of Count Basie, Glenn Miller, Jimmie Lunceford, Duke Ellington, Artie Shaw, Harry James, and the Dorseys, and the big-band singer Sinatra.[8] That Kerouac was a Sinatra fan at a time when Sinatra fans were legion is not special. It seems clear though that Kerouac found points of identity in Sinatra's performances and, although they were very different in style and personal aesthetics, that he emulated Sinatra. Nicosia describes how, in the late 1950s, Kerouac courted Helen Weaver by singing her Sinatra tunes, such as "Chicago" and "Why Try to Change Me Now?"[9] In the early 1960s, Kerouac reported to a friend that the tunes that he recalled while secluded in the mountains of Washington state were mostly ballads and included a Sinatra song he recalled as "Last Night." He was most likely referring to "Last Night When We Were Young" from *In the Wee Small Hours,* the album to which he read when recording:

I sang Embraceable You You Silk and Laceable you to all the stars of mountaintop night, scaring the bears, altho my real first favorite song is "I Love You" by Irving Berlin. No. 2 is "Embraceable You" and No. 3 at the time was "Last Night" as sung by Sinatra but now I stick to "Moon River" as No. 3. Of course, I'm not forgetting No. 4, "Lady of the Evening" by Duke Ellington.[10]

He also used his friend Jerry Newman's recording studio to record Sinatra songs with professional musicians, occasions that were, in Nicosia's words, "an excuse for an endless and deliberately self-destructive celebration," which I take as a euphemism for drunken playtime.[11]

The home recordings Kerouac made may just as likely have been alcohol-fueled exercises in melancholy. Maybe on other occasions he read along with *Come Fly with Me* or *Songs for Swingin' Lovers,* but on the tape that survives, he accompanies himself with ballad albums, which Kerouac does not simply leave to play in the background. In a rudimentary fashion, Kerouac engineers his readings in relation to the recording, pausing and moving the microphone closer to the speaker to provide musical interludes. Perhaps most radically, he does not read through one full text and then another, but patches together segments, as if he were sequencing an album himself. The two texts are one of his novels of childhood in Lowell, *Dr. Sax,* a dreamlike fantasy of memory and local history, inspired in part by the mysterious radio hero The Shadow, and the more experimental—in Michael McClure's words—"long breath of bop prose," *Old Angel Midnight.*[12] Kerouac alternates segments of *Doctor Sax* and *Old Angel Midnight,* weaving his own words and voice with Sinatra's and the Nelson Riddle and Gordon Jenkins arrangements. A number of minuscule but significant associations can be drawn out of the tape. On the tune "Glad to Be Unhappy," for example, the lyric "Unrequited love's a bore" arises, a phrase that forms a keystone of the *Pull My Daisy* soundtrack that Kerouac had recorded not long before. The texts that Kerouac reads on the tape suggest regression and perhaps the unconscious mechanisms that Kerouac prized in his writings, even though here he is not spontaneously weaving prose, but performing previously written materials.

Like Ginsberg, Kerouac did occasionally weave reference to Sinatra into his own writing. Where Ginsberg alludes to Sinatra's music and persona, Kerouac tends to restrict himself to the songs that pass through his mind. His recollection of Sinatra in relation to his stint as a fire spotter, isolated on a mountain in Washington, is borne out in the novels he constructed from that episode, *The Dharma Bums* and *Desolation Angels.* Both novels strongly represent confrontations, typical of Kerouac, Ginsberg, and the Beat Generation in general, of the sacred, particularly to be found in the alternative of Eastern religions, and the secular, with which they engaged every day in the post–World War II United States. In *The Dharma Bums,* the tension and equilibrium in Kerouac's own voice can be found in his account of his protagonist (surrogate) Ray Smith's visit with his mother and family:

Sunday afternoons my family would want me to go driving with them but I preferred to stay home alone, and they'd get mad and say "What's the matter with him anyway?" and I'd hear them argue about the futility of my "Buddhism" in the kitchen, then they'd all get in the car and leave and I'd go in the kitchen and sing "The tables are empty, everybody's gone over" to the tune of Frank Sinatra's "You're Learning the Blues." I was as nutty as a fruitcake and happier.[13]

As if to underscore the point, Kerouac reused the allusion and the connection to Buddhism in *Desolation Angels,* which recounts his and protagonist Jack Dulouoz's memory- and fantasy-filled isolation on a mountaintop, his "Desolation in Solitude," and their "Desolation in the World" on returning to community and, here, a San Francisco poetry reading:

"The tables are empty, everybody's gone over," I sing, to Sinatra's "You're Learning the Blues"—
    "O that empty business," laughs David. "Really Jack, I expect you to make a better show of what you really do know, than all these Buddhist negatives—"
    "O I'm not a Buddhist anymore—I'm not anything anymore!" I yell and he laughs and slaps me gently.[14]

In each novel, Kerouac scatters references to Sinatra, and other musicians of the mid-1950s that he documents and reimagines: the line, "Don't let the blues make you bad," he attributes to Sinatra; another memory of "In the Wee Small Hours"; "I sang 'I'm a Fool' the way home in the cab."[15] As in Ginsberg's poems, Kerouac's references to Sinatra and other examples of mass culture mark his work in time and lend them a recognizably historical dimension. For Kerouac, however, the roots of his personal affection for and emulation of Sinatra also filter through his fictional references.

The connotations and meanings that Ginsberg and Kerouac found in Sinatra were rather different from those cultural consumers of the 1950s and early 1960s might have drawn. As avatars of that cultural awareness generally encompassed by the term "hip," Frank Sinatra and the Beat Generation might seem to go together hand-in-glove, but the types that were generated around Sinatra and the Beats respectively were quite different. Sinatra was urbane, trim, and adult in both personality and appeal by comparison with his image of the 1940s. As a band singer, a solo performer, and Hollywood star, he held a distinctive place in a cultural mainstream. By contrast, the Beats were represented as unkempt, unorthodox, and unruly. Although Kerouac and other writers sought success in the mainstream, and his success was marked by achievement there—when *On the Road,* published by the respectable Viking Press, made the standard bestseller lists—Beat culture was also marked as ground-up, built around personal style, including dress and demeanor, and the activity of individuals and groups in such colonies as Greenwich Village, San Francisco's North Beach, Venice in Southern California, or communities in cities around the world.

The properties that the Beat generation, as a widely dispersed subculture distinct from the more concentrated literary movement, employed for self-definition were also adopted, appropriated, and co-opted. In the movies, television, cartoons, and other mass media, Beats became beatniks, and the diffusion of an image heralded the diffusion of a cultural activism.

A 1960 *MAD* magazine parody of the hit Broadway musical *My Fair Lady,* titled "My Fair Ad-Man" explicitly sets the beatnik at a pole opposite Madison Avenue.[16] Advertising executive Henry Higginbottom, represented by Cary Grant, bets colleague Charles Pickerwick, portrayed by Charles Laughton, that anyone can write advertising copy, even a beatnik he pulls from the gutter. Depicted as Frank Sinatra, aspiring novelist Irving Mallion (the supposed musical is based on the book, *You're a Pig, Mallion,* by George Bernard Schwartz, in the typically Yiddishized *MAD* world) wants only to publish his manuscript, *Son of On the Road.* In this case, a fictive Sinatra emulates Jack Kerouac and celebrates him in song—although imagining these lyrics in either Sinatra's or Kerouac's voice demands some imagination and work:

> All I want is a pad somewhere
> Way downtown near the Village Square,
> Without a phone or care . . .
> Oh, wouldn't it be Kerouac . . .
> Oh, so Kerouac caring nothing
> How the world lives on;
> I would never budge till it
> Was gone, like I mean real gone!

MAD, no. 54, "Son of On the Road." (© E. C. Publications. Used with permission. All rights reserved.)

MAD, no. 54, "My Fair Ad-Man." (© E. C. Publications. Used with permission. All rights reserved.)

But Higginbottom transforms the beatnik into a model man-in-a-gray-flannel-suit, and in the end, Mallion renounces his bohemianism and decides to burn the novel because, singing of Madison Avenue, he has "grown accustomed to this place."

As a beatnik, itself a stereotype, Mallion dresses in beret, coarse-woolen sweater, jeans, and sandals, and he wears a small goatee. His speech is littered with "man" and "like." When he arrives at the BVD & O agency, he is preceded by his odor. What transforms him into an ad-man is not "a little bit of luck," but "a little bit of soap." In the satire, the beat style is cluttered and dirty, the people naïve and idealistic. Madison Avenue is orderly and clean, but the ad-men remain opportunistic, facile, and idealess "yes-men." Ultimately, this is simply a matter of styles, and Mallion exchanges one style for the other, as easily as he gives up his "threads" for a Brooks Brothers suit.

Why cast Frank Sinatra—or a caricature of him—in this role? Arguably, this is less the Sinatra of 1960, the period of *Ocean's 11,* and more the pre-Beat, hipster-era Sinatra of wide-shouldered suits and floppy bowties who is attached to the part. Even more likely, it is the Sinatra of *The Man With the Golden Arm* (1955) five years before, the card-dealer/junkie/drummer Frankie Machine, who forms the strongest link with the Beat subculture, a character who combines associations with drugs, poverty, the underworld, and the promise that modern music might represent. Reading "My Fair Ad-Man," allowing for all the brilliantly juvenile parody characteristic of *MAD,* it is possible to hear the voice of the Sinatra persona speaking such lines as Mallion's opener: "Man, like I've been on an all-night kick, and I'm nowhere, Dads! So clue me in! Where am I?" A means of determining inclusion and exclusion in subcultures, lingo was one of the significant features of the Beat generation, as it was one of the ways that Sinatra defined his persona and the constitution of his inner circle. Anyone who could not understand what was being said was not part of the crowd. Many extended commentaries of the Beats contemporary to the movement, which could be seen as touristic guidebooks as much as social or cultural inquiries, included a discussion of jargon, generally with a dictionary to define such terminology as "to blow," "to bug out," or a "pad" or a "chick."[17] Similarly, commentators from Arnold Shaw to Bill Zehme have included glossaries or discussions of Sinatra's verbal codes and the appeal of a "gasser" and the distinction (if there is one) between a "Harvey" and a "Clyde."[18] There were, then, correspondences between moments in Sinatra's fictional and public personas that made his casting in this cartoon fiction plausible despite the differences between the character types.

It is perhaps only when we look at the start of the story of "My Fair Ad-Man," when Irving Mallion is the unwashed beatnik, that the dissonance appears prominent. At the end, Mallion winds up clean and erudite. He sings (to the tune of "I've Grown Accustomed to Her Face"):

> You see, I've grown to be dependent
> on my clothes from Italy;
> The snide remarks and insults
> I now make so wittily;
> I've grown accustomed to the life;

> Accustomed to the dough;
> Accustomed to this place.

In other words, Irving Mallion has been transformed from a beatnik, with whom we may draw correspondences to properties in the Frank Sinatra who portrays him, into an image consistent with the more recognizable Frank Sinatra. It is a transformation that Mallion's mentor grows to lament, recognizing distinctions with which Allen Ginsberg and Jack Kerouac might have agreed. "We ruined him . . . ," Higginbottom laments. "[H]is mind was fresh and clean, free of the falseness of our world. And we threw him into it . . . chin deep."[19]

Notes

1. Roy Carr et al., *The Hip, Hipsters, Jazz and the Beat Generation* (London: Faber and Farber, 1986), 11.

2. Carr et al., *The Hip, Hipsters, Jazz and the Beat Generation,* 39.

3. Allen Ginsberg, *Collected Poems 1947–1980* (New York: Harper and Row, 1984), 371.

4. Ginsberg, *Collected Poems 1947–1980,* 468–69.

5. Ginsberg, *Collected Poems 1947–1980,* 720.

6. Ginsberg, *Collected Poems 1947–1980,* 195.

7. Blaine Allan, "The Making (and Unmaking) of *Pull My Daisy," Film History* 2 (1988): 185–205.

8. Gerald Nicosia, *Memory Babe: A Critical Biography of Jack Kerouac* (New York: Grove Press, 1983), 42, 66, 77.

9. Nicosia, *Memory Babe,* 538.

10. David Perry, booklet article, "The Jack Kerouac Collection," 7, in *The Jack Kerouac Collection,* Rhino, CD R 70939, © 1990.

11. Gerald Nicosia, "Off the Road: A Portfolio of Kerouac Photos," in *Beat Angels,* edited by Arthur Knight and Kit Knight (California, PA: Unspeakable Visions of the Individual, 1982), 69.

12. Michael McClure, "Jack's *Old Angel Midnight," Old Angel Midnight,* by Jack Kerouac, edited by Donald Allen (San Francisco: Grey Fox Press, 1993), xx.

13. Jack Kerouac, *The Dharma Bums* (New York: New American Library, 1959), 112–13.

14. Jack Kerouac, *Desolation Angels* (New York: G. P. Putnam, 1980), 187.

15. Kerouac, *Dharma Bums,* 118, 187; *Desolation Angels,* 295.

16. Anon. [and Mort Drucker], "My Fair Ad-Man," *MAD* 54 (April 1960) [reprinted in *William M. Gaines's Three Ring MAD,* edited by Albert B. Feldstein (New York: New American Library, 1964), 99–125].

17. See for example, Lawrence Lipton, *The Holy Barbarians* (New York: Julian Messner, 1959); and Francis J. Rigney and L. Douglas Smith, *The Real Bohemia: A Sociological and Psychological Study of the "Beats"* (New York: Basic Books, 1961).

18. Arnold Shaw, *Sinatra: Retreat of the Romantic* (London: W. H. Allen, 1968), 367–68. See also, Bill Zehme, *The Way You Wear Your Hat: Frank Sinatra and the Lost Art of Livin'* (New York: Harper Collins, 1997), 35–39.

19. Anon [and Drucker], "My Fair Ad-Man," 121.

9

Sinatra in (Lyrical) Drag

Philip Furia

In his book, *Sinatra! The Song Is You: A Singer's Art,* Will Friedwald cites "Some-one to Watch over Me" as the kind of song Sinatra sang to project a poignant, vul-nerable persona so that "bobby-soxers wanted to mother him as well as wrestle him in the back of a DeSoto."[1] There are two significant facts about that choice of song that I want to explore in this chapter. First, at the time he recorded it, "Some-one to Watch over Me" was an old song from an almost forgotten Broadway musi-cal, *Oh, Kay!,* which George Gershwin wrote with his brother Ira in 1926. Second, it was written for a female performer—Gertrude Lawrence.

So many of the songs Sinatra has helped transform into standards—"April in Paris," "The Lady Is a Tramp," "Little Girl Blue," "My Funny Valentine," "I Get a Kick Out of You," "Just One of those Things," "It Never Entered My Mind," "But Not for Me," and "Bewitched, Bothered and Bewildered"—were also written for fe-male performers—Ginger Rogers, Vivienne Segal, Ethel Merman—in Broadway shows of the late 1920s and 1930s. By contrast, Sinatra has recorded relatively few songs from Broadway musicals from his own era, the so-called age of "integration" that was launched with the 1943 Rodgers and Hammerstein production of *Oklahoma!* Why did Sinatra choose to sing songs from these old shows and why did he confine himself almost exclusively to songs written for women? Finally, how did the singing of such "female" songs help define his singing persona?

While Broadway songs before *Oklahoma!* may have lacked full integration into the characters and story of the book, theater songs of the 1920s and 1930s had a re-lated quality, sometimes dubbed "particularity," which sets them apart from the more banal products of Tin Pan Alley. "Someone to Watch over Me," for example, takes the standard Alley cliché of a girl longing for the boy of her dreams but gives it a fresh twist that defines it apart from other songs cast in this mold. Although the singer is yearning for an unnamed "someone," instead of innocence she exudes a world-weary sophistication. Although she has not found her lover yet, she says, with an air of hardened experience, that he is her biggest, most unforgettable, and only regrettable love affair. Similarly, while she portrays herself as a poor, lost lamb, she is also aggressively seeking the man of her dreams and demanding that he speed up his arrival, adding a dimension to her character that is considerably unlamblike.

Within the musical *Oh, Kay!*, the song "Someone to Watch over Me" had little relation to character or plot. In fact, it was so lacking in integration that the star, Gertrude Lawrence, sang it in the middle of act 2, long after she had met, kissed, and cavorted with the leading man. Audiences of the time, however, cared more for the song than the story. To showcase the song, Lawrence, instead of singing it directly to the audience from center stage, as was customary, stood off to the side and sang to a rag doll she cradled in her arms. With that introspective, dramatic delivery, "Someone to Watch over Me," as one critic put it, "wrung the withers of even the most hard-hearted" and provided the audience "with an experience they would remember and relate for years.[2] Those same words could describe the effect of a Sinatra performance on a nightclub audience. It was to such particularized songs that Sinatra was drawn, songs where he could place himself, even without scenery, costume, or props, into the character and dramatic situation evoked by the lyrics, creating what he liked to call "saloon songs."

But why was he drawn to songs written for women? In the formulaic boy-meets-loses-then regains-girl plots of the day, romantic ballads of longing or lament were assigned to female characters on the conventional assumption that women were more given to wistful or melancholy effusions, while male characters were more often given songs of romantic importunity. In the Gershwins' *Girl Crazy* (1930), for example, Ginger Rogers sang the mournful "But Not for Me," while Alex Kearns had the more forthright plea of "Embraceable You." By singing both kinds of songs from Broadway shows of this era, Sinatra extended the emotional range of his singing persona, and when he did an album of romantic laments such as *Only the Lonely,* the lyrics defined subtle emotional facets of that character.

In order to adapt songs written for female characters in Broadway musicals, however, Sinatra usually had to alter the lyrics, sometimes quite extensively. What is striking about his rendition of "Someone to Watch over Me" is that he did not sing the "male" version of the lyric which Ira Gershwin, as lyricists typically did, wrote for male vocalists who wanted to perform or record the song apart from the musical as an independent number. In rewriting the lyric for a male singer, Gershwin eliminated his rhyme of *handsome* with *man some,* but Sinatra chose to sing the female version, changing "he" to "I" but keeping the clever rhyme.

In such adaptations, Sinatra only compounds the gender crossings already present in the original lyric, which, like many Broadway songs written for female performers, gets some of its particularity by having the woman sound like a man. When Ginger Rogers sang "But Not for Me," for example, Ira Gershwin gave her pugnacious lines and gritty invectives. Similarly, in "Someone to Watch over Me" he had the supposedly little-lamb-like persona assume an aggressively "masculine" posture by demanding that her lover follow her lead. By adapting previously feminine lyrics that had been masculinized, Sinatra used songs like "Someone to Watch over Me" and "But Not for Me" to project, beyond his streetwise, tough-guy stage presence, a poignant, vulnerable, and "lost" persona.

The era that produced such richly "particular" Broadway songs for him to draw upon might have been very short-lived. Already in 1927, Oscar Hammerstein and Jerome Kern moved beyond "particularity" toward "integration" when they wrote *Show Boat.* Hammerstein himself adapted Edna Ferber's novel into a libretto that closely wove songs like "Ol' Man River" and "Can't Help Lovin' Dat Man" into the story and its characters. Yet the age of the fully integrated musical was still some fifteen years away. While Hammerstein wanted to move further in the direction of integration, other songwriters, such as Porter, the Gershwins, and even Kern himself still thought more in terms of the song than the story. More than anything else, however, it was the crash of 1929 and the Depression that retarded the evolutionary development of the Broadway musical. Beginning with *The Little Revue* of 1929, "book" shows gave way to the loose format of "little revues" with their self-contained songs and sketches where the emphasis was upon wit and sophistication rather than huge casts and lavish sets. That emphasis increased the need for "particularity" in songs, where a lyric created its own sense of character and dramatic situation. When a producer was fortunate enough to get a beautiful set—even a second-hand set from another show—she wanted a song that would take full advantage of it. Thus when the producer of the 1932 revue *Walk a Little Faster,* inherited a Parisian set, he summoned his songwriters to create a number around it. The composer, a Russian émigré named Vernon Duke (formerly Vladimir Dukelsky) had lived in Paris and easily tossed off a sophisticated, haunting melody. However, the lyricist, E. Y. "Yip" Harburg, who had grown up wretchedly poor on New York's Lower East Side, had to go to Cook's travel agency, grab some brochures, and, seated at Lindy's restaurant in New York, wonder what Paris was like. It would have been easy for him to conjure up the hackneyed theme of "Paris in the spring," where one thinks of a lost lover from youth. What Harburg came up with, however, was a clever twist to that cliché—a woman who has never been in love but is so moved by Paris that she wishes she *had* been in love so that now she *could* have such memories of springtime charms and warm embraces.

Because Harburg had designed his lyric to be sung by a female performer, Evelyn Hoey, Sinatra had to omit the verse for the song. Harburg's feminine verse details April wearing a gown, waltzing along a Parisian street, and getting drunk on the mere whiff of wine. Verses were a holdover from the nineteenth century, where songs alternated between verse and chorus, but by 1920, the verse served merely to introduce the chorus (or, as it is sometimes called, the refrain). Pop singers frequently omitted the verses of songs, but Sinatra retained them when they suited his purpose (he even made a separate recording of the verse—and only the verse—from Mitchell Parish and Hoagy Carmichael's "Stardust").

While verses were not important in pop performances of songs, they were a critical component of Broadway songs (and thus for Sinatra's adaptations of theater songs). The melody of a verse was usually less opulent than that of the chorus, and the lyric was closer to speech, so that a verse served to ease the transition from dialogue to singing as performers "talked" their way into the full-throated lyricism of the chorus. In romantic stage duets, there was often a "boy's" verse and a "girl's" verse, while the chorus, which the romantic leads usually sang together, was "unisex." That androgynous chorus, where a genderless "I" croons to an equally ambiguous "you," meant that a song could receive maximum exposure beyond the show by male and female singers through radio and recordings. In the case of "April in Paris," however, there was only a "girl's" verse, so that all Sinatra could do was omit it. However, he created the feel of a verse by taking a section from the chorus, the part usually called the "bridge" or "release" (since it differs musically from the other three sections of songs built on the common AABA formula) and making it introduce the song as well. Thus, his version of "April in Paris" starts out with the bridge, lamenting his ignorance of springtime's charms, then leads into the chorus with the song's title line.

Sinatra performed a similar restructuring of "Little Girl Blue" from Rodgers and Hart's 1935 production of *Jumbo*. Written for Gloria Grafton, the song had no verse but did have a "Trio Patter" section that served as a transition between the chorus and its reprise. Hart wrote the trio patter as the woman's memory of her youth, when the world seemed like a circus tent strung with stars. In the chorus, Hart has her address herself in the second person—as if she were her own naughty child who had to be told to sit down and count on her fingers. That second-person address made Hart's chorus appropriate for male as well as female vocalists, and Sinatra's choice to sing the "Trio Patter" section had the advantage of making his own persona seem more sympathetic toward the woman he addresses, empathizing with her childhood dreams but also offering the brutally honest advice that she recognizes that her love affair is over, so that he seems a paternal friend who commiserates with, rather than chides, his "Little Girl Blue."

By the mid-1930s, "book" musicals like *Jumbo* had begun to return to Broadway, but songs remained "particular" rather than integral, providing Sinatra with more of the kind of self-contained lyrical drama he could adapt for his own performances. In addition to "Little Girl Blue," *Jumbo* gave him "The Most Beautiful Girl in the World" and "My Romance." He found an even richer store in Rodgers and Hart's 1937 musical, *Babes in Arms,* which provided him with no fewer than four superb standards—"Where or When," "I Wish I Were in Love Again," "The Lady Is a Tramp," and "My Funny Valentine." The first two numbers were done as duets, so he could sing them with little or no alteration, and all he had to do with "Lady Is a Tramp," originally written as a solo for Mitzi Green, was change "I" to "she" in lines about not waiting to eat dinner too late or arriving late at the theater. Arguably, Sinatra's version is more effective as a man's defense of the unconventional woman he loves than the original, in which the woman herself pugnaciously flaunts her disdain for affectation.

A more profound change occurs when he sings "My Funny Valentine," which in the show was sung by Mitzi Green to Ray Heatherton (who played a character named Valentine). Like Shakespeare's sonnet, "My mistress' eyes are nothing like the sun," Hart's lyric overturns traditional romantic compliments and deals realistically and ironically with a lover lacking in any apparent charm. Instead of praising her beloved's features, the singer mocks his laughable looks, less-than-Greek figure, and weak mouth that when he speaks betrays his dim-witted thoughts. Such imagery is conventionally more applicable to a male rather than a female character, as is the formula of a beautiful woman in love with a homely man. For Sinatra to sing such a lyric *to* a woman required a complete recasting of the tone of the song. Instead of singing it with coy, tongue-in-cheek mockery, Sinatra rendered "My Funny Valentine" with straightforward, almost solemn, sentiment.

To do so, he again had to eliminate the verse that was so critical in balancing the lyric's ironies in the Broadway production. For one thing, the verse contains definite indications that the singer is female, such as her calling her lover a "gent." However, the verse was also laced with archaisms, such as "thou" and "thy," which allowed the singer to temper her mockery while holding her real emotions at bay with romantic hyperbole. By omitting the flippant verse and starting in directly at the chorus, with a hushed and reverent invocation of the title phrase, Sinatra brings out the song's understated sentiment. By the time he reaches the plea that his lover, for all of her faults, not even change a hair to please him, the line comes off not as an affectionate afterthought but a passionate climax.

He performed a similar transformation on Cole Porter's "Just One of Those Things," which in *Jubilee* (1935) was sung as a duet by the romantic leads. Again, the verse, with its allusions to Dorothy Parker and Abelard and Eloise, made the singers too literate and sophisticated for Sinatra's taste. Moreover, when Porter has Juliet tell Romeo to wake up and realize that their affair was merely a casual fling, it makes the singers dismiss the break-up of their romance with coolly casual aplomb. By starting in at the chorus, Sinatra again makes the lyric more passionately remorseful at the passing of an affair that, as a gossamer-winged trip to the moon, was hardly as trivial as the title phrase implies.

When a verse suited his persona, however, Sinatra retained it. For Porter's "I Get a Kick Out of You," from the 1934 *Anything Goes,* he sings the verse exactly as Porter had written it for Ethel Merman. Although it had touches of urbane elegance, such as the singer's lament that she is battling a chronic case of ennui, the verse leads into the chorus with a vernacular punch as she suddenly sees her beloved's face. For the unmiked Merman, the line was an invitation to blare a perfectly enunciated compliment to the last row of the balcony; Sinatra, however, delivers the line more as speech than song, an understatedly spoken declaration of love at first sight that then launches him into the chorus.

It was there that the lyric underwent major surgery. Some of Sinatra's alterations, such as "You give me a boot," were probably his own improvisations. It may have been such liberties that supposedly prompted Porter to say to Sinatra, "If you don't like my songs as I wrote them, please do not sing them." Nonetheless, the "boot" line gives the lyric a slangy kick that offsets Porter's more archly elegant phrases.

More problematic are the lyrics that Sinatra frequently sang in place of Porter's own lines about sniffing cocaine. Sinatra sometimes sang Porter's original lyric, as

Merman did, with a deliciously ironic pause that underlined the rhyme between *sniff* and *terrif—ically* and suggested that perhaps a sniff of cocaine might not be as kickless as the lyric asserts. In other versions, however, he sang lines Porter did not write, about a "whiff" of a "perfume from Spain" and a "riff" from a bop refrain. The alterations probably were made to avoid problems with censors, but it is more interesting to speculate about who made them, as well as who made the many other changes in lyrics that Sinatra sang. Some have suspected that it was lyricist Sammy Cahn who refashioned lyrics for Sinatra. Cahn, who wrote many original songs for Sinatra, such as "I Should Care" and "My Kind of Town," claimed to have guided the singer toward the work of the generation of superb songwriters who had preceded him. "I take great pride in the fact that I introduced Frank to a lot of the great, great songs," Cahn said. "That was our love, all of us. We loved the great standards. How are you not going to love them? Whenever we'd be around someplace, we'd always play the great songs . . . I [would say] Frank, there's a song . . . Because he's got a good sense of music, you can lay a song on him, [and he'll say], 'Oh, geez, that's good. Let me have that!' "[3] With his tremendous admiration for the artistry of lyricists like Hart, Gershwin, and Porter, Cahn, if it was his work, must have taken a secret delight in revising their words to suit Sinatra's persona. In most cases, the revisions are so astute that they go unnoticed, though at times they mar the original, such as substituting "gal" for "guy" in a skein of rhymes that included *guy, sky, fly*ing, *high,* and *i*-dea.

If Sinatra did have Cahn's help, it might help explain why he was able to take one of those lengthy, allusive Porter "catalog" song of the 1930s and edit it down to enough lines of enduring significance to turn it from a period piece into a standard. The title song from Porter's 1934 *Anything Goes* listed many contemporary figures, from Sam Goldwyn and Anna Held to wealthy families, such as the Vanderbilts and Whitneys, who had been impoverished by the Depression to illustrate the point of the title phrase. "Anything Goes" also referred to the moral abandon of the era, and Porter had Ethel Merman catalog the shocking goings-on in newly opened bars after the lifting of Prohibition and nudist parties in Hollywood studios.

Ignoring all of the contemporary allusions and the sophisticated flaunting of convention, Sinatra carved out lines from different parts of the catalog to create a persona who is not a frenetic participant in the mad revels of the age but a bemused observer of them. By adding a line not in any of Porter's versions of the song—"when most guys today that women prize today are just silly gigolos"—Sinatra further distances himself from the moral abandon. He concludes his version of "Anything Goes" with a marriage proposal, saying that while he knows he is no great lover, in a world where "anything goes," he is sure his beloved will accept this most traditional of propositions.

No catalog song of the period underwent a greater sea change in Sinatra's hands than "Bewitched" from Rodgers and Hart's 1940 production, *Pal Joey.* The show, which was based on a series of satirical stories by John O'Hara about a small-time gigolo, was attacked by critics for its gritty departure from the usual frothy formulas of musical comedy. "Bewitched," in particular, was singled out by critic Brooks Atkinson as a "scabrous" lyric.[4] In the show, it was sung by Vivienne Segal in the role of a horny, hard-nosed, and well-heeled ex-stripper who finances a night club for Joey, played by a young Gene Kelly in his first starring role on Broadway. After a drunken romp, Segal wakes up to find the diminutive Joey still out cold on the floor, and she sings "Bewitched" as a cynical commentary on their affair. The verse begins with her astonishment that after drinking a quart of brandy, she does not have the shakes, and she attributes her lack of a hangover to Joey's sexual prowess. Through a series of choruses, she celebrates her new-found joy even though she realizes it is based purely on lust. She lists his faults—he's a ridiculous gigolo who is just sleeping with her for her money—yet she admits he makes her feel like a sexually hungry schoolgirl again. As originally written, "Bewitched" is one of most unsentimental—even antisentimental—songs Hart or any lyricist ever wrote, and its acerbity is heightened by the fact that it is sung by a female character who is far removed from the typical Broadway ingénue.

In Sinatra's hands, however, "Bewitched" becomes a tender ballad of romantic enthrallment. Selecting bits and pieces from its four choruses, Sinatra, presumably again with Sammy Cahn's expert help, pieced together a lyric that bears little resemblance to its original. Where Hart's character vowed to worship the trousers—and clearly what's in the trousers—that "cling" to Joey, Sinatra's persona longs for the "day" he will chastely cling to his beloved. The original line where Segal calls Joey a laugh then adds that "the laugh" is "on" her is a naughty pun on "on," but in Sinatra's tender "male" version of the lyric the sexual innuendo disappears. "Bewitched" even loses its catalog character and becomes a streamlined love song. Its particularity inheres in the persona who mocks his infatuation even as he delights in it, yet Sinatra's version of the verse begins not with downing a quarter of brandy but the gently self-deprecating recognition that he is a romantic fool.

Pal Joey was one of the last Broadway shows Sinatra was able to mine for "particular" songs, and "Bewitched" is so much a part of the story and characters of the show it actually anticipates the era of the "integrated" song. That era arrived in full force in 1943, when Richard Rodgers turned from Lorenz Hart to Oscar Hammerstein as his collaborator on *Oklahoma!* After *Oklahoma!*, songs had to be integrated into the dramatic situation of a musical and be closely tied to the character who sang them. The role of the lyricist in a musical also changed after *Oklahoma!* Ira Gershwin, Lorenz Hart, and Cole Porter saw themselves as pure lyricists and never attempted to write the book of a musical, a task they invariably left to a playwright. Cole Porter, in fact, always puzzled over why anyone would want to "write book," because the story of a musical was usually nothing more than a clothesline for hanging songs. For these lyricists, a good show was a show with many good songs, and they measured success of the show by the number of songs from the score that went on to become independently popular through sheet music and record sales.

In the era of integration, by contrast, Broadway marquees usually carried the phrase "Book and Lyrics by . . ." Oscar Hammerstein, Alan Jay Lerner, or Frank Loesser. Such lyricist-librettists adapted existing literary works—James Michener's *Tales of the South Pacific*, George Bernard Shaw's *Pygmalion*, Damon Runyon's *Guys and Dolls*—into a libretto where they could create the dramatic context for their songs. Despite their integral relation to the book of a musical, such songs frequently went on to become independently popular. *Oklahoma!* was one of the first musicals to produce an original cast recording—a boxed set of 78 rpm records—so that even people who had not seen the show could listen to the score. Consequently, some of the most integral songs from the show—"The Surrey with the Fringe on Top," "I'm Just a Girl Who Cain't Say 'No,'" "Kansas City"—became hits. With the advent of the LP in the 1950s, the cast album could fit on a single disk. At the same time, Hollywood turned away from creating original film musicals, such as *Top Hat* and *Meet Me in St. Louis,* and instead merely made cinematic versions of Broadway shows, thus making the scores even more familiar. By the mid-1950s, such integral songs as "The Rain in Spain" from *My Fair Lady* and "Trouble" from *The Music Man* could be heard on radio's Top 40.

Significantly, however, Sinatra recorded relatively few songs from the era of the integrated Broadway musical. To be sure, he did "Almost like Being in Love" from *Brigadoon,* "Luck Be a Lady" from *Guys and Dolls,* and "I Could Have Danced All Night" from *My Fair Lady.* However, most integrated songs from this era, such as "Bali Hai" from *South Pacific* or "Maria" from *West-Side Story,* are so recognizable as "show tunes" that it would have been difficult for him to transform them into saloon songs. Occasionally, as with "Send in the Clowns" from Stephen Sondheim's *A Little Night Music,* he found a song with the kind of particularity he sought, but after *Oklahoma!,* the Broadway musical was no longer a treasure house of songs for him.

In going back to the musical theater of the 1920s and 1930s, Sinatra was actually turning to the lyricists who had preceded his own contemporary songwriters such as Johnny Mercer and Sammy Cahn. Those lyricists, who primarily wrote for Hollywood films, continued to create songs with particularity long after Broadway lyricists, such as Sheldon Harnick and Stephen Sondheim, had embraced the principle of integration. Mercer's "One for My Baby" and "Something's Gotta Give," Cahn's "I Guess I'll Hang My Tears Out to Dry" and "Call Me Irresponsible," are squarely in the lyrical idiom of Hart, Porter, and Gershwin. Neither Mercer nor Cahn had success on the Broadway stage, even though their collaborators, such as Harold Arlen and Jule Styne, went on to triumph with other lyricists on shows such as *House of Flowers* and *Gentlemen Prefer Blondes.* Along with such lyricists as Tom Adair ("Everything Happens to Me") and Carolyn Leigh ("Witchcraft"), Mercer and Cahn maintained the tradition of the particular song that evokes its own sense of drama and character.

By directing Sinatra to his own lyrical forebears, Sammy Cahn did a double service. Not only did he provide Sinatra with superb material, he helped songs from forgotten Broadway musicals of the 1920s and 1930s to become standards. If it was indeed Sammy Cahn who artfully altered the lyrics of the great masters, his service was even more valuable. Had it not been for his changing a line about singing a *maiden's* prayer to singing a *lonely* prayer, Sinatra might never have recorded a gem like "It Never Entered My Mind," which Rodgers and Hart wrote for Shirley Ross in the 1938 musical *Higher and Higher.* Although Sinatra could not sing lines about wearing makeup, having a hairdo, and putting a mudpack on his face, he could salvage enough from the catalog of choruses, to add yet another poignant, sophisticated, and subtly "female" dimension to his singing persona. He, in turn, did equal wonders for the songs he took from Broadway. If they supplied him with literate wit, urbane elegance, and tender vulnerability, he rendered them with a sensuous, vernacular, emotional power that they often lacked in their original stage performances. To paraphrase Katherine Hepburn's famous (and probably apocryphal) remark about Fred Astaire and Ginger Rogers, if these Broadway songs gave Sinatra "class," he gave them "balls."

Notes

1. Friedwald, *Sinatra! The Song Is You: The Singer's Art*, 156.
2. Wayne Shirley, "Introduction," *Oh Kay!* Smithsonian Collection Recording, LP R 0085, 1928.
3. Friedwald, *Sinatra! The Song Is You: The Singer's Art,* 156.
4. Dorothy Hart, ed., *Thou Swell, Thou Witty* (New York: Harper and Row, 1979), 155.

10

Sinatra Meets Television:
A Search for Identity in Fifties America

Ron Simon

After he died on May 14, 1998, Frank Sinatra was eulogized as the personification of American show business. His conquest of the entertainment industry was glorified in what *Entertainment Weekly* editor David Hajdu labeled "a grand media memorial," the most effusive since the assassination of President John F. Kennedy. Most commentators agreed with art critic John Rockwell's assessment that Sinatra's life "touched on innumerable facets of our culture" for more than fifty years.[1] In all the countless articles, one question that haunted Sinatra was never fully answered: Why did America's most successful entertainer have so much trouble with America's most popular medium of entertainment, television, in the fifties? In fact, *TV Guide*'s 1954 criticism became a prophesy for the whole decade: "TV has been a sour note in the Sinatra symphony of success, which includes juke box, variety, stage, night club, and, as his recent Oscar attests, movies."[2]

Frank Sinatra embraced television at two distinct periods in his fifties career—the first in the early fifties when he was in the depths of unpopularity and commercial failure and the second, in the late fifties, when he was at the height of his recording artistry and financial security. During each period, he presented a new persona to the public and, although conditions in his career and the circumstances in television were vastly different, both series failed to connect with the general audience. At one point, even the indefatigable Sinatra declared the "TV racket's too tough!"[3]

In the early fifties, television was a frightening medium to even this country's most seasoned performers. In December 1950, *Variety*'s lead article underlined the anxiety engendered by the demands of live television.[4] Four from show business's all-time pantheon—Fred Allen, Jack Benny, Eddie Cantor, and Jimmy Durante ("The A-B-C-Ds of Comedy")—all agreed that television was a confusing medium and that there was no set pattern to a successful weekly series. These four giants, headliners since the twenties, decided to limit their exposure before the appetite of television devoured them. These veteran vaudevillians, who appeared on countless stages throughout the country, were wary of appearing one night a week in a television studio.

Two months before that *Variety* report, Frank Sinatra, with less than ten years under his solo belt, began hosting his own variety series, seen live every Saturday night. From the earliest days of television, following the convention established in vaudeville and radio, the variety show had been marked by the dominance of the host. Whether it was the energetic slapstick of Milton Berle or the down-home folksiness of Arthur Godfrey, the host personified the essence of the show, serving as connective tissue for the entire proceedings. Especially crucial to the role of the host was the opening monologue, in which the master of ceremonies defined his character each week. For instance, Berle's opening remarks were a combination of insults, wordplays, and running gags about his mother and brother Frank. In this way, Berle and other masters, like Bob Hope and Jack Benny, created a character with whom the audience would identify each week—Berle, the urban trickster; Hope, the breezy wise guy; and Benny, the vain cheapskate.

When Sinatra began hosting his series on October 7, 1950, it was the beginning of his self-confessed dark period. Instead of bringing a well-defined character to television, Sinatra was using his series to discover himself. He had just lost three crucial individuals who had helped foster his public identity in the forties: Emmanuel "Manie" Sacks, who had masterminded his recording persona, left Columbia Records in January; later that month, George Evans, Sinatra's trusted public relations agent, died; and in April, Louis B. Mayer, who had engineered his movie image, fired him from MGM. Without his mentors, Sinatra could not even count on the one thing that never failed him, his voice. In April, he cancelled the last two days of his Copacabana engagement because of a vocal-cord hemorrhage.

Having suffered momentous setbacks in the recording studio, nightclubs, and the movies, Sinatra was hoping to salvage his career in the upstart medium of television. Most biographers have deemed the turning point in Sinatra's comeback to be *From Here to Eternity* (1953). Sinatra, however, in a September 14, 1956 interview with Edward R. Murrow on *Person to Person* attributed his redemption to an appearance on a Bob Hope television special on May 27, 1950. This was Sinatra's first performance on the small screen, and, according to Sinatra, the industry was watching "to see if I could get off the canvas." Sinatra chose an unusual number to mark his inaugural appearance, "Come Rain or Come Shine," a song he had not yet officially recorded and would not record for eleven years. In his later years, Sinatra would call this Harold Arlen–Johnny Mercer standard the greatest in the American treasury of song. Perhaps, in selecting the classic "Come Rain or Come Shine," he was making a personal statement, committing himself to a new maturity and confidence. We can only speculate whom (or what) Sinatra, at his nadir, would love despite the inclement weather: perhaps Ava Gardner, with whom Sinatra was conducting a scandalous romance; perhaps his loyal audience, who always stood by Frankie no matter what; perhaps his talent, which always got him through the messy times. Sinatra also sparkled in routines, even spoofing the singer who inspired him, Bing Crosby. He credited his unexpected success to Hope's writers for building sketches around his limited comic abilities. *Variety* declared Sinatra a "video natural."[5]

This guest appearance gave Sinatra a psychological boost and a revived presence in the business. William Paley, chairman of CBS, certainly took notice and signed him to a multiyear contract, worth $250,000 a year. Sinatra was contracted to host a weekly television variety show and star in a radio series, *Meet Frank Sinatra*. Paley had also signed such talent as George Burns, Red Skelton, and Amos 'n' Andy, betting that the established stars would continue to generate advertising dollars on radio, while giving legitimacy to his new television network. Not a good sign, Sinatra's radio program, a curious mélange of singing and chatting with the audience, was canceled after nine months. CBS was not a great innovator in the production of television variety shows. The network lagged behind NBC in the development of color technology and, consequently, did not encourage elaborate production numbers or lavish sets. Paley paid big money for the talent and required his stars to carry the show—not the best premise for a man still struggling with his identity and self-esteem.

Not Ready for Prime Time

There were great expectations for *The Frank Sinatra Show* for the 1950 fall season. With stars of Sinatra's magnitude making their debut, the pre–Walter Annenberg *TV Guide* proclaimed that the week of September 16 augured "The Dawn of TV's Golden Age!" (perhaps the first use of that Augustan term). Sinatra's one-hour show was telecast live from New York at 9:00 p.m. and sponsored by the Bulova Watch Company. The songs would be the key to the series—usually presented straightforward in front of a curtain. Comedy bits were interspersed throughout the program, making it feel like an old-time Broadway revue. A supporting company of regular comedians, including Ben Blue, initially helped Sinatra with the routines. His long-time Columbia arranger, Axel Stordahl, recognized for his lush strings and romantic ballads, supervised the music. Nevertheless, the onus of the entire series rested on Sinatra's thin frame.

Behind the scenes, the writers grappled with the essential elements of the Sinatra character, trying to figure out how the romantic singer of the forties fit into postwar America. Of course, there were constant jokes about his skinniness, but they wore very quickly. That fact was visually apparent and was not compelling to nourish a well-rounded character, week in and week out. Besides that, the boy singer in a bow tie had grown up and so had his public, no longer in bobby socks. Sinatra was now competing against mature voices for a grown-up male and female audience. There were new and more popular sounds in the air—the relaxed style of Perry Como and the melodramatic belting of Frankie Laine. How do you define Frank Sinatra for a new generation, especially when he was not the hottest recording artist in town? One strategy was to make jokes made about the singer's dwindling fortunes. In sketch after sketch, Sinatra was always trying to make extra money. In one routine, Sinatra, his clothes torn, is running away from his fabled bobbysoxers—his lament is "they thought I was Frankie . . . Laine." The producers defined Sinatra by his past, targeting girls who grew up with him during the war. When he introduced one of his songs that was currently on the charts, Sinatra acted surprised and said, almost in shock, "Guess what . . . *I* have a hit."

Mocking his lowly status in show business is not a quality associated with Sinatra. He was always the cocky welterweight from Hoboken, not one to walk away from a fight with self-deprecating humor. There were certainly other options in constructing a viable persona: What if the series had been called *Sing and Dance with Frank Sinatra* after his little appreciated 1950 Columbia recording? Here Sinatra was engaged in the sounds and moods of the day, totally up-to-date. But no one in Sinatra's camp conceived him yet as a free and easy swinger, appealing to women and men alike, so they continued to struggle to make him relevant to an early fifties female audience. Sinatra even grew a thin, Cesar Romero-style moustache, but the suavity of a Latin lover was not his personality. And there was also no need to create an unattainable romantic fantasy because Sinatra's adolescents were now married women. In later shows, Sinatra dispensed with the facial ornaments and the awkward opening monologues, where he could have revealed new sides to himself, and just sang his old hits. To make matters worse, the producers were never able to correct the faults that *Variety* criticized in the initial review of the show: "Production wise, those responsible for getting the program before the camera kept throwing some inexcusable curves at Sinatra. It was bad pacing, bad scripting, bad tempo, poor camera work and an overall jerky presentation."[6]

The writers were most effective in connecting Sinatra with his forties accomplishments. Several times, they recreated Sinatra's filmed ode to brotherhood, *The House I Live In* as a live dramatic sketch. Six years after being recognized with a special Academy Award, the piece by blacklisted writer Albert Maltz still had sting, but certain changes were necessitated by the Cold War atmosphere. The final two countries in Sinatra's plea for tolerance—"Should I hate your father 'cause he came from Ireland or France or Russia?"—were altered to Sweden and Holland. The year 1950 marked the beginnings of McCarthyism, and persecution of Nordics was not the issue of the day. No wonder the sketch and stirring song by Lewis Allen and Earl Robinson did not generate the controversy it did in 1945, when Sinatra was denied a visa because of alleged Communist associations. The additions of Sweden and Holland made the whole segment innocuous, probably just the way the network wanted it. Early in the run of Sinatra's series, CBS was the first network to institute loyalty oaths and the legal department, which was also managing the blacklisting effort, would have rejected any positive mention of Russia. Politics notwithstanding, Sinatra was certainly having trouble with the current "house" he was living in, the Columbia Broadcasting System, and began referring to himself, in rhyme no less, as "Paley's bad guess on CBS."

The producers tried to help energize the show by finding guest stars who would be compatible with Sinatra and had a flair for television. Some guests were from his distant past—Rudy Vallee, the Pied Pipers, the Andrew Sisters—who had little relevance for the emerging television generation. Others were hot for the moment in the new medium—Faye Emerson and the curvaceous Dagmar (whose comic rapport with Sinatra would inspire Mitch Miller to have them record the notorious "Mama Will Bark")—but their fame quickly faded. There was even a summit meeting of sorts with the new singers on the block, Frankie Laine and Perry Como. Sinatra not so secretly resented sharing the billing with Laine and Como; it was in no way an antecedent to the "Three Tenors," but a desperate attempt to get publicity for the show. With no Hope or Crosby, Sinatra's guests underlined his fall from commercial grace.

The one performer who ignited the show and made Sinatra comfortable was the future Great One, Jackie Gleason. Gleason brought an outrageousness and fun that relaxed Sinatra and the writers—a burden was lifted from Frank of carrying the show. With Gleason, the writers experimented with the form of the series, even creating a mini-musical. At this time, Gleason was in the minor leagues, under contract to DuMont, hosting a low-budget variety series, *Cavalcade of Stars.* However, on the Sinatra show he literally burst on the scene, impressing the network and audiences alike. Everyone recognized the potency of a Sinatra-Gleason combination, agreeing with *Variety* that the duo had "a lot of fun with their kidding and transmitted that fun neatly to the audience."[7] Sinatra and CBS negotiated in vain with DuMont to free the corpulent comedian from his contract. Unfortunately, it was not until the fall of 1952, when Sinatra was off the air, that CBS signed Gleason. Almost immediately, the Great One proved to CBS that Saturday night was not the loneliest night of the week.

Occasionally, allusions to the real-life imbroglios of Sinatra crept into the show. During a boisterous New Year's Eve sketch, a stranger wandered in and was greeted by Sinatra as "Mortimer." The guest was then manhandled by the Sinatra's hired "servants," the Three Stooges, and forced to drink a cocktail without a glass. This viciousness of the routine left little doubt that this was a covert reference to Lee Mortimer, the gossip columnist Sinatra punched in 1947. Even more personal was a commercial pitch that Sinatra gave on February 3, 1951. Guest star June Hutton, wife of orchestra leader Axel Stordahl, asked him who was getting his Valentine this year. There was an immediate, palpable hush in the studio. Would he publicly admitted his love for Ava Gardner, even while he was married to his Hoboken sweetheart, Nancy? (Sinatra did not officially divorce Nancy until November 1951). Ready to answer, Sinatra's eyes twinkled and he blurted out, "Bulova, of course." Stepping out of the ad for a second, he added to the inquiring minds in the studio audience and everyone at home, "Fooled you!" For that instant Sinatra was real, not a character concocted for a television series. Unfortunately, those moments of a flesh-and-blood Sinatra were all too rare.

Throughout its two-year run, the producers tinkered with *The Frank Sinatra Show.* One problem was that the series was on opposite Sid Caesar's *Your Show of Shows,* one of the strongest on-air and behind-the-scenes productions teams ever assembled. *Your Show of Shows* also had a contemporary relevance, satirizing current trends in suburban America. It was witty and up-to-date, unlike the Sinatra show which was most comfortable in the previous decade. During the second season, the series was moved to Tuesday night at 8:00 p.m., opposite Milton Berle, an old-time comedian who successfully retooled himself for television. Later that season, the show was relocated to Hollywood so that, in Sinatra's words, it could attract the caliber of talent of Bob Hope and Lucille Ball. Unfortunately, not much money was poured into production and the show throughout its run, continued its "jerky presentation."[8] The Los Angeles version never featured Hope and Ball, and when the show did have stars such as Louis Armstrong and the Three Stooges, they reused tired scripts from the New York days. The final show was on April 1, 1952, and, later, a *TV Guide* headline asked the question that was dogging the singer: "Can Sinatra Make Good in TV?"[9]

Sinatra Finds Himself

As he campaigned for the role of Maggio in *From Here to Eternity* in late 1952, Sinatra was open to other possibilities in television. He considered playing a jazz musician in a filmed series for Desilu Productions, called either *Blue in the Night* or *Downbeat,* both titles, perhaps, reflections of Sinatra's mental state. Contrary to the circulating wisdom in the industry, Sinatra could succeed in television if given the right inspiration and the right production team. His renewal on television can be attributed to the vision of NBC president Sylvester "Pat" Weaver. Weaver envisioned a new form of programming, the spectacular, which brought a team of creative individuals across the board, from producer to star, to create a one-time event for television. Spectaculars gave well-known artists the opportunity to stretch themselves and the medium without interfering with their normal careers.

Sinatra's potential was immediately grasped by NBC after he was let go from CBS. Within six months, he was a guest on *All Star Revue: The Jimmy Durante Show* (October 18, 1952) and *The Buick-Berle Show* (October 7, 1953), two NBC comedy cornerstones. In both shows, Sinatra displayed a comic flair totally absent from his CBS series. On the Durante program, critics were amazed by his hidden ability at mimicry, especially his dead-on impersonation of his friend Jackie Gleason. Berle devoted his whole program to making fun of Sinatra's failed attempt at series television. Berle, in jest, created possible television programs for the singer, including a situation comedy, *I Hate Miltie*, in which thin Frank plays the rotund Fred Mertz role, and a puppet show where Frank was dressed and acted suspiciously like Burr Tillstrom's Kukla. Inspired by these madcap pairings with legendary vaudevillians, Sinatra was engaged by the material and revealed his comic, spontaneous side. There was a joyous revelry, a party atmosphere, which permeated these live productions.

Even before the 1954 Oscar telecast, when Sinatra received the Academy Award for his *Eternity* role and his comeback became official, NBC producers wanted to capitalize on the multifaceted talents of Sinatra, which were hidden for so many years. He was cast in a lavish, color production of *Anything Goes* (February 28, 1954), supervised by Leland Hayward and featuring the original star, Ethel Merman. This is the only record of Sinatra in a live Broadway musical, ironically playing the role his idol Bing Crosby made famous in the 1936 movie. How timely and appropriate the part of Harry Dane is; Sinatra gets to perform two Cole Porter songs that would define his new mature style, "I Get a Kick Out of You" and "Just One of those Things," the latter reworked into his 1954 film *Young at Heart.* Both recordings were also essential to his commercial and critical renaissance at Capitol Records, where, according to John Rockwell of the *New York Times,* Sinatra transformed "songs by others into the most immediate of individual statements."[10]

This led NBC impresario Max Liebman (the mastermind behind *Your Show of Shows*) to make Sinatra the centerpiece of two extravaganzas, *Fanfare* (November 7, 1954) and *Kaleidoscope* (April 4, 1958). Both shows, originating live in New York, cut away to Hollywood to present the newly revived Sinatra performing his current Capitol recordings. In *Fanfare,* director Bob Banner brought to life the cover of *Songs for Young Lovers*—the iconic lamppost, the lonely street, and the haunted singer in a Cavanaugh with cigarette. This moody, film noir-like set piece literally "stole the show," according to *Variety,* from the otherwise colorful proceedings.[11] For *Kaleidoscope,* Sinatra introduced his biggest hit of the fifties, "Learnin' the Blues," with full orchestra supervised by Nelson Riddle. The staging, again by Banner, highlighted Sinatra, in front of the musicians on a bare stage. This composition became the signature mise-en-scène of Sinatra's specials in the sixties and seventies. Sinatra was finally defined in the moment, not in the glorious but distant past.

That left one great NBC producer that Sinatra had not yet worked with, Fred Coe—the man who had earlier seized the potential of live drama with his production of Paddy Chayefsky's *Marty.* He got his chance in September 1955, when Coe presented one of television's most ambitious undertakings, a musical version of Thornton Wilder's *Our Town* for *Producers' Showcase* (September 19, 1955). Sinatra was cast as the stage manger and one-man Greek chorus, who introduced the simple townspeople of Grover's Corner, New Hampshire. His folksy paeans to rural life were augmented with such Sammy Cahn and Jimmy Van Heusen songs as "Impatient Years," "Look to Your Heart," and "Love and Marriage." There was plenty of turmoil behind the scenes. Everyone connected with the show, from producer Coe to director Delbert Mann to floor manager Dominick Dunne, was rankled by Sinatra's missed rehearsals with costars, Paul Newman and Eva Marie Saint. However, Sinatra came alive in the telecast from Los Angeles, and *Our Town* today endures as a classic of live television. Sinatra's dexterity in interweaving dramatic dialogue and tender song with a warmth and charm earned the singer accolades ("unquestionably his peak TV performance" proclaimed *Variety*[12]). In addition to the rave reviews, Sinatra earned one of his biggest hit records of the fifties, "Love and Marriage," a song that spoke directly to family-obsessed America. Sinatra could play a character on specials; but could he play himself on a weekly series?

With his film and recording careers in full gear, Sinatra did not undertake any ambitious television projects during the next two years. On October 10, 1956, he was the guest star in a special for his friend Dinah Shore, in which they recreated their early days at WNEW during the late thirties. Critics compared their live duet, directed by Bob Banner, with that of Ethel Merman and Mary Martin on the *Ford*

50th Anniversary Show. The possibilities in television for Sinatra seemed endless; he was triumphant as a soloist, comedian, dramatic actor, and musical star.

Another Persona, Another Show

In 1957, he signed an unprecedented deal with ABC, then the distant third network, to do it all. The network signed Frank Sinatra to a $3 million contract to produce a weekly series that would encompass: one live special, thirteen half-hour musicals, thirteen half-hour dramas starring Sinatra, and ten half-hour dramas hosted by Sinatra. This *Frank Sinatra Show,* sponsored by Chesterfield cigarettes and the Bulova Watch Company, would be the most expensive thirty minutes in television history and owned by the star himself. So much money was involved that *Variety* wanted to know if Sinatra was a singer or a salesman: "Sinatra isn't the first and won't be the last of the entertainers to become a dollar-happy commercial pitchman, though rarely has an actor or singer of his stature (and he's on the upstairs level in both depts.) gone so heavy in personalizing the pitch. Does he need the money? Does Rockefeller?"[13] The established networks, NBC and CBS, thought that this deal was financially risky. However, ABC, flush with the recent success of *Disneyland* and the western *Cheyenne,* needed a world-class entertainer to give the network star power. They were betting on Sinatra as actor and singer to lock up Friday nights for the 1957–1958 season.

Unfortunately, there was no tradition of variety entertainment at ABC. The executive producer assigned to the project was noted for his work in such genres as science fiction and westerns. The director hired for the premiere episode specialized in Toscanini and opera. There was no showman, like a Hayward or a Liebman, to create innovative set pieces and, as importantly, keep the rehearsal process running smoothly. Within several weeks, the ambitious concept was scrapped because the star did not have time or the desire to devote himself to dramas, which were cheaply produced anyway. Sinatra wanted to concentrate on music performed before a live audience, with Nelson Riddle conducting the orchestra. However, it was too late. *TV Guide* demanded to know: "What's Happening to Sinatra?"[14]

Sinatra was being torn apart by success. The *New York Times* reported that the has-been, who struggled to find work seven years ago, was now "perhaps the highest-paid performer in the history of show business." He expressed different sides of his volatile personality in different undertakings. His raffish charm and romantic longings were revealed in such concept albums as *Come Fly with Me* and *Where Are You?* His dramatic skills were reserved for the movies; his role as a disillusioned writer in *Some Came Running* was one of his most complex performances. Dividing himself on each new endeavor, Sinatra chose a more limited persona, the high-rolling swinger, to project on his second series, again simply called *The Frank Sinatra Show.* Each musical program began with the Riddle strains of "The Tender Trap" as Sinatra in hat debonairly strolled down in the theater aisle with raincoat in hand à la Joey Evans. The El Capitan Theater in Hollywood became the nightclub that "Pal Joey" dreamed about. When Sinatra hit the stage, two budding starlets greeted him and obediently took his accessories. This Sinatra spoke the lingo of a hipster. He called his guests "charlies" and dames; the bachelor Sinatra was throwing a party. His softer, more vulnerable side of *Wee Small Hours* was little on display. This weekly soirée marked the first time that the hedonistic philosophy of Hugh Hefner entered the average American home via television.

Too Hip for the Home

The nation, however, was not ready for such a cultural revolution. Jack O'Brian of the New York *Journal American* complained about his "wise Guyisms" and double entendres.[15] *Variety* concurred and stated the "worst attribute of the show . . . is the dialog, with Sinatra spouting a torrent of flip expressions that presumably are supposed to be sophisticated and hip, but come across in a completely affected manner."[16] In fact, the Sinatra show was counter to the entire ABC philosophy. ABC programs were produced for the young housewife and her children, the former bobbysoxer who now was ensconced in the suburbs; *The Adventures of Ozzie and Harriet* and *Rin Tin Tin* were the norm on Friday nights. America seemingly did not want a high-living roué disrupting its baby-boom values. Against weak competition, the most dominant entertainer in the history of show business ran a distant second or third in the ratings.

Television was now America's favorite pastime; approximately 80 percent of the nation had sets as compared with 9 percent when Sinatra hosted his first series. The variety show, which was popular with the largely urban television audience in 1950, was replaced in loyalty by the western, now enjoyed by the entire nation. America was enthralled with James Arness, whose *Gunsmoke* would begin its four-year reign at the top of the Nielsen ratings. The demographics were not right for Sinatra. He failed to connect with city viewers earlier (the core of his audience), and he did not have the mainstream appeal to win over the heartland and the suburbs, especially with his ring-a-ding-ding insouciance.

In retrospect, the second series was laying the groundwork for the emergence of Sinatra's Rat Pack. Earlier in the year, Humphrey Bogart had died, and Sinatra was assuming leadership of the informal club. Although the programs are formulaic—Sinatra alternating songs with a guest star, culminating in a duet—the leader was auditioning his friends. During his series, Sinatra welcomed individually Dean Martin; Sammy Davis, Jr.; and Joey Bishop. Each was developing an aspect of his persona to dovetail with the leader—the affable, boozy Dean; the loquacious and obsequious Sammy; and the sarcastic sycophant Joey. Frank was visibly relaxed in their company and with all, encouraged improvisation from the tired scripts. Ironically, the fourth Rat-to-be, Peter Lawford, was enjoying greater ratings success with his detective series, *The Thin Man,* which followed Sinatra's program at 9:30 p.m. on NBC. The Rat Pack would be officially christened in January 1960 when the gang was filming *Ocean's 11* by day and performing at the Sands in Las Vegas at night.

Sinatra's other guests ranged the gamut from established stars, including Ella Fitzgerald, Eddie Fisher, and Ethel Merman to such entertainment oddities as Spike Jones and Stan Freberg. The most disappointing show was the Christmas special with Bing Crosby. Sinatra discovered his calling as a vocalist at a Crosby concert in the mid-thirties and the pair had recently joined forces in the exuberant musical *High Society*. In 1957, Sinatra had released *A Jolly Christmas,* one of the most spirited holiday albums ever, and the hope was that these good feelings could be translated to television. The series was now on the rocks, and Sinatra decided to take things in his own hands and make his directorial debut. He went against convention and recorded the program on film, without an audience. As a result, neither rapport nor spontaneity was generated with Bing. Also, the flippant dialogue between the traditional carols made the atmosphere even more strained. If you cannot bring warmth to "White Christmas," the end is certainly near.

The second *Frank Sinatra Show* lasted only one season, and the biggest deal in television history was a bust. For a year, Sinatra did not perform on television except for a tribute to his friend and adviser Manie Sacks (*Some of Manie's Friends,* March 3, 1959), in which he and Dinah Shore recreated their electrifying duet. In the fall of 1959, he signed a deal with Timex to produce a series of irregularly scheduled specials on ABC. He went back to the concept that Pat Weaver articulated early in the fifties: bring together great artists and create something unique for television.

Television, Sinatra's Way

For the first two specials, Sinatra hired one of television's most tasteful producer/directors, Bill Colleran, who set the style for *The Bell Telephone Hour* and *Your Hit Parade.* Colleran took Sinatra away from a theatrical setting that confined his first two series and dreamt up elegant settings for encounters between Sinatra and his guests. There was nothing routine or formulaic about these specials. Among the highlights: Sinatra, Dean Martin, Bing Crosby, and Mitzi Gaynor performing an energetic tribute to Jimmy Durante (October 9, 1959); Sinatra swinging with Red Norvo's jazz combo (December 13, 1959); and Sinatra and Ella Fitzgerald relishing an inimitable Gershwin medley (December 13, 1959). With the attitude held in check, we again see a multifaceted performer: Sinatra as comic singer, as jazz artist, and as upholder of the American song tradition.

More unusual pairings were devised for the 1960 specials. On February 15, Sinatra hosted a salute to some special women, singing with the legendary Lena Horne and chatting with one of his political idols, Eleanor Roosevelt. In a spectacular taped in Miami, and broadcast May 12, Sinatra, with fellow Rat Packers, Davis, Bishop, and Lawford as well as daughter Nancy, welcomed the King of Rock 'n' Roll, Elvis Presley, back from the Army. Sinatra's duet with Presley was the only performance with his pop rival in any medium. There is a freewheeling sense of camaraderie and fun as each sings the other's hits (the Voice croons "Love Me Tender," and the Pelvis belts "Witchcraft"). All told, these four specials during the 1959–1960 season exploited Sinatra's many moods and personalities, paving the way for his future involvement in television. However, that would take five more years, and Sinatra would reinvent himself once again.

When he turned fifty in 1965, Sinatra contemplated his life and profession. He released the album *September of My Years,* which was one of his most personal works, a touching reflection on the joys and anguishes of his younger years. Sinatra also compiled and narrated a retrospective record, *A Man and His Music,* which highlighted his unprecedented career in thirty-one songs. Both projects received the Grammy Award, anointing Sinatra as elder statesman of the industry. *A Man and His Music* also inspired a companion television special (November 24, 1965), which marked Sinatra's return to the medium after limited guest appearances on such series as *The Judy Garland Show* (September 19, 1962) and *Hollywood Palace* (October 16, 1965). This special, which revealed the tender, nostalgic side of Sinatra, was honored as the television event of the season, receiving the coveted George Foster Peabody medallion and the Emmy Award for Outstanding Program. Sinatra continued to star in television specials, ensuring he remained a force in contemporary music; but the shows were produced annually and featured almost all music. Sinatra and his producers realized that he was most comfortable communicating his emotions and thoughts through song.

As host of his own fifties series, Sinatra went from tepid loser to cocky winner in five years. Neither personae were well-rounded enough to sustain a show, week in and week out. Television hosts, especially in the fifties, were easygoing and friendly. Middle-class America wanted to welcome into its collective living room someone who embodied its traditional values, like a Perry Como or a Garry Moore. Frank Sinatra was in no way average. His life and music were bigger than life, the stuff of legend. He worked best in television when he came on his own terms and was not made to be a weekly guest in the home.

When Sinatra began his ABC series, he asserted that "If I fall on my face, I want to be the cause. . . . All of the years when I was taking advice from others they told me wrong 50% of the time."[17] Sinatra would eventually be proven right, but it would take more than forty years. In desperation, he decided to film before a live audience to keep the series afloat. Those film clips would prove to be a bonanza for the Sinatra family after the singer's death. If Sinatra was too hip for a fifties audience, he was perfect for the cocktail culture revival at the dawn of a new century. Those old black-and-white clips have been the source of two PBS specials, *Sinatra Duets* (2002) and *Vintage Sinatra* (2003). The filmed songs also served as the basis for a theatrical presentation in New York's Radio City Music Hall (2004) and a revamped show is slotted for London in 2006, which will eventually tour the United States and settle in Las Vegas. Even, the Christmas show, *Happy Holidays with Bing and Frank,* found a belated redemption. A color film of the special was found in the vaults and released on DVD in 2003. What *Variety* deemed as "studied, pretentious and awkward" in 1957,[18] became an ironic, colorful foretelling of a twenty-first century hipster Christmas, complete with spiked eggnog.

In retrospect, Sinatra was always the personification of that Pat Weaver concept, the spectacular, and best presented on television when he had something to say. In his later specials of the sixties and seventies, he continually transformed himself as a delicate balladeer of bossa nova, accompanied by the legendary Brazilian composer Antonio Carlos Jobim (November 13, 1967); as a rejuvenated song-and-dance man, working with his first costar, Gene Kelly, in yet another comeback special *Ol' Blue Eyes Is Back* (November 18, 1973); and as the heavyweight champion of song in the live spectacular from Madison Square Garden, *The Main Event* (October 13, 1974). In the eighties, his persona gained gravitas as the icon of show business (*Sinatra: The First Forty Years,* January 30, 1980) and the ambassador of song in cable presentation *Sinatra: Concert for the Americas* (November 1981). Although it took some time, Frank Sinatra finally learned to do television, his way.

Notes

1. John Rockwell, *Sinatra: An American Classic* (New York: Rolling Stone Press, 1984), 12.
2. "Can Sinatra Make Good on TV," *TV Guide,* April 4, 1954, 5.
3. "Frankie Says: 'TV Racket's Too Tough!," *TV Guide,* September 17, 1955, 5.
4. "The A-B-C-D's of Comedy," *Variety,* December 13, 1950, 1, 43.
5. *Variety,* June 5, 1950.
6. *Variety,* October 11, 1950.
7. *Variety,* January 17, 1951.
8. *Variety,* October 11, 1950.
9. "Can Sinatra Make Good on TV," *TV Guide,* April 4, 1954, 5–7.
10. Rockwell, *Sinatra,* 141.
11. *Variety,* April 27, 1955.
12. *Variety,* September 21, 1955.
13. "Sinatra: Singer or Salesman?," *Variety,* November 6, 1957.
14. "What's Happening to Sinatra?" *TV Guide,* February 8, 1958, 8–10.
15. Jack O'Brian, "To Be Frank—A Long Show," *New York Journal-American,* October 19, 1957.
16. *Variety,* December 23, 1957.
17. Hal Humphrey, "Sinatra Is Calling Own Signals Now," *New York World-Telegram,* August 13, 1957.
18. *Variety,* December 23, 1957.

11

Frank Sinatra and Elvis Presley: The Taming of Teen Idols and *The Timex Show*

James F. Smith

It can be argued that the popular success of musical performers is a commercial commodity to be made and sold, but the cultural importance of Frank Sinatra and Elvis Presley transcends the millions of dollars they earned. In each case, a single artist came to be symbolic for the youth of an era, an idol representing not only contemporary taste but also, perhaps, a generation's desire for recognition in the present and their collective hopes for achieving the American dream in the future. Each performer carried his original cohort of fans and added new acolytes as his music moved through time and evolved stylistically. Both ensured their success as recording artists through live performances and through motion picture appearances. Coming from backgrounds that were simultaneously different (northern urban versus rural southern) and similar (humble but with middle class aspirations), they symbolized movements in mass culture touched by specific time and place. As they broke from traditional standards and boundaries, they appealed to the emerging self-awareness of youth in mid-century America. Through their contributions to American popular culture, Sinatra and Presley came to be identified with their respective eras—not only at their genesis as pop icons but throughout their lives. Within the first decade of their careers, both Frank and Elvis transcended the teenage market: The teen idols became pop stars through media exposure, film careers, public acceptance by the mainstream of their personal images and of their chosen musical forms, and the aging of their original fans.

During the post–World War II age of abundance, the United States experienced unprecedented material prosperity and population growth. The "teenager," originally a social and economic cultural phenomenon identified during the war years, became increasingly important in American popular culture. For the teens, as well

Sinatra and Elvis Presley: *The Timex Show*, 1960. (Courtesy of Photofest. Used with permission.)

as their parents, material well-being was seen as an entitlement of the expanding middle class, and whether or not their individual circumstances placed them in the comfort of white suburbia, as a generation they took a level of material satisfaction for granted. However, they wanted something more. In his analysis of the bobby-sox adulation of Frank Sinatra in the 1940s, Bruce Bliven argued " . . . we have left [teenagers] with a hunger still unfulfilled: a hunger for heroes, for ideal things that do not appear, or at least not in adequate quantities, in a civilization that is so busy making things and selling things as ours."[1] Thus, in the war years, the young invested their passion in the skinny crooner from Hoboken who so clearly articulated their collective dreams and desires. Passion was more important than prosperity, at least for the young, both during the 1940s and a decade later when the comfortable formulas of the popular music world were again turned upside down by the coming of Elvis Presley and rock 'n' roll.

In many respects, celebrities have assumed a conspicuous and significant role in American culture during the last half of the twentieth century. For one thing, Americans have become increasingly skeptical of the "traditional" hero, such as a political leader or athlete, with the harsh glare of media attention revealing that great people may not always be as noble as their public image. Needing replacements for the visible role models and the cultural glue that hold a civilization together, we have seized upon contemporary examples of well-known people who reflect the values and aspirations of our changing cultural environment. People whose fame rests primarily on being well known, rather than on genuine greatness, are celebrities. In addition, as social structures become more diverse and fragmented, certain public figures may come to represent the values and aspirations of a cultural subset more than those of the mainstream do. A careful examination of our celebrities reveals that they fall into two basic categories: "citizen" celebrities, whose adulation is in the mainstream, reinforce mass cultural values; and rebel or "rogue" celebrities, whose fame rests on the admiration of a cultural subgroup, embody the particular tastes and values of their admirers, often in opposition to mass cultural values. In either case, the celebrity can assume the role of popular hero, making the adulating group feel good about itself and offering both a model to imitate and a vision of success toward which to strive.

During this same half century, media-dominated America has also witnessed the growing cultural significance of its young people. The teenager as social and cultural force, and important economic market segment, is a fairly recent historical phenomenon. Freed by the personal mobility and the relaxed restrictions on behavior of the home front during World War II, teenagers often assumed roles earlier generations had reserved for adults. With many adults absent due to military service or extended and irregular work schedules in defense industries, young people had more freedom and responsibility. At the same time they remained *young*. As adolescents, their interests centered on finding, testing, and asserting their own identities in a rapidly changing world. Their growing affluence in the context of a booming wartime economy and available jobs or increased allowances, enabled them to display that identity as a well-defined style.[2] Once unleashed in the 1940s, the genie of youth culture could not be put back in its bottle after the war any more than the world could retreat from the coming of the nuclear age. With scarcely a hitch, the postwar economy continued to grow, satisfying the pent-up demand for consumer goods in a society characterized by middle class aspirations and the pro-creation ethic. With a single-mindedness reminiscent of wartime patriotism, family life, and affluence became cultural touchstones at least through the early 1960s, and once again young people were afforded the luxury of self-definition and self-indulgence. Buttressed by the growing baby-boom population, more than 75 million strong by the mid-1960s, youth culture seemed here to stay, and so became a focus for cultural commentators and for shrewd market executives.

As cohorts of teenagers sought to define and assert their collective identities, they naturally chose personae to admire who embodied their collective tastes and aspirations. So-called "teen idols" were most likely to be found in the media, and a medium that beat close to teen hearts, particularly since the 1940s, was popular music. Both live and recorded performances were widely available; the music was portable and pervasive, an accessible and repeatable reinforcement of their style. Through their devotion to their music and their idols, teens were no longer "disconnected individuals" but shared a common interest.[3] The popularity of Frank Sinatra and Elvis Presley was not an accident, but a logical product of the intersection of mass media with an audience yearning for something to claim as its own. In each case, we find an expression of the values of a cultural subset whose importance is now taken for granted. In each teen idol, we find a celebrity who embodies characteristics of both the citizen and the rogue.

Todd Gitlin explains the tension between the adult mainstream's fear and loathing and teenagers' generational defiance in this way:

[Earlier] generations of parents had also been disturbed to see their children writhing with abandon, treating their bodies like erotic instruments, screaming at idols like Frank Sinatra. Popular music often serves to insulate young people against the authority of previous generations, and the commercial search for The Latest makes generational tension over music virtually automatic. But in rock's heyday there was a special intensity on both sides. When teenagers screamed themselves hoarse at Frank Sinatra in the forties, whatever quality it was that teens celebrated and editorialists deplored was the possession of a single skinny singer. Now both sides agreed that rock was all of a piece, love it or leave it.[4]

By the 1950s, the mainstream found cause for alarm not only in the antics of the young but in the music itself, and Elvis was only its most notorious example. The "noise" that parents deplored became magnetic to youth because their parents could not comprehend or appreciate it. However, in the case of both Frank Sinatra and Elvis Presley, age and the passing of time succeeded in doing what the parents, press, and preachers could not do. Failing to suppress the menace in its heyday, the mainstream eventually absorbed both performers.

Mainstream acceptability for Frank Sinatra came at a price: he had to "die," at least in one persona, in order to recreate himself. The "boy next door" had become a song-and-dance movie star, then an outspoken advocate for racial and ethnic tolerance, and then a singer-on-the-skids who had seen his audience drift away to Perry Como, Frankie Laine, Tony Bennett, and the newcomers who followed him while he made few truly satisfying recordings and even fewer hits. His personal life was the subject of scandal sheets, and in April of 1950, his throat hemorrhaged. However, within three years, he was back on top again with a Best Supporting Actor Oscar, a contract with Capitol Records, and a new image to go with his new sophisticated "older" sound. From the 1950s onward, Frank would be the swinger instead of a heartthrob, a dangerous but likable rogue who ran with the hipsters of the Rat Pack and whose persona appealed to women and men alike. As always, his music was squarely in the popular mainstream, but it now would never be really *square,* except perhaps to later unsophisticated teenage audiences. Instead, he and his sound seemed to define the "cool" of the adult postwar world, as dry martinis became the drink of choice in the cities and suburbs of mid-century America. Both Frankie, now more worldwise than boyish, and the bobby-soxers had grown up.

Elvis, too, experienced a reincarnation in the late 1950s, though perhaps less by his own hand than by the skillful manipulation of the Colonel and the timely intervention of Uncle Sam. In March of 1958, Elvis was inducted into the Army, and in August, his beloved mother Gladys died. Though he was only twenty-three, the trauma of losing Gladys and the ordeal of leaving the public eye at the height of his fame to become a soldier caused Elvis to do a great deal of growing up. But his uncomplaining acceptance of military service—which was always portrayed as standard government-issue rather than a celebrity gig—as well as the identifiable grief at his personal loss warmed the public to the rock 'n' roller, and mainstream culture sighed in relief as the Pelvis proved to be the All-American Boy after all. In hindsight, it is amusing to discover the very real anxiety that Elvis, and many of those close to him, felt about the effect his absence from his public would have on his career. Compounding his lack of visibility was the fear that rock music itself would turn out to be the passing fad that cultural pundits and mainstream performers such as Frank Sinatra were predicting. However, thanks both to Tom Parker's strategy of encouraging RCA's releasing a carefully controlled stream of stockpiled records every few months to keep Presley hits on the charts and to the endurance of rock 'n' roll itself, Elvis need not have worried. Nevertheless, either by accident or by design, the rogue would soon be mainstreamed, and while teenagers looked elsewhere for singing idols, the rest of America would come to embrace Elvis as an icon.

A symbolic juxtaposition of these two mid-century music idols occurred when Frank welcomed Elvis on a Timex television special aired in May of 1960 to celebrate his return from the Army. Though he was just beginning to define his 1960s movie persona, the subdued Elvis was evident from the start.[5] For his part, Frank, who had no taste for rock 'n' roll and whose show persona clearly represented the mainstream popular music establishment (by his choice of songs), Rat Pack cool (in antics with his cronies), and responsible fatherly affection (toward daughter Nancy), was a generous and gracious host and seemed to enjoy clowning and singing with Presley.

The "Welcome Back Elvis" show, which aired May 12 on ABC, was the fifth (and last) in a series of programs sponsored by Timex (of which four aired during the 1959–1960 television season). Taped on April 1 at Miami's Fontainebleau Hotel, this show marked the first time that Frank hosted a guest appealing to a "young audience." Previous specials in the series had featured Bing Crosby, Nat Cole, Dean Martin, Ella Fitzgerald, Lena Horne, and even Eleanor Roosevelt. Without a doubt, Elvis was on Frank's turf, and his appearance with Sinatra clearly presented the "good boy" Elvis image to the mainstream, even as parts of his performance caricatured elements of his early appeal. Once during an appearance on the *Steve Allen Show* in the 1950s, Elvis was forced to dress in formal attire and sing "[You Ain't Nothin' but a] Hound Dog" to a basset hound in order to tone down his performance and soothe the critics who had found an appearance on Milton Berle's show the prior week crude and offensive. On the *Timex Show,* Elvis again appears in a tuxedo, but he no longer needs toning down. He "imitates" Sinatra mannerisms in his rendition of his newly recorded song, "Fame and Fortune," as well in his "Love Me Tender/Witchcraft" duet with Sinatra. Nevertheless, Elvis is clearly an apprentice and somewhat uncomfortable in Sinatra's world. Writing for *Billboard,* Ron Grevalt observed that "Presley has much to learn before he can work in the same league with pros like Sinatra, Joey Bishop, and especially Sammy Davis, Jr. . . . [He] had a disturbing tendency to swing his arms back and forth . . . which gives the impression that he's never at ease."[6] Awkward or not, the music and the man were tamed and glossed for a mainstream audience, and this appearance of the two *former* teen idols together heralded the culmination of RCA's and Tom Parker's mass-marketing of a teen phenomenon into a mainstream star at the same time it confirmed Sinatra's status as *the voice* of contemporary American popular music.

The multifaceted incoherence of the pop music scene of 1960 provides an instructive context in which to place the "Welcome Back" program. Members of the first wave of rock renegades, except for Elvis, were virtually absent from the scene, as Frankie Avalon, Paul Anka, Ricky Nelson, and other "teen idols" replaced Little Richard, Chuck Berry, and Jerry Lee Lewis on the charts. Pop single releases seemed to be looking for an identifiable style, vacillating between teen-pop and novelty songs, with occasional throwbacks to middle of the road pop of the previous decade. Nevertheless, it is safe to say that the pop single market continued to reflect the tastes of young listeners in 1960, since by the late 1950s, most of the single releases were being purchased by teenagers. During the months preceding *The Timex Show,* number one singles included songs by Frankie Avalon ("Why"), Marty Robbins ("El Paso"), Johnny Preston ("Running Bear"), and Mark Denning ("Teen Angel"). The longest-standing number one song of the year was Percy Faith's "Theme from *A Summer Place,*" which topped the *Billboard* chart from February 28 through the end of April, when it was replaced by Elvis's "Stuck on You" for four weeks.[7] Presley would provide the most consistency among number one hits in 1960, scoring a total of three during the year. It is also noteworthy that during the six weeks between the taping and broadcast dates of *The Timex Show,* the Congressional "payola" hearings, which had already devastated rock patriarch Alan Freed, climaxed with Dick Clark's testimony and simultaneous divestment of his financial interests in the recordings he had featured on American Bandstand. Clark had made his peace with Congress, but the rock business was still suspect.

Mainstream pop musical taste, that is "adult" taste, was reflected in long-playing albums, and there was considerably less volatility at the top of the album charts, reflecting perhaps album consumption by more mature (and therefore less fickle) listeners. The Kingston Trio was all the rage, on home phonographs as well as on college campuses, having three albums reach the top of the *Billboard* chart. The soundtrack to Broadway's *Sound of Music* (twelve weeks) and Bob Newhart's *Button-Down Mind* comedy album (fourteen weeks) had the most longevity, with the latter capturing the Grammy for Album of the Year.

When he was discharged on March 5, 1960, Elvis was reborn as a civilian and as a performer. In April, he received the National Association of Record Merchants first annual award for best-selling male artist (Connie Francis, a Dick Clark protégée, was the female winner). As a singer, his repertoire began to include more of the pop tunes he had tried to record in Sam Phillips's studio.[8] Then his career took another turn: on April 20, he went to Hollywood to shoot *GI Blues,* and in quick succession, he would make two more movies and complete three extensive recording sessions between his discharge and the end of the year. Elvis might have been back, but he was a different Elvis; in fact, except for two charity performances in Memphis during early 1961, he would not perform again on stage until the summer of 1969 and the triumphant Las Vegas concert appearances, which heralded the start of the last phase of his career. His appearance had changed; "sharkskin" Elvis of the 1960s had a sleek pompadour with moderated sideburns, and the infamous Presley sneer was now a smile. The rock 'n' roll energy could still be detected in a record or two, but his style was shackled in the more than thirty formula movies (far cries from Oscar vehicles) and soundtrack recordings he made.

For his part, Frank Sinatra had settled firmly into a pattern of consistent excellence, thanks to his status as a bankable film star and to his remarkable association with Capitol records, Billy May, and Nelson Riddle. Recognized by the Film Exhibitors of America as their Top Box Office Star in 1960, Frank appeared in *Can-Can* and *Ocean's 11,* the latter film signaling his ascendancy to the dominance of the Las Vegas entertainment scene, while the former won a Grammy for Best Soundtrack Album. He would also make his first concert tour of Japan and begin a highly visible association with John Kennedy and the Democratic Party that would extend through the inauguration the following year. In 1960, as they had each year since 1957, the readers of *Playboy* voted him Top Male Vocalist (and they would continue to do so each year through 1966, and again in 1968 and 1969). In 1959, he had won Grammys for Album of the Year and Best Male Vocal Performance for *Come Dance With Me,* and his album of the year in 1960, *Nice 'n' Easy,* would remain on the *Billboard* charts for eighty-six weeks and reach the top position for one week in October (though it would lose to Newhart's comedy album in the Grammy awards). With the exception of the fickle (and juvenile) pop singles charts, the popular music scene was clearly Frank's domain, and his definition of turf is seen in the setting, guest list, and repertoire of *The Timex Show.*

The "Welcome Back" special (produced by Sammy Cahn and Jimmy Van Heusen and under the musical direction of Nelson Riddle) was set at Miami Beach's Fontainebleau, an unmistakable locus of adult chic and a favorite East

Coast venue for Sinatra. The showbiz establishment headliner guests—Joey Bishop and Sammy Davis—were joined by Nancy Sinatra, and later (unannounced) Peter Lawford, while the Tom Hansen Dancers provided floorshow interludes. The Cahn and Van Heusen opening number "It's Nice to Go Trav'ling" had come from Frank's *Come Fly with Me* album. Sinatra was joined by Nancy, Joey, and Sammy in singing modified lyrics as Elvis in uniform was unveiled and joined briefly in song before leaving the stage. His departure was trailed by wisecracks from the adults noting that Fabian and Ricky Nelson were not so happy that Elvis had resumed civilian life, and that Frank had reached into his deep pockets to welcome Elvis home (the price tag was widely reported as $125,000). Clearly, the impression is left that Frank is generous to Elvis, welcoming him back to join *his* world with a tidy paycheck. At the same time, he had taken pains to reassure the press that his critical attitude toward rock 'n' roll had not really changed, "But after all, the kid's been away two years and I get the feeling that he really believes in what he's doing."[9]

The next extended segment of the show, nearly forty minutes, reflects just how marginal Elvis is with respect to the "real" world. Rather than Joey Bishop's comic suggestion that an appropriate gift to Elvis would be a Conway Twitty album (Twitty had just begun his career as an Elvis "clone"), Sinatra and company proceed to offer the ex-soldier a musical present of the two years he had been away. Framed by a "time machine" motif presented by Nancy and Tom Hansen's dancers, the audience is treated to selected musical highlights from 1958 and 1959: Frank sings "Witchcraft" (to be reprised by Elvis later); Sammy does "There's a Boat Leaving Soon for New York" (from *Porgy and Bess*); the dancers pay homage to "Japanese" influence on culture and later to the Chipmunk-style novelty records; Frank makes observations on album cover art (noting his own *Only the Lonely* award) and sings "Gone with the Wind"; and finally Sammy takes the lead with imitations of leading pop stars (Nat Cole, Tony Bennett, Louis Armstrong, and Dean Martin) singing the Sinatra classic "All the Way," culminating with the surprise appearance of Peter Lawford, replete with dancing, jokes, and Rat Pack shenanigans. Does this extended interlude whet the appetite for Elvis's "real" appearance? Or does it firmly stake out the territory where Elvis is a minor player? I suppose the answer depends on the viewer's reason for tuning in.

Approximately two-thirds into the show, Elvis reappears—sporting his "transitional" hairdo, pinky ring, and tuxedo. He opens his set, accompanied by the Jordanaires (who had helped tame his sound on RCA from the raw rockabilly style he had recorded for Sam Phillips on Sun Records) and a combo featuring two members of his original trio, Scotty Moore and D. J. Fontana. The first number, "Fame and Fortune," is a harbinger of the new Elvis song, owing at least as much to the American popular song tradition as to rock 'n' roll, and his performance of the number *sans* guitar has been likened to the Sinatra-style of presentation. "Stuck on You" (which reached number one the week before airdate) is next. While the song is closer to Elvis's rock style, the Pelvis is reduced to shaking his head, and slightly flopping his cowlick, suggesting rather than performing his trademark gyrations. Joined at the close by Frank and Joey, Elvis smiles at Sinatra's quip that he is "glad to see the Army hasn't changed you"—an ironic jab, to be sure, since the change is obvious to everyone. Bishop's second banana role continues as he muses that he has never heard such screaming from women before, only to be chided by the boss, "What about me, Charlie?" Again, the master asserts his sovereignty.

The assimilation of Elvis to the mainstream is cemented when Frank orchestrates the "duet." While the combo and Jordanaires stand silent in the shadows almost off-screen, Nelson Riddle and the orchestra accompany the superimposed "Love Me Tender"–"Witchcraft" number. Peter Guralnick argues that Sinatra "parodies himself" in his rendition of "Love Me Tender," while Elvis "shows utter respect" for "Witchcraft," indicating "by a shake of his shoulders, the limp extension of his wrist, his bemused acceptance of a task which he is prepared to perform with elegance and humility."[10] The duet culminates in the "That's pretty!" harmonizing on the last two lines of "Love Me Tender." Then Frank observes that "We work in the same way, only in different areas" (shoulders versus hips). In fact, the harmony is *so* pretty that the lines are reprised before Frank dismisses his guest in the company of his recently engaged daughter, with the paternal admonition: "She's spoken for."

The show's denouement is all Sinatra with a focus on his closeness to Nancy and his ambivalence regarding her growing up. Another duet of sorts on "You Make Me Feel So Young" [So Old], sets the stage for reminding us that Frank is now about to be a father-in-law and that Nancy (who then joins the dancers for a featured number) has actually outgrown things like crushes on teen-idol singers, though husband-to-be Tommy Sands was, in fact, one of many Elvis replacement idols during the 1958 to 1960 hiatus (his hit: "A Teenage Crush"). A reprise of "It's Nice to Go Trav'ling" contains the thanks and acknowledgments, and Frank bids farewell to television specials for five years.[11] Elvis, too, eschewed television until his 1968 "Comeback Special," though both performers would continue to appear on the big screen and on the record charts for the rest of the decade. By all measures, the program was a success, earning a 41.5 Trendex rating, representing a 67.7 percent audience share.[12]

Within the first decade of their respective careers, both Frank and Elvis transcended the teenage market. Teens continued to seek the latest musical forms to distinguish themselves from adult tastes and sensibilities.[13] In their later careers, there is a kind of anachronistic quality attached to the success of the two idols. Sinatra became the hip organization man for the adult generation cashing in on postwar prosperity. Always the consummate swinger and epitome of self-confidence, Frank stood in sharp relief against the musical and cultural pyrotechnics of the 1960s; the shallow preening of disco; and the sensitivity of male singer-songwriters in the 1970s, though it could be argued that his vulnerability, most often seen in saloon songs, was always a part of his appeal to both sexes. Regardless of his forays into contemporary material, such as songs penned by George Harrison, Jimmy Webb, or Rod McKuen, his greatest success continued to rest with the standards. Presley, first the flamboyant rebel of postmaterialistic rejection of the mainstream and then an exaggeration of the excesses of style and appetites in his later years, seemed to be somewhat out of tune with changing times. If Sinatra could be seen as a relatively unchanging model for a particular kind of male identity or lifestyle, celebrated in the "cocktail culture" of the 1990s, Presley became first a formula "boy next door" in his films and soundtrack recordings and then a kind of burlesque or caricature of 1970s excess in his grooming, sequined clothes, elaborate staging and orchestration, drug abuse, and slaking of other appetites. If anything, Frank always remained a hip figure, even as he aged. Elvis was the wild "hillbilly cat" in his youth, but in the 1960s, he was tamed beyond the wildest dreams of his critics, and when he reemerged as a live performer in the 1970s, the polished showman was no longer dangerous, at least in public. By the end, he would become pathetic.

The debate over which image of Elvis would appear on his commemorative postage stamp is significant. The young, rebellious Elvis won hands down over the older, bloated pop star, suggesting that his greatest influence and most memorable significance was as a teen idol. It will be much harder to fix a single iconic image of Sinatra on a postage stamp, since representations from each stage of his career—"Bones" with his bow tie, the cocky hipster of *Pal Joey,* the suave leader of the Rat Pack, the Reaganite solid citizen, and the tuxedoed master of the pop music form—say something worthy of memory to the American audience. Elvis had his greatest musical significance as the harbinger of a new music form, the key to his enduring popularity. Sinatra, however, evolved as a performer and cultivated a personal image that seemed to relate more consistently to changing times and expanding audiences.

Neither Frank Sinatra nor Elvis Presley set out to exploit teen hysteria, but both found that their popularity among teens was a useful vehicle to propel them to stardom and give them the influence they needed to succeed. At the same time, in each artist's journey to stardom and in their respective musical articulation, the teenagers found ways to express their identities as well as their hopes for the future. Although Elvis Presley's contribution is most associated with a particular era and Frank Sinatra's music and style is timeless, both singers lived and sang stories fundamental to the human spirit and the American dream. The teens may have outgrown their idols, just as Frank and Elvis outgrew the teens, but their relationship has had a lasting impact on American cultural history and on the course of our musical heritage.

Presley died before his appeal was exhausted; Sinatra fades into peaceful fulfillment away from the public eye. Both did it Their Way, but Sinatra finished the song. There is still speculation on what Elvis would have been had he lived. There always will be Sinatra music in our popular imagination, much as there will always be Presley music, but will there be a Sinatra equivalent to Graceland as a destination for faithful pilgrims on important anniversaries?

Notes

1. Bruce Bliven, "The Voice and the Kids,: *The New Republic,* November 6, 1944, 593.

2. The popular press began to pay considerable attention to the young during the war years. The cover story of *Life* magazine August 23, 1943 is a good example. Focusing on the swing dance form of jitterbug or the Lindy Hop, a pictorial document stylized the steps of

youthful dancers acting out "American impatience with the restrictions of conventional forms," 95. Similar pieces in other issues looked at hairstyles, clothing fashions, and makeup as youngsters created a subculture. Accordingly, George Frazier's "Frank Sinatra" in *Life,* May 3, 1943, 54–62, places the singer in this context.

3. Landon Jones, *Great Expectations: America and the Baby Boom Generation* (New York: Ballantine Books, 1980), 72.

4. Todd Gitlin, *The Sixties: Years of Hope, Days of Rage* (New York: Bantam Books, 1987), 43.

5. An article in *Newsweek,* May 30, 1960, asked the question "Is This a 'New' Presley?" observing "The sideburns and 15 pounds of flesh were gone. . . ." In the piece, Elvis states, "I'm ambitious to become a more serious actor, but I don't want to give up the music business . . . ," 91. He also observes that his fans have matured, but they are sticking with him.

6. Ron Gevalt, "Elvis Projection Needs Face-Lift," *Billboard,* May 16, 1960, 38.

7. Elvis would be unseated by the Everly Brothers ("Cathy's Clown"), return to the top spot with "It's Now or Never" (four weeks), and close the year with "Are You Lonesome Tonight?" Other artists with top hits that year included the Hollywood Argyles ("Alley Oop"), Brenda Lee ("I'm Sorry" and "I Want to Be Wanted"), Brian Hyland ("Yellow Polka Dot Bikini"), Chubby Checker ("The Twist"), Connie Francis ("My Heart Has a Mind of Its Own"), Larry Verne ("Mr. Custer"), The Drifters ("Save the Last Dance for Me"), and Ray Charles ("Georgia").

8. In his liner notes for *Elvis: From Nashville to Memphis: The Essential 60's Masters,* © 1993, Pete Guralnick notes that Elvis's first recording session following his army stint included "Fever" (made popular by Peggy Lee), "It's Now or Never" (patterned after "O Solo Mio"and a 1949 Tony Martin song), and "Are You Lonesome Tonight" (a favorite of the Colonel's wife and a hit in 1927 by Gene Austin). The latter two sides had success as pop rock singles, both reaching number one on the charts during the summer and fall of 1960.

9. Rick DuBrow, "500,000 Await Elvis Today," *UPI* Report, March 5, 1960.

10. Peter Guralnick, *Careless Love: The Unmaking of Elvis Presley* (Boston: Little Brown, 1999), 63.

11. His next show would be in the fall of 1965 when he hosted the ABC *Hollywood Palace.*

12. Guralnick, *Careless Love,* 63.

13. At the height of their fame in the 1960s, the Beatles paid homage to Elvis during a visit to Graceland even though the teens of the era had pretty much abandoned him.

12

Frank Sinatra: Dancer

Jeanne Fuchs

Dance has to look like the music.

—George Balanchine

Crooner, teen idol, song stylist, sex symbol, actor, innovator, consummate artist are all labels that come easily to mind when Frank Sinatra's name is mentioned. Frank Sinatra dancer, however, does not immediately surface in our consciousness. Nonetheless, Frank Sinatra did dance early in his career in film, and my purpose is to examine that aspect of his career and demonstrate the impact it had; how at the time his dancing represented a transitional moment of great importance. It would not be an exaggeration to say that the dancing experience contributed to Sinatra becoming a movie star. The quality of his dancing remains an equally important matter as well as how the films and dancing fit into what was happening in the Hollywood musical during the period.

Three MGM musicals will be examined: *Anchors Aweigh* (1945), *Take Me Out to the Ball Game* (1948), and *On the Town* (1949). All of the films were made with Gene Kelly as costar and with choreography by Kelly and Stanley Donen. The films coincide with the period in which Sinatra was a teen idol and already a national celebrity. He was young, energetic, ambitious, and immensely gifted. The transition from band singer to movie star was aided in large measure by his appearance in these three musicals.

Sinatra was a nondancer when he went to Hollywood. Not only would he end up dancing, but he was also paired with one of the great film dancers of all time, Kelly. While there is a tendency to look at Kelly during the numbers they do together, it seems certain that the Sinatra fans were not focusing exclusively on Frank's partner. In any case, even if one person actually has better training than another does, and if this becomes evident to the audience, it undermines the entire number. The studio, Kelly, or Sinatra would not have consented to his looking amateurish next to Kelly. The result is that he does not. While not as polished or as exuberant as the ever brash and extroverted Kelly, Sinatra holds his own, and his naïve and boyish qualities in most of the dances serve to complement the nature of the character he plays in the film—usually the uninitiated (especially about women) and impressionable sidekick of the aggressive, experienced (especially about women), and sex-obsessed mentor, Kelly. Sinatra's passiveness presents the perfect foil for Kelly's aggressive character in all three films.

The question of how a nondancer metamorphoses into a performer who can hold his own on camera with someone who is a superb dancer is one that bears examination. There is a two-part or even a three-part answer: the body is important, musicality is crucial, and self-confidence becomes imperative. On all counts, Sinatra proves himself well equipped. One could say that what made him a success as a singer also greatly aided in his dance efforts: he possessed a thin, compact, flexible body. His breath control, which he had refined by swimming and running, remains a crucial factor.[1] He was young, willing, and physically agile. As to musicality, he wins hands down. His musical talent remains unchallenged; his incredible timing and phrasing provided him with a distinct edge in learning routines. As to self-confidence, Sinatra not only had it, he projected it throughout his entire career. In 1942, Harry Meyerson at RCA observed that when Sinatra first came to a recording session he was not like other band vocalists: "He came in self-assured, slugging. He knew exactly what he wanted. Most singers tend to begin with the humble bit. . . . Popularity didn't really change Sinatra. On that first date he stood his ground and displayed no humility, phony or real."[2] Later in his career, many would refer to Sinatra's self-confidence as arrogance. What remains indisputable is that his sense of self-worth, as a performer, existed from the beginning and became a key element in his success. He had the self-assurance of a champion—the one who rises to the challenge and wins the event because of psychological fortitude.

In addition, Sinatra carried himself with an innate grace; never clumsy or physically awkward, although depicted as socially backward in these films, Sinatra moves through his own space with ease and is comfortable with his persona. He embodies musicality and self-confidence. Another critical quality for dancer, actor, or singer, and one understood by the best performers, is the value of stillness. Garbo knew it, Kelly used it, and Sinatra possessed a natural intuition for it, especially in the delivery of a song, but he carries this quality over into his body movement as well. Of course, an overriding and crucial quality for screen success that both Kelly and Sinatra exuded is physical magnetism, that is, sex appeal. Kelly bubbles over with animal magnetism in all his films, and while Sinatra's is more understated, it remains present in his overall affect as well as in the dancing. Again, the shyness and introverted nature of the roles he played adds to his sex appeal and provides as well a contrast with Kelly's aggressive physical presence.

Fortunately, there exists a record of what his fellow artists thought of Sinatra's work and it bears quoting. Jerome Delamater in *Dance in the Hollywood Musical,* interviews, among others, Gene Kelly and Betty Garrett, to whom he poses the question directly: "What did Kelly do about working with non-dancers?" Betty Garrett responds, "When Gene worked with somebody like Frank, he scaled himself down to things the person could do. He didn't give you something impossible to do, but Frank is a natural. Whatever he had to do, he could do very presentably. He's just very quick and had a certain style about the way he moved. I think he looks marvelous in the things he does, and he worked very hard; he was right there with us all the time."[3] Gene Kelly's answer to the same question is more detailed and reveals an aspect of the transitional elements of the musical in Sinatra's career alluded to earlier. Kelly states, "Very hard work and a great willingness . . . to be beaten and insulted a lot. . . . A fellow like Frank, he had made two pictures and had really not unglued his hands from the microphone yet, and he was anxious to move around and improve his motion picture image. He certainly was the idol of teen-age America. We all know that. He was an avid worker. He practiced very fervidly. It's very tough for a non-dancer."[4] Kelly also knew that the choreography had to fit the performer's ability. He worked on what made the individual look good and he succeeded. The transition from band singer to musical comedy star in Sinatra's career is a hallmark as important as his transition from singer-movie star to actor in *From Here to Eternity.* Both mark defining moments in the development of what came to be one of the most enduring careers in all of show business.

At this point, it is important to demonstrate how the particular thinking at MGM, and in Hollywood, fit quite neatly into the notion of a nondancer becoming a dancer. Hollywood musicals placed a premium on the impression of spontaneity, on group choreography, and on a natural looking technique.[5] While Fred Astaire at RKO often played characters who were professional dancers, MGM usually preferred transforming ordinary folk—soldiers, sailors, baseball players, farmers—into "spontaneous" dancers. The studio embraced a kind of "folk art" or "mass art," thus professionals such as Judy Garland were often depicted as ordinary people who just suddenly and spontaneously burst into song or dance or both. A compelling parallel with Sinatra can be made with Kelly himself. He was not a singer and as a nonsinger sang all his own material in a tiny voice. The same can be said of Fred Astaire. Being untrained never prevented either from singing most effectively. (Actually, this whole mind-set forms the basis of Woody Allen's film, *Everybody Says I Love You.* Allen exploits the traditional Hollywood philosophy: He and the other actors actually cannot sing and—except for Goldie Hawn—nobody can dance either. The viewer, having been conditioned by old Hollywood musicals, is not completely shocked by the irony that Allen underscores, but the comedy resides in the fact that the "stars" cannot sing or dance.)

This basic studio philosophy worked in Sinatra's (and others') favor, but he never looks amateurish. Although cast in the role of an "ordinary" guy, when Sinatra begins to sing, he transcends this status instantly. Jane Feuer in *The Hollywood Musical,* notes, "The frequent casting of non-dancers in Hollywood musicals leads to the creation of routines in which a thin line separates normal from choreographed movement."[6] In the case of the three musicals under examination, the statement is not completely accurate. While Kelly and Donen's choreography may be "scaled down," there are some difficult passages that could never pass for "normal" movement. The point is to pretend that everyone can sing like Judy Garland and dance like Gene Kelly even though that remains an impossibility. (In Woody Allen's version, because it is an affectionate parody, they sing and dance but they are mediocre—again, Goldie Hawn excepted.)

The idea that "we're all just regular folks who can naturally sing and dance" emerges as a most American notion. The basic illusory nature of the classic Hollywood cinema reinforces that view; it also coincides with the commonly held view that anyone can act and that actors make up their lines as they go along. The whole perspective that anyone can perform such difficult feats remains linked to the ever-present problem in the musical genre and in movie musicals of integrating the musical numbers with the narrative elements in the film. For a musical to seem more "real," abrupt transitions or no transitions must be avoided when songs and dances begin and end. Kelly and Donen were especially focused on this problem.[7] An example of how this integration can be achieved smoothly occurs in *Anchors Aweigh.* Instead of a hot night on the town that the two sailors on shore leave had planned, they spent the whole time babysitting for Dean Stockwell, a child who has run away from home to join the navy. To save face with the guys back at the canteen and hostel they fabricate the evening's exploits. They sing and dance the message to their peers. Most notable is the smooth transition into the song ("I begged her, I pleaded") that shows how the story line and the song are integrated into the plot, but above all, it is Sinatra's film debut as a dancer and that is important. The number is short (approximately one and a half minutes) and performed in a small area thus restricting the movements of the dancers. The dance is made up of simple tap steps that move from side to side. There are occasional full stops as the sailors sing lines from the song and hold a pose as they do so. Sinatra looks at his feet frequently, and if one watches closely, as he and Kelly move "upstage," Sinatra is counting to himself. The finale of the number is exciting, using a technique that Kelly was to develop in all of his film choreography. The dancers charge forward directly *at* the camera. In this way, Kelly hoped to capture a three-dimensional quality that one experiences when seeing a dance on the stage. Not only does this provide a brilliant effect as Kelly and Sinatra jump from cot to cot moving directly toward the camera, but it also has the added attraction of enhancing the "adolescent" quality of the scene (boys whooping it up at sleepaway camp) with the two sailors jumping like schoolboys on the furniture much to the pleasure of the onlookers. Frank's movie dancing debut is a marked success.

Nondancers will always be at a disadvantage in executing certain steps, primarily jumps. Dancers are trained when they jump to remain suspended in the air for a few seconds. Because dancers have mastery over their bodies even as they leave the floor, they control both ascent and descent. The ability to remain in the air—to show the picture as it were—is called "ballon." Therefore, in jumps, Sinatra is at a disadvantage, but since most of his numbers involve tap and some movements from jazz, he is not often shown in the air. The alert viewer and, of course, dancers

Sinatra and Gene Kelly: *Take Me Out to the Ball Game*, 1949. (Courtesy of Photofest. Used with permission.)

will notice this problematic area of controlled elevation, which takes years to master. Photographic stills, however, reveal his lack of ballon. (See above from *Take Me Out to the Ball Game* in which Kelly has a distinct "pose" in the air and Sinatra is already nearly on the ground.)

Robert Joffrey used to say that only dancers look at the feet of those dancing; more often than not, spectators look at the upper body. I would add that the audience looks more often at the rapport between the dancers and/or their props and surroundings. This phenomenon ensures that nondancers will not risk unseemly comparisons with their partners, and Sinatra ultimately did not. No one expected him to be as proficient as Kelly. The fact that Sinatra never dances alone gives this emphasis. He needs the professional to shore up his own efforts.

Sinatra's dancing improved with each subsequent film. The numbers became more complex with more dancers; they are longer and, whereas in *Anchors Aweigh* he dances only once, he is included in more than one number in the other films. He never seems wanting and, in fact, adds a great deal to the overall ensemble dance numbers because of his obvious enjoyment in executing them.

After the success of *Anchors Aweigh,* the studio was eager to have another vehicle for Sinatra and Kelly, thus, *Take Me Out to the Ball Game* was conceived by Kelly and Donen. Since O'Brien and Ryan are baseball stars, who moonlight as vaudevillians off-season, *Take Me Out to the Ball Game* begins with a musical number. The scenario accents the song-and-dance-man side of the Hollywood musical with its roots in vaudeville, and in the first and last numbers in the film, the stars even appear on a proscenium stage. The first number shows a confident Sinatra, holding his own with his partner, looking almost as exuberant as the irrepressible Kelly, and incidentally, he no longer looks at his feet. Only the jumps remain problematic. Sinatra displays a professional dancer quality in the vaudeville sequences. His thin, flexible body and his stage presence add to the notion that he is both a song *and* a dance man.

In the "Nelly Kelly" number that opens the film, both men wear white pants, red and white striped jackets, straw boaters, and carry a cane. All of the steps are taken from standard vaudeville routines. The dancers move toward the camera doing time steps, then side to side with various grapevine movements; they strut with hats held aloft, do bell jumps (Sinatra's weak point) and they have one moment when they plant their canes on the stage and waltz around them. The most difficult step is one in which they place their bodies on a diagonal, while supporting themselves on one arm on the floor and pump the free arm up and down while bending and extending their legs. Kelly's athleticism shows here and Frank looks polished during this strenuous sequence.

Another scene in *Take Me Out to the Ball Game* that accents Kelly's love of athletic movement (with many steps borrowed from folk or "character" dances such as the mazurka, the czardas, the Irish jig, sailor's hornpipe, and flamenco) is the O'Brien to Ryan to Goldberg number. (Goldberg is played by Jules Munshin.) In this uproarious pas de trois, the dancers do variations on some of the above types of dances and charge the camera, this time sliding forward on their stomachs. This number, which gives the folk-musical impression of spontaneity, showcases the "triple threat" hamming it up in the best song and dance tradition. For the finish, they run upstage and form a human pyramid (à la circus) with Sinatra jubilantly at the pinnacle, supported by Kelly and Munshin.

Not all of the scenes that require movement in this film are dance sequences. For example, "It's Fate Baby It's Fate," the song that Garrett sings to Sinatra at the ballpark, is not a dance number per se; however, it is choreographed. She pursues him as he runs up and down in the stands and ends up carrying him off in her arms. This segment requires timing, control, and grace (while conveying the impression of being a bit awkward). Sinatra has to be running away from his pursuer but cannot trip or fall through the bleachers. Garrett as an experienced dancer (and despite her long skirt) carries her role off perfectly while Frank provides just the right combination of fear of and fascination with his suitor.

The final scene in the film pairs off Kelly and Williams, Sinatra and Garrett as they should be according to the script. The characters, however, drop their film/script identity and use their real-life names. There is a pre-Fellini feeling to this ploy; the characters in the film have become the "stars" and his or her name denotes a transformation that underscores the celebrity aspect of each actor. Introducing Esther Williams as herself and not as K. C. Higgins and Sinatra as himself and not Denny Ryan and so forth creates a new and unexpected slant for the spectator. We see everything but the cameraman shooting the scene. While this may be an attempt to unmask and demystify the players, it also clearly intends to cast them in a new light. Nonetheless, one cannot believe that Gene Kelly loves Esther Williams anymore than one can cope with Sinatra and Garrett as a permanent couple. The device to break down the barriers between players and audience, although fanciful, distracts from the ending of the film. It breaks out of the established framework and presents the viewer with an odd surprise. On the other hand, the ploy does serve to underscore the star status of all of the principals and is especially advantageous to Sinatra.

The final film, *On the Town,* may be considered in many ways, the best of the trilogy, even though it has some weak points. The male trio, Kelly, Sinatra, and Munshin, are reunited and pursue (or in Sinatra's case is pursued by) Vera-Ellen, Betty Garrett, and Ann Miller. Adapted from the Broadway musical, *On the Town,* which itself originated from the ballet, *Fancy Free,* by Jerome Robbins, with music by Leonard Bernstein, it has a more varied story line, better songs, and a better script than the two preceding musicals. The technical brilliance of the filming of the musical numbers and the megawatt energy of the cast are enough to ensure this film's place in history. Being filmed on location, in New York City, only added to its frenetic pacing. With the possible exception of the dream sequence, "A Day in New York," the film offers an integrated whole in which musical numbers flow naturally from the narrative. Once again, Sinatra has made strides as a dancer, and Jules Munshin, another nondancer, looks pretty agile too. The three women in the film are all dancers, adding considerably to the overall power of the ensemble numbers. The first is Betty Garrett, a female cab driver, who pursues Frank Sinatra with even more determination than in *Take Me Out to the Ball Game.* The second, Vera-Ellen, represents the struggling young dancer trying to forge a career in the big city—she even moonlights as a cooch dancer on Coney Island. The third, Ann Miller, a wealthy socialite, bordering on nymphomania and under psychiatric care, displays a reckless pursuit of men in general and of Jules Munshin in particular.

As to the males, Kelly plays his usual Lothario role until smitten by the "real" thing in the person of Vera-Ellen. Sinatra, often referred to as "Junior," portrays the choirboy sailor who has ingenuously mapped out a sightseeing tour for his buddies, but who proves to be a fast learner (in switching gears) under the tutelage of the cab driver. Jules Munshin, while a bit more subtle than Kelly, is more interested in finding a woman than in seeing the town from Yonkers on down to the Bay: in just one day! He has the luck to link up with the lustful Miller.

Oddly enough for all the musical razzmatazz of *On the Town,* it was not easy to pin down a segment in which Sinatra's improvement as a dancer is clearly seen. That could mean that his performance has become more seamless. In the opening montage, which shows the sailors exploring the "town" and singing its praises, there is little or no dancing, but a lot of choreographed movement. In the Museum of Natural History, the first big number, prehistoric man, becomes a showcase for the specific tap-dancing talents of Ann Miller. The three sailors and the female cabby literally become her props. Then Sinatra has two songs with Garrett: one in her cab and one on top of the Empire State Building. Kelly has a dance number with Vera-Ellen in a Carnegie Hall studio and then the big "A Day in New York" sequence in which Kelly gets to do some virtuoso dancing. Still even the sequences listed above (as in *Take Me Out to the Ball Game*) require agility and various kinds of staged movements including "Come up to My Place," "You're Awful," and even the Coney Island segment. The only clip in which Sinatra and Munshin really dance full-out is the number that includes all six principals (a pas de six). It forms the dancing finale of the film and remains a stirring example, indeed, a classic example, of triumphant film dancing and choreography. The three couples begin on the top of the Empire State Building singing "On the Town." The whole number is complex and athletic; at one point, the sailors jump over their dates' heads. Again, the technique of having the dancers rush toward the camera is used effectively as the six dancers charge out of the doors of the Empire State and turn onto 34th Street. The tempo is fast and furious and not a beat is missed; every note has a step—no pauses at all. The joyous procession moves back and forth along the street, singing all the way. Sinatra fits into this ebullient number and looks as professional as Kelly or any of the other dancers. He has clearly entered the musical comedy ranks with ease and, incidentally, never looks at his feet. Those days are over.

Actually, *On the Town* has less dancing than one remembers. Stanley Donen himself made the same comment. He said he regretted that there was not more dancing in it.[8] Moreover, despite Kelly and Garrett's accolades about Sinatra's hard work in rehearsals, when it came to shooting and multiple takes, Sinatra was often not cooperative; he disliked intensely having to do more than *one* take especially on the narrative or book part of the script.[9] He said too many takes made him stale; hence, Donen, Kelly and others dubbed him "One-take Charlie."[10] His reputation for disliking rehearsing stayed with Sinatra throughout his career. In *Guys and Dolls,* for example, he would retire to his dressing room and tell Joe Mankiewicz to call him when he finished rehearsing with "Mumbles," his nickname for Marlon Brando.[11] (Many critics pointed to his slipshod rehearsal habits as the reason for the failure of his television series for ABC in the 1970s.) Sinatra's attitude toward takes and rehearsals seems at odds with his perfectionist tendencies in his music. He believed that a recording was forever, so his music was obviously more important to him than any other aspect of his career. Movies were not his priority, but stardom was.

In many ways, Sinatra's work at Metro-Goldwyn-Mayer taught him a great deal—not just how to dance. The studio system taught him fundamental lessons and enriched his already extraordinary talent. Part of that enrichment was learning to perform as a dancer for the first time. Another part of that enrichment consisted in his exposure to a wide network of artists—writers, designers, directors, musicians, other singers, actors and dancers—collaborators in a collective effort to produce a superior product; they all helped enlighten Sinatra about his own strivings toward perfection. Despite the stories about his displeasure with repeated rehearsals and takes, at this stage in his career, he did them, at least in the dance sequences. The experience added to his already self-confident stance; the ease with which he would later execute movement in films, on the concert stage, on television, and in nightclubs attests to the effectiveness of his training at MGM. The three musicals examined here demonstrate the kind of intensity, energy, and even innocence that went into the formation of Sinatra and other nondancers and nonsingers from the same period.

Clearly Sinatra's life and career took varied routes after the 1940s. The disarming, innocent character he portrayed in the musicals disappeared. Artistically, he developed immensely in the intervening years. Sinatra the man has always posed more questions than can be answered. He inspires daydreams and fantasies in his fans and friends alike. He represents the strange phenomenon of the enigmatic, elusive celebrity. There have been a handful who grip the imagination but are difficult to fathom: Garbo, Valentino, Tracy, Hepburn, and Sinatra to name a few. In the spotlight, they are superstars who shun publicity; they seem to possess a split personality—a contradictory nature. The characterization of a double life seems accurate if one compares the boyish, all-American roles Sinatra played in the forties musicals, with his later dramatic and darker roles. The staggering length of his career, and his sheer endurance, toughened him. He learned that the only event that surely ends the "act" would be "the final curtain." The intense interest that he still inspires proves that in spite of his absence, he will never be silent. He remains one of the most fascinating figures ever to grace the world stage.

It seems appropriate to accord the final comments to a long-time associate of Sinatra's, Sammy Cahn. He stressed the enigmatic side of the star's personality when he said, "There are three questions about Sinatra no one can ever answer at any given moment: What is he like? Where is he now? Will he show up tonight?"[12]

Notes

1. David Hanna, *Sinatra: Ol' Blue Eyes* (New York: Random House Value Publishing 1998), 16 [original copyright, Starlog Communications International, 1990].

2. Steven Petkov and Leonard Mustazza, eds., *The Frank Sinatra Reader* (New York: Oxford University Press, 1995), 15.

3. Jerome Delamater, *Dance in the Hollywood Musical* (Ann Arbor: UMI Research Press, 1981), 200.

4. Delamater, *Dance in the Hollywood Musical,* 216.

5. Jane Feuer, *The Hollywood Musical,* 2nd ed. (Bloomington and Indianapolis: Indiana University Press, 1993), x.

6. Feuer, *The Hollywood Musical,* 9.

7. Delamater, *Dance in the Hollywood Musical,* 133.

8. PBS Broadcast (Channel 13 in New York City), *The Movie Makers: Stanley Donen,* March 1996.

9. Stephen M. Silverman, *Dancing on the Ceiling: Stanley Donen and His Movies* (New York: Alfred A. Knopf, 1996), 95.

10. Silverman, *Dancing on the Ceiling,* 95.

11. Hanna, *Sinatra: Ol' Blue Eyes Remembered,* 37.

12. Petkov and Mustazza, *The Frank Sinatra Reader,* 161.

Mikhail Baryshnikov and Elaine Kudo in Twyla Tharp's *Sinatra Suite*. (American Ballet Theatre production. Courtesy of Martha Swope. Used with permission.)

13

Dancing to Sinatra:
The Partnership of Music
and Movement in Twyla Tharp's
Sinatra Suite

Lisa Jo Sagolla

The notion of "dancing to Sinatra" immediately calls to mind images of World War II–era GIs and their sweethearts dancing cheek-to-cheek to the crooner's ballads or couples jitterbugging to "Five Minutes More." A provocative presence among social dance music makers of the swing era, Sinatra's songs have also inspired the dancing of professional choreographic artists in ballet and modern dance. It can be argued that the most important and popular choreography created for the concert stage to Sinatra's music is Twyla Tharp's *Sinatra Suite* choreographed in 1983 for Mikhail Baryshnikov and Elaine Kudo of American Ballet Theatre.

The roots of this ballet extend back to the 1970s when Tharp choreographed *Once More, Frank,* a duet to three Sinatra songs. She created the work for a television special she was directing and intended it to be a small, intimate dance for her and Baryshnikov. However, because the Russian star's salary and the rehearsal space were being provided courtesy of American Ballet Theatre, *Once More, Frank* was also performed at the ballet company's star-studded gala at the Metropolitan Opera House on July 12, 1976. It was disastrous! While Tharp and Baryshnikov looked to the piece as an opportunity for avant-garde experimentation and agreed to eliminate all virtuosic elements from the choreography—they pledged Baryshnikov would not leave the ground even once—the audience expected the great danseur to astonish them with his by then legendary classical technique. In her autobiography, Tharp lamented: "We were roundly boo-ed by the $500 a ticket crowd. Misha, who had never been boo-ed in his life, was delighted. However, I had [been], and I was miserable and humiliated as he kept dragging me out for more calls."[1]

At the time, Tharp was an extremely popular modern dance choreographer. She had begun her dance-making career in the 1960s creating serious, formalistic, experimental works. By the 1970s, however, she had rebelled against the minimalist aesthetic of her postmodern contemporaries and established a reputation for making entertaining dances, featuring comedy, wit, spectacular costumes, and popular music. At the end of the decade, though, she turned to choreographing narrative works that darkly explored human relationships, often portraying bitterness and confusion. As a result, her popularity decreased dramatically. It was then that she decided to revisit Sinatra's music. She felt she "needed something wholesome, something American" and said, "I need something I can believe in. . . . I need fidelity, loyalty, trust and love."[2] She chose arrangements of Sinatra's songs from the late 1950s and early 1960s, the period, she says, "when all parents were together, the last time we assumed as a culture that of course men and women lived together and loved for a lifetime."[3]

On October 14, 1982, at the Queen Elizabeth Theatre, in Vancouver, Tharp regained her popularity when her company danced the premiere performance of her new work *Nine Sinatra Songs.* Costumed in 1950s-era evening attire designed by Oscar de la Renta, lit by a twirling mirror ball, and accompanied by Sinatra recordings, seven couples offered variously styled ballroom dance duets that depicted the many faces of romance—infatuation, adolescent awkwardness, seduction, intimacy, and domination.

The following year, Tharp created *Sinatra Suite.* Performed by one couple only, it included four of the duets from *Nine Sinatra Songs,* plus a new solo choreographed especially for Baryshnikov. Unlike *Nine Sinatra Songs* of which there is no film or video recording available to the public, *Sinatra Suite* was aired October 5, 1984, on PBS as part of the Emmy Award–winning special "Baryshnikov by Tharp," which was subsequently made commercially available on a videocassette titled "Baryshnikov Dances Sinatra."[4] Though some may argue that the original *Nine Sinatra Songs* is the more fully realized and artistically interesting work, *Sinatra Suite* is, by far, the more influential in that it has reached, via television and video, many more viewers than have seen, or probably will ever see, *Nine Sinatra Songs* performed live on the concert stage. *Sinatra Suite* is the work that has been preserved and will, therefore, be shown, studied, and referenced as the documentation of the conjunction of Tharp and Sinatra.

Among the critics, the most talked about and controversial aspect of both *Nine Sinatra Songs* and *Sinatra Suite* was the choice and use of Sinatra's music. Of *Nine Sinatra Songs,* Clive Barnes wrote in the *New York Post:* " . . . the audience was practically screaming its approval . . . whether the vociferous reception was for Tharp, the recorded Sinatra, or a bit of both, I don't know . . . despite the wit and off-beat charm of the venture, it only adds up to the sum of its music. It is, after all, Sinatra's way, not Miss Tharp's."[5] In a later magazine article, Barnes opined; "I suspect almost anyone . . . could have a hit with a Sinatra ballet."[6]

The *New York Daily News* reported: "*Nine Sinatra Songs* is a knockout, a runaway hit, a rafter-ringing delight. And who would have guessed it? Even with the canny and unpredictable Tharp at the helm, how could a bunch of tired ballads by

Ol' Blue Eyes be turned into a suite of dances with a cutting edge this sharp? . . . For music which is at its best dull and old-fashioned, Tharp has shaped dances that are breathtakingly stylish, innovative and up-to-the-moment."[7] The *Christian Science Monitor* explained: "Tharp takes the various personae of the Sinatra voice—tough, tender, crooning, yet suggestive—and extends those qualities to a level more intense than Sinatra himself can manage, showing them up for being a little silly."[8] Choreographer and critic Gus Solomons, Jr., wrote: "Tharp is the only person who could get me to sit still for Frank Sinatra's singing."[9] A critic for the *Dancing Times,* a British publication, confessed: "till now Sinatra has been a singer I've always enjoyed without stopping to listen carefully. Tharp, catching the emotion and the line of his singing, shows the eloquence with which he utters single phrases, the lyricism with which he shapes an entire song. So casual, yet such authority."[10]

Of *Sinatra Suite,* the *New York Times* dance critic Anna Kisselgoff wrote in 1983: "To say Frank Sinatra's songs can be shallow would seemingly invite revolution from every bobbysoxer who ever lined up outside the Paramount, were it not for Mr. Sinatra's own reflections at a concert last week. To like one of his classics, 'Strangers in the Night,' he said, 'You have to like pineapple yogurt.' . . . and [so Kisselgoff claims] *Sinatra Suite* could then be called a pineapple yogurt duet."[11]

An analysis of how Tharp's choreography relates to Sinatra's music in each song of the suite reveals much about the varied relationships that can occur between music and dance, particularly if the listener's notion of music encompasses not only rhythm and melody, but also the dramatic implications of the orchestrations and the lyrics. Such study also serves to illuminate the sophisticated subtleties of phrasing and dynamics inherent in Sinatra's vocal style. It could even be argued that Tharp's movement phrases and kinesthetic dynamics enhance how we hear Sinatra in these songs. To illustrate these points, one can use the ballet's loosely suggested narrative as a framework.

Whereas in *Nine Sinatra Songs* different couples present positive and humorous portraits of romance, and all remain partnered forever, *Sinatra Suite* tells a bittersweet tale of a couple who grows apart and culminates with a solo for the male dancer. The ballet begins when the couple meets as "Strangers in the Night" to which they dance a formal tango. During the introductory music, Baryshnikov remains relatively still while his partner circles around him. The moment we hear Sinatra's voice, the couple is seen in a gliding movement of which the focal point is Baryshnikov's hand pressing firmly against Kudo's scapula as if propelling her forward—just as Sinatra is using the lyric to take control of the music, Baryshnikov is taking kinesthetic control of the dance.

When Sinatra reaches the end of the phrase that culminates with a high note on the word "through," he significantly lightens his tone quality, a change that is mirrored by the dancers who forsake the percussive quality of their initial choppy, "talking" movements, and take on the weightlessness of the ballet aesthetic as Kudo opens her long legs and is lifted into a beautiful fan kick. The way Sinatra holds the next long, high note on the word "you" and, without taking a breath, charges directly into the following "strangers in the night" is cleverly underlined by the choreographer. Again, a light balletic lift happens on the high note, but this time, though it appears as if this move will be the endpoint of the phrase, Tharp understands that what is really the highlight here is the wonderful way Sinatra segues nonstop into the next vocal phrase. Therefore, she never allows the lift to end. As Kudo's feet touch the ground, the choreography flows seamlessly through skillfully designed circling patterns into a low-level phrase by Baryshnikov, which the dancer ends powerfully in sync with Sinatra's voice as it lands solidly on the word "night," finally finishing his marvelously long vocal line.

Throughout the song, Tharp repeatedly and inventively marries musical and terpsichorean phrasings. By creating choreography that fits so closely with Sinatra's musical styling, Tharp has made a dance that conveys the feeling of "rightness" a couple experiences when they first sense themselves being transformed from "strangers" into partners.

In the ballet's second section, danced to the lushly sung, yet tenderly orchestrated ballad "All the Way," the couple's intimacy blossoms. The dancers function more like actors in this segment performing choreography that utilizes subtle gestures and glances to convey the emotional intensity Sinatra packs into the lyric.

After an opening sequence of sensual lifts, twirls, and extensions, danced to Sinatra's full-voiced singing about the requirements of real romantic love, the couple winds up on their knees, gazing almost reverently into each other's eyes. Sinatra then illuminates the importance of the verse's final lyric, "if it's real," by softening his volume, at which point the couple slowly stands and the choreography takes on a quiet, less dancelike style. As Baryshnikov walks plainly toward his partner, it appears as though he is being pulled magnetically, as if mesmerized by her. The design of their movements becomes subservient to their emotional connection and to his desire to keep his gaze constantly fixed upon her.

When Sinatra arrives at the lyric, "who knows where the road will lead us, only a fool would say," he places such unusual affection on the word "fool" that the term is amazingly robbed of any derogatory association and the dancing couple simply stops and embraces each other comfortably. As Sinatra starts into the new musical phrase, however, and it is clearly time to dance again, the couple seems unready to step apart and move into new choreography. Instead, they impulsively repeat their embrace and then, belatedly join Sinatra's swelling rendition of the song's ending phrases with an open-legged lift and swooping skater's spin.

By the next song, "That's Life," the couple has begun to conflict. Using an apache dance as her inspiration, Tharp created a comic portrayal of the couple's disaccord and actually received protest letters in response to the presentation of this duet in *Nine Sinatra Songs.*[12]

Tharp again worked hand-in-hand with Sinatra to conjure the drama. The singer begins to set the abusive tone of the number by barking out the lyrics in short, clipped phrases. He then calls attention to the most disturbing word in the passage by extending the "shh" sound in his pronunciation of "shot." Tharp emphasizes "shot" by starting the first actual lift of the piece—a rapid, spinning move—on this word. Kudo is swept up by Baryshnikov on the elongated "shh" sound. She then slices her leg aggressively backwards into a neat, sharp line while the couple rotates angrily through the remainder of the phrase.

As Sinatra continues to sing of his acceptance of life's injustices in an incongruously ranting tone, and Baryshnikov pushes, shakes, drops, and drags his partner around the stage, an arresting arrhythmic sensibility pervades that supports the depiction of an askew situation. Sinatra seems propelled not by any temporal dictates of the music, but by the need to persuasively communicate the meaning of the lyrics. Though he sometimes throws the words out squarely in rhythm—like darts aimed pointedly at the beats—just as often he will pace, accent, or elongate the phrases in a decidedly conversational fashion. Likewise, Baryshnikov puts his partner through a series of awkward maneuvers that begin when he wants her to move and end when he grows tired or irritated and wants to do something else. Sometimes his intentions are confounded by her initiative, which contributes to the overall disharmony. The resulting choreography is not synchronized with the musical rhythms of the singer's delivery, but shares in Sinatra's freewheeling approach.

Probably the most memorable moment in the entire suite is the daring, keenly timed ending of this section. Kudo runs full speed across the stage and throws herself into the air. Miraculously, Baryshnikov turns around just in time to catch her. Then, it is as if Sinatra had been watching the dancers' astounding feat and sings his final lyrics, "My, my" in amazement.

In the next piece, a closely partnered ballroom dance to "My Way," Tharp uses Sinatra's rousing anthem to individualism to illuminate the growing desire for separation within the couple. While a ballroom-dancing couple represents the epitome of romantic oneness—two people moving in perfect harmony with each other and the music, one leading, the other agreeably following, both continually adjusting their movements so as to work as a unified entity—in Tharp's choreography, one sees the dancers reveling in their individual movements. For example, just as Sinatra sings, "the end is near" for the first time, Baryshnikov plants himself in a lunge at his partner's side, their arms linked at the elbows. Suddenly, she lets go of him and does a quick turn alone. The motion sends a small jolt through his body. He tolerates the movement and immediately reconnects and resumes dancing with her, yet one imagines it was not an action he liked or had planned. Throughout the song, the dancers politely take turns developing or supporting each other's phrases, yet as the dancing grows increasingly more passionate, it remains driven by impulses that emphasize each dancer's singularity, not their togetherness. By the end of the dance, she has gone.

The ballet ends with a beautifully lonely solo for Baryshnikov to "One for My Baby," in which he ruefully physicalizes his sorrow. The movement language Tharp has developed for the dancer draws upon his physical genius as both a ballet technician and a dramatic movement artist.

As Sinatra begins to sing, Baryshnikov simply stops moving and listens—he has already loosened his tie and removed his jacket, which he slings over his shoulder while gracefully spinning a skater's turn that runs out of steam just before the lyric starts. The dancer drops his jacket during the first instrumental interlude and proceeds casually to noodle around the space, initiating movement phrases that go no-where—a perfect complement to the singer's relaxed rendition. However, when Sinatra reaches the words "brief episode," Tharp choreographs a markedly con-trasting movement that allows us to hear the lyric in a different way than we other-wise might. Sinatra emphasizes the word "brief" and softens his voice through the word "episode" until it delicately fades to nothing. Baryshnikov, on the word "brief," steps strongly into a rapidly spinning back *attitude*—the first clearly clas-sical position of the piece. But, as Sinatra fades into "episode," Baryshnikov lifts his arms up into a rounded overhead position that strengthens, rather than dissi-pates the shape, and makes us hear a beautifully rounded "oh" sound; suddenly, we realize Sinatra has not thrown away this word, but has, instead, carefully shaped the vowel within it, slyly telling us, perhaps, how precious the episode really was.

As the piece progresses, Baryshnikov continues to underline many of the nu-ances of Sinatra's brilliant phrasing and treatment of melody and lyrics. When the singer seems almost to be falling off the edge of the pitch as he squeezes out the word "easy" on a long held note, Baryshnikov does an inward turn while inclining his torso forward, as if he, too, is perilously close to falling. The choice to turn *in-ward,* rather than *outward,* also creates a feeling of tension or strain—mirroring the tight sound of Sinatra's "e" vowel—as the dancer spins by drawing energy into himself rather than opening out into the breeziness of an outside turn.

It is also during this solo that the viewer becomes aware of the degree to which Baryshnikov's performance throughout the suite can be seen as an embodiment of Sinatra the man, as well as Sinatra the singer. The dancer's kinesthetic attitude so boldly suggests the Sinatra persona that while watching Baryshnikov, it feels as though one is "seeing" Sinatra. In the most spectacular moment of the dance, it could be argued that Baryshnikov actually manages to out-do Sinatra in terms of his characteristic "cool-guy" casualness; after completing eight astonishing pirou-ettes, the dancer off-handedly strolls out of the spins as if he had done nothing at all remarkable.

Finally, it is hoped that this analytic highlighting of a few of the noteworthy re-lationships between the music and choreography in this enormously popular ballet has enhanced one's understanding of how a choreographic artist might hear and utilize music to support or inspire her expressive efforts. Perhaps one's own hear-ing of these Sinatra songs has also been enriched or altered. As a videotape of *Sina-tra Suite* is commercially available for purchase or rental, the reader is advised to view the entire ballet with eyes and ears attuned to unearthing the full extent of the rich and intriguing partnership that exists between the dance and music of Tharp and Sinatra.

Notes

1. Twyla Tharp, *Push Comes to Shove* (New York: Bantam Books, 1992), 270–71.
2. Twyla Tharp interview, John Gruen, December 8, 1983, Manuscript collection, Dance Research Collection, The New York Public Library of the Performing Arts.
3. Tharp, *Push Comes to Shove,* 270–71.

4. *Baryshnikov Dances Sinatra and More with American Ballet Theatre,* directed by Don Mischer and Twyla Tharp, produced by Don Mischer (West Long Branch, NJ: KULTUR International Films, 1984), 60 minutes, color.

5. Clive Barnes, "Tharp Dances to Sinatra's Beat," *New York Post,* January 26, 1984.

6. Clive Barnes, "Twyla Tharp and the Modern Classicism," *Dance and Dancers,* September 1987.

7. Rob Baker, "Tharp's Delightful Sinatra Songs," *New York Daily News,* January 27, 1984.

8. Nancy Goldner, "An All-Around Triumph for Twyla Tharp," *Christian Science Monitor,* February 6, 1984.

9. Gus Solomons, Jr., "Twyla Tharp and Dancers," *Dance Magazine,* May 1992.

10. Alastair Macaulay, "Twyla Tharp Dance," *Dancing Times,* February 11, 1984.

11. Anna Kisselgoff, "American Ballet Theatre Performs Twyla Tharp's Sinatra," *New York Times,* December 13, 1983.

12. Tharp, *Push Comes to Shove,* 276.

Sinatra as Tony Rome, 1967. (Courtesy of Photofest. Used with permission.)

14

From Sam Spade to Tony Rome: Bogart's Influence on Sinatra's Film Career

Walter Raubicheck

Frank Sinatra's recording and film careers reveal interesting parallels and divergences. In the forties, his music and his movies served to create a unified persona: the fresh-faced young innocent of *Anchors Aweigh* (1945) seemed to be a perfect physical embodiment of the Voice that his audience heard on records and the radio. However, during the fifties and sixties, Sinatra created new film images that occasionally contradicted the lush romanticism of the Capitol and Reprise recordings. The psychopathic killer in *Suddenly* (1954), for example, could not be easily reconciled with the singer of *In The Wee Small Hours of the Morning* (1955). This was the kind of role—the tough, violent yet strangely appealing social outcast—that his friend Humphrey Bogart had originated in *The Petrified Forest* (1936) and developed in a variety of gangster movies and films noirs in the thirties and forties.

Interestingly, the "swinging" Pal Joey character—perhaps Sinatra's signature role in the fifties—is rooted in the forties, in John O'Hara's popular sequence of stories. It is not difficult to imagine Joey against the backdrop of a classic film noir. An unmistakable romanticism marks these movies: under the tough, hard-boiled surface, actors like Bogart and Cagney conveyed a hidden but potent sensitivity and a wounded but still active idealism. This is the quality that Sinatra seems to understand: toughness is often the necessary shell to protect tenderness. The beauty of the fifties and sixties recordings in no way cancels out the cynicism of Sinatra's "tough" films or the "swinging" ones with the Rat Pack. (Sinatra also played roles in which his ethnicity and his comic talents accompany his streetwise toughness.) Like Bogart's, Sinatra's appeal lies in his implicit assumption that toughness does not exclude feeling, that a sense of irony does not preclude a sense of honor.

It is a truism when discussing Sinatra's film career that he had one ten-year period of major work, from *From Here To Eternity* in 1953 to *The Manchurian Candidate* in 1962. After that, it is said, he walked through his films as "one-take" Sinatra, reserving his creative energy for his true art, the singing of American standards. However, I would like to suggest that the films he made after 1962 are consistent with his basic goal as a film actor: to carry on the persona created by his friend and mentor Humphrey Bogart. For the sensibility of the characters Bogart created in the forties and early fifties is one that appealed so strongly to Sinatra that it influenced all his film work.

The biographical data, of course, is fascinating. Bogart's last film, *The Harder They Fall,* was made in 1956, just as Sinatra's film career was reaching its first artistic high points. The two were close friends, Sinatra was a major player in Bogart's Rat Pack, and after Bogart's death in 1957, Sinatra came close to marrying his widow, Lauren Bacall. *Suddenly* shares a remarkable number of plot and thematic elements with Bogart's *The Desperate Hours,* released a year later in 1955. Clearly some kind of torch was being passed on to Sinatra from the older actor, one he desired and treasured.

The Bogart screen sensibility is perhaps best described by Forster Hirsch in his wonderful book on film noir, *The Dark Side of the Screen:* "Bogart balances astringency with a fleeting sentimentality and romanticism in a way that no other actor ever has. [He] has the face of a man of enormous feeling kept in check: he is clearly a man with churning insides beneath the still mask. His gaze is direct yet wary; the scornful twist of the lips does not belie the sense of honor that turns him into a hero no matter what kind of role he is playing."[1] Hirsch's emphasis on the romanticism of the Bogart hero is essential to our understanding of Sinatra's attraction to the role. For it is this element that unites his film and recording careers: Bogart's "fleeting sentimentality and romanticism" are brought to prominence in Sinatra's music, while the "astringency" and "sense of honor" are the qualities he strove to attain in his acting roles.

Interestingly, Bogart's career reveals a very different arc from Sinatra's. He began by playing villains in the 1930s Warner Brothers gangster series. With the exception of his astounding portrayal of Duke Mantee in *The Petrified Forest* (1936), the memorable hoodlum in Robert Sherwood's play who represents all the forces of chaos and disorder, the characters Bogart played in this period were one-dimensional tough guys who were often killed at the end of the pictures by heroes played by James Cagney and George Raft. In 1941, this pattern was changed forever by *High Sierra* and *The Maltese Falcon.* In these two films, Bogart proved that he could play the protagonist and not only the antagonist in the crime films that came to be known as film noir. In both these pictures, Bogart proved he could play a romantic lead as well, as intense, erotic scenes with Ida Lupino and Mary Astor demonstrated. As Sam Spade in *The Maltese Falcon* and Philip Marlowe in *The Big Sleep* (1946), Bogart brought Hammett's and Chandler's private eye heroes to indelible life on the screen.

In the period from 1941 to 1947, Bogart played the archetypal tough loner, even when he was not a private eye. In *Casablanca* (1943), *Dead Reckoning* (1947), and

Dark Passage (1947), Bogart refined the 1941 persona, which became an enduring aspect of American popular culture. Beginning in 1948, he tried to expand his range with mixed results: astoundingly successful as a man destroyed by greed in *The Treasure of Sierra Madre* (1948), but merely interesting as a wealthy businessman in *Sabrina* (1954). He played no more private eyes and only returned once to an earlier model when he played the Duke Mantee-like convict in *The Desperate Hours.*

Sinatra's career is markedly different. From the juveniles he played in the forties musicals, Sinatra emerged full-blown in the mid-fifties as a major screen presence. In the sixties, he moved closer and closer to Bogart's tough private eye persona, finally adopting it completely in *Tony Rome* (1967). Indeed, five of Sinatra's last six screen characters are detectives. Clearly Sinatra felt that he had finally reached his personal goals as an actor as he settled into the tough private eye or police detective he portrayed in *Tony Rome, The Detective* (1968), *Lady in Cement* (1968), the television film *Contract on Cherry Street* (1977), and his last feature film, *The First Deadly Sin* (1980). In these neo-noirs, he played either the incorruptible police detective or the loner private investigator walking down the mean streets of Miami or New York in the swinging sixties and the cynical seventies.

In the fifties, Sinatra played in a wide variety of genres, from musicals such as *Guys and Dolls* to romantic comedies such as *The Tender Trap* to harrowing dramas such as *The Man With the Golden Arm,* all released in 1955. But any discussion of his film work in that decade must begin with *From Here to Eternity* (1953), not only because of the legends that surround Sinatra's casting, the impetus it gave to his stalled career, and his subsequent Academy Award, but primarily because it established all the characteristics of his own film persona of the next decade, some of which he would draw on for each role. First of all, Angelo Maggio is an Italian American from Brooklyn, the only clearly defined ethnic character in the film. Second, he provides the film's best humor during his drunk scenes, and Sinatra here proves that he possesses some genuine talent for comedy. Third, he is tough, stubborn, and defiant, all traits that Sinatra would portray quite effectively in the films to come. In the company of conflicted, introverted characters such as Burt Lancaster's Warden and Montgomery Clift's Pruitt, Sinatra's Maggio injects his scenes with the movie's real energy and passion. Maggio's pugnacity and violent reaction to insults are reminiscent of Bogart's tough guy, but the humor and the ethnic traits are Sinatra's own. He gave up these distinctive characteristics in the later "Bogart" films of the sixties and seventies. Somewhat ironically, his evident desire to replace Bogart on the screen did not result in his greatest achievements as a movie actor.

His ethnicity in *From Here to Eternity* marks him as a working class immigrant, and although the character as written does exhibit some stereotypically "crude" behavior, this Italian-American identity became part of the Sinatra persona in the fifties, in marked contrast to Bogart's classless, existential image. Sinatra was often cast in roles that utilized his Northern-Jersey working class accent and manner, roles that revealed a subtext in the scripts involving social snobbery and class barriers that Sinatra the singer undermined with the beauty and perfect diction of his singing voice. For example, in *High Society,* Sinatra gives Mike Connor a proletarian spin that differs from his predecessor James Stewart's cockiness in *The Philadelphia Story* (1940), the film based on Philip Barry's play that is the basis for the musical, and makes him a perfect foil for the blue-blooded arrogance of Tracy Lord (Grace Kelly). Their mutual, class-based suspicion of each other, however, is broken down when Sinatra serenades her with the ballad "You're Sensational": Kelly's character finally responds ardently to the sensuality of the song and Sinatra's directness and rough charm. In *Pal Joey,* Sinatra's Joey Evans is a saloon singer who yearns to be a supper-club entertainer complete with French repartee. As a result, he is easily seduced away from Kim Novak's chorus girl by the "class" and money of Rita Hayworth's socialite. Ultimately, of course, he rejects social climbing for love. In *Some Came Running* (1958), Sinatra plays the middle-class writer Dave Hirsch, but the class issue is foregrounded by his growing affection for the working class floozy played by Shirley Maclaine and his disenchantment with the cultured professor played by Martha Hyer. Bogart would not have fit these roles as well as Sinatra, whose immigrant ethnicity gave him the requisite authenticity.

In addition, Sinatra also played a variety of lighter roles in the fifties that would have been beyond Bogart's range. As the irresponsible but charming hotel owner in *A Hole in the Head* (1959), Sinatra displays a genuine talent for light romantic comedy and domestic melodrama. To cast Bogart in this role would have substituted intensity for the good-natured swagger of Sinatra's womanizer. Frank Capra, who directed the film, had never cast Bogart throughout his long career. In fact, Sinatra's playing here recalls the comic touch that Clark Gable gave to *It Happened One Night* (1934): both actors possessed a particularly American insouciance that marks Capra's style of humor. The scenes with the boy (Eddie Hodges) are particularly affecting, since Sinatra's raffishness keeps the sentimentality in check. Tony Manetta is not that different from Danny Ocean, the character Sinatra would play the next year in the first Rat Pack film, *Ocean's 11,* although the Rat Pack Sinatra sacrifices Tony's vulnerability to extend the hipster cockiness.

Critical consensus holds that Sinatra's last great performance was in *The Manchurian Candidate.* Certainly nothing he had done before and nothing he would do later prepares us for the character of Bennett Marco, the strung-out Army intelligence major whose nightmares about murder in the military turn him into the epitome of a man headed for what was then called a "nervous breakdown." His famous scene on the train with Janet Leigh, as she watches him fumbling unsuccessfully to light a cigarette, brings out a vulnerability in Sinatra that we do not associate with either him or Bogart. Laurence Harvey's Raymond Shaw is really the protagonist of the film, but Sinatra's Marco once again supplies its genuine touch of cold war paranoia.

This is not to say that Sinatra was a "greater" actor than Bogart, but to point out that during his most prolific and popular screen period, he often played against the Bogart type he would later embrace. Sinatra had the lighter touch: even if the movie were done as a nonmusical drama, Bogart would have given Joey Evans's struggle to maintain his integrity such conflicted energy that the film would have been more like an adaptation from Hemingway than from O'Hara. (Gene Kelly, who starred in the Broadway musical version, would not have possessed the appropriate screen presence for the role: by the fifties, his movie persona was simply too nice.) Sinatra is able to give Joey just the right combination of character flaw and personal charm to make him attractive, not tragic.

When Sinatra moves into Bogart's own territory, he does a credible job, but, like everyone else, he can never quite convey the depths of feeling beneath the stoicism that Bogart projected so effortlessly. In *Suddenly,* for example, Sinatra is entirely convincing as the homicidal psychopath, but he wears the character's psychosis on his sleeve. The menace is therefore not as great as it would have been had Bogart played the part, for he would have been more in control: the hints of madness would have made the family's situation that much more terrifying. In the private-eye movies of his later career, Sinatra is unable to reach the hard-won sense of self-sufficiency that Bogart conveys as Spade or Marlowe: Sinatra cracks wise as he looks on the corruption around him, but he never communicates the feeling that his personal integrity has been tested or questioned. Part of the problem, of course, is in the material: Marvin Albert, who wrote the Tony Rome series, is no Dashiell Hammett or Raymond Chandler. Part of the problem also lies with the genre: the tough-guy private eye seems out of place in the late sixties of Raquel Welch and Jill St. John, and the filmmakers are not giving the archetypal characters the postmodernist spin of Robert Altman's *The Long Goodbye* (1973) or the Watergate sensibility of Roman Polanski's *Chinatown* (1974). Sinatra is solid in these movies and he clearly relishes the parts, but he is unable to give them the psychological weight of Bogart's noir classics.

Contemporary critics were quick to see the Bogart connection behind the Tony Rome films. *Time* called *Tony Rome* "a blatantly inept, uncredited remake of Humphrey Bogart's 1946 *The Big Sleep*."[2] Bosley Crowther in the *New York Times* commented that "This sort of business is familiar, and if Sinatra chooses to go in for it in a style that emulates Humphrey Bogart's to a certain extent, that's his affair. Although he quite clearly endeavors in this film, as he has done before, to galvanize the character of a me-first loner as Bogart so frequently and effectively did, he comes up with a callous, cool-cat character somewhat short of old Bogey's."[3] The *Saturday Review* pointed out that "[Sinatra] has had to fit himself into a type molded long before by Humphrey Bogart and, before him, by Dashiell Hammett . . . *Tony Rome* is lively and entertaining, and for this we must thank both the capable Mr. Sinatra and the persistent ghost of Mr. Bogart. In fact, the film makes no bones about its purpose—that of updating the Bogart "Shamus" formula, which still can cast its spell."[4] While many of his contemporaries such as Dean Martin and James Coburn were jumping on the James Bond bandwagon to play international spies, Sinatra preferred to stay within the older forties tradition. Part of the reason may have been his physical appearance at fifty-two: his added weight, graying hair, and lined face gave him the suitable hard-bitten look required for the part. He had turned fifty in 1965, and the movie he made that year, *Von Ryan's Express,* was the first one in which he truly looked his age; the new maturity gave his portrayal of Colonel Ryan a tough authority—it is also a role that Bogart would have relished in his prime. Certainly one gets the sense from *Tony Rome* and *Lady in Cement* that Sinatra is playing a part he feels extremely comfortable in, a part he had always wanted to play.

Sinatra's Tony Rome is an anomaly in the "swinging" mid-to-late sixties Miami Beach world of the films. As he moves among the druggies, free-sex swingers, posh hotels, and tawdry strip clubs, Sinatra conveys the image of a fifties throwback: When he is working on a case, he is dressed like a typical private eye from a decade and even two decades earlier, complete with suit, tie, and hat. (In the interior scenes, he always needs to find a place to put down this ubiquitous hat, while no one else in the films still wears one.) It is as if Sinatra used these rather thin vehicles to reassert the stoic, tough-guy values of Sam Spade or Phillip Marlowe amid the amorality of the contemporary scene. When he is not working, Sinatra's Rome lives on a house-boat and dresses like Bogart in the sailing outfits he wore on his beloved boat in the years he spent socializing with Sinatra in the original Rat Pack.

The three police detective films, of course, have a different tone from the *Tony Rome* films. The cop he plays in *The Detective, Contract on Cherry Street,* and *The First Deadly Sin* certainly shares Tony Rome's toughness and sense of integrity, but he is also more burdened by guilt and suffering and much less prone to wisecracking his way into the arms of beautiful suspects. In *The Detective,* shot in the same year as the second Tony Rome film, Sinatra plays police detective Joe Leland, who is strug-gling with the corruption of the department, the chronic infidelities of his wife, and his own guilt in contributing to the execution of an innocent man. Instead of standing apart from the sordidness of his environment through his dress and his sardonic wise-cracking, Sinatra's character in this film is deeply implicated in it, and the actor here is able to convey the tarnished morality of the protagonist with a seriousness of pur-pose and accomplishment that surprised many critics who had written him off since the Rat Pack films. Sinatra is authentically New York circa 1967 here, not a throw-back to earlier models of the noir shamus.

Sinatra's last feature film, *The First Deadly Sin,* is probably the best example of this more somber detective. The scenes with his dying wife, played by Faye Dunaway, bring out his compassion and extreme sensitivity, while the scenes of his confrontation with the police bureaucracy emphasize his honesty and sense of justice. It is a good example of color film noir: many scenes are shot on rainy, dark Manhattan streets, and the movie stresses psychological aberration in the character of the psychotic serial murderer. Thematically, the film reaches for more than it grasps: the religious symbolism (the movie is simply filled with crucifixes) never quite explains satisfactorily Lieutenant Delaney's lonely fight against physical evil (his wife's unnamed illness), insanity (the killer), and human vanity (the cor-ruption of the police department and the justice system). Sinatra was clearly drawn to the Lawrence Sanders novel, as he served as executive producer on the project. Whether the film's preoccupation with resisting all these various kinds of evil had a personal resonance for him or he simply realized that the aging cop was a great part, he did choose a fitting vehicle with which to end his film career. He is superb as Delaney, and he powerfully conveys, in Forster Hirsch's description of Bogart's character, a man with "churning insides beneath the still mask."

As an actor Sinatra, like Bogart, rejected the method approach of Brando and his Actors Studio contemporaries. He was a natural actor, both in his singing and in films, as many have noted. He interpreted lyrics by temporarily becoming the character who was experiencing those feelings, not simply by fitting notes to words. One always senses that Sinatra is thinking about the meaning of the lyrics as he sings them. In movies, he also displayed the requisite ability to become his character, as long as it did not stray too far from his own personal style and sensibility, and he did so with an urgency and energy that rarely failed him. Even in a film like *Some Came Running,* in which he plays the unlikely role of a novelist, Sinatra is able to find common ground with the character, not only because Dave Hirsch is a drinker and occasional womanizer, but also because Sinatra could empathize with Hirsch's struggles as an artist and his unwavering personal integrity. He always performed in films with a particular model in mind, that of his friend Humphrey Bogart—who on screen and in life embodied integrity for Sinatra. "There'll never be another performer like Bogey was," Sinatra once said. "His characters had a lot of fun in them. They had cynicism, and they had honesty, and he was a seedy character but he had honor all the time."[5]

As a singer, Sinatra was deeply affected by Bing Crosby's music, but he gradually grew away from Crosby's style and forged his own—particularly in the dark, brooding balladry of the Capitol years—while as an actor he grew ever closer to the Bogart image as his career developed. The singer and the actor in Sinatra complemented each other, never more clearly demonstrated than in 1968 when he was simultaneously shooting *Lady in Cement* by day in and around the Fontainebleau hotel on Miami Beach while performing in the hotel's La Ronde lounge at night, despite singing difficulties created by a bout with the flu. One journalist at the time reported that "it's not difficult to tell when Sinatra has had a bad night, when the show at La Ronde has not met his standards. He is strained, tense. But on days when the previous night's show has gone well . . . his mood is so high that everyone on the set is up with him."[6]

Again, Sinatra's sensibility as an artist was a unified one, the Tony Rome acting persona he inherited from Humphrey Bogart was always fed by the singer who captured the essence of romanticism. Ultimately Sinatra possessed a noir sensibility: like the heroes of these enduring American films, he projected both a surface stoicism and a deeply sensitive core that enabled him to convey genuine emotion without lapsing into sentimentality. Sinatra the singer is in no danger of being underappreciated, but it is now time to recognize his achievements as a screen actor and to understand the intimate connection between the artistry of the vocalist and that of the movie star.

Notes

1. Foster Hirsch, *The Dark Side of the Screen* (New York: Da Capo, 1981), 150.

2. *Time* review quoted in Gene Ringgold and Clifford McCarty, *The Films of Frank Sinatra* (New York: Carol, 1993), 230.

3. Bosley Crowther, *The New York Times,* quoted in Ringgold and McCarty, 230.

4. *Saturday Review.* Quoted in Ringgold and McCarty, 230.

5. Frank Sinatra, *Newsweek* quoted in Steven Petkov and Leonard Mistazza, *The Frank Sinatra Reader* (New York: Oxford University Press, 1995), 134.

6. Roy Newquist, "Sinatra Power," quoted in Petkov and Mustazza, 134.

15

Sinatra Satire:
Fifty Years of Punch Lines

Patric M. Verrone

Frank Sinatra was satirized for as long a period, and in as many different media, as anyone in the twentieth century. From animated cartoons of the 1940s through television sketches of the 1990s, these parodies were both a reflection of, and a force behind, the public perception of Sinatra. They also speak to the dramatic way American comedy changed over that fifty-year period.

When Sinatra came to prominence in the late 1930s, his concerts included bobby-soxers who rushed the stage, screamed, and even fainted. The earliest Sinatra jokes were based on his phenomenal effect on young women. A print cartoon from the early forties showed a G.I. on a ladder outside his girlfriend's window, ready to elope. She kept him at bay saying, "Do you mind waiting a few minutes, Henry? I'm listening to Frank Sinatra."[1] Another depicted a teenager in a plaid skirt and saddle shoes weeping over her record player. Her father asked her mother, "Isn't she feeling well, or is that Frank Sinatra?"[2] A Frank Beaven cartoon showed three literally wild women clinging to the bars of a cell as a guard tells a visitor, "This is our Frank Sinatra ward."[3]

These cartoons were as innocent as Sinatra satire would ever get. They commented on the "Sinatra phenomenon" rather than on the man and did so in a flattering way. The mere name "Frank Sinatra" is the punch line in all three cases. There is no actual rendering of Sinatra in any of them and, considering that his fame was derived from recordings and radio, no rendering was necessary. This would soon change, however, when animated cartoons developed a comedic "Sinatra look."

Between 1944 and 1950, at least seven animated cartoons from three different studios[4] depicted characters based on Frank Sinatra. "Frankie" (as he was called in many) was typically a bone-thin crooner who sang into a stand-up microphone, wore a huge bow tie, and made females squeal and faint. Although Sinatra never lent his voice to any of these cartoons and the name "Sinatra" was never used, there was no doubt (then or now) who was being parodied.

Warner Brothers created six Sinatra cartoons. In "Swooner Crooner,"[5] Porky Pig's egg farm runs afoul when his bobby-soxer hens leave their posts to swoon over "Frankie"—a crooning rooster singing "As Time Goes By." Porky hires a new rooster (a pipe-smoking Bing Crosby–type) and the two roosters have a crooning contest that produces mountains of eggs, including an unexpected pile from Porky himself.

In "Book Revue,"[6] characters from book jackets come to life, including "The Voice in the Wilderness" (a wheelchair-bound Sinatra pushed by a muscular orderly). His version of "It Had to Be You" knocks out "Little Women," "The Lady in the Dark," and "Mother Goose." Later, when the Big Bad Wolf escapes from a "Life" sentence, the Voice reappears and the (male!) wolf passes out into "Dante's Inferno."

"Hollywood Canine Canteen"[7] features musical dogs (ranging from Kaynine Kiser to Leopold Bowowsky) putting on a United Service Organization (USO) show. One sequence includes a Bing Crosby "bowser" wooing Dorothy Lamour only to be interrupted by a Sinatra dog. His serenading causes Crosby to pass out, allowing Lamour to carry Sinatra off in her arms.

In a Bugs Bunny cartoon called "Slick Hare,"[8] a young (and human) Sinatra makes a quick appearance at the bar of the Mocrumbo Restaurant. He draws at the straw of his drink with all his might, only to be sucked back in, his feet flailing helplessly.

In "Catch as Cats Can,"[9] a Bing Crosby–based parrot (with pipe and racing form) encourages Sylvester the Cat to pursue a Sinatraesque canary. This canary wears a bow tie, makes she-canaries faint off a windowsill, and has a physique so gaunt he eats birdseed from a box marked "Vitamins A, B, C, D, E, and Z." After the clever canary foils several schemes, Sylvester tires of plotting and simply eats the Crosby parrot (incongruously taking on his leisurely mannerisms and the ubiquitous pipe).

The final Warner Brothers appearance was "Curtain Razor"[10] in which talent agent Porky Pig auditions the bird trio of Bingo, Frankie, and Al (as in Crosby, Sinatra, and Jolson). During a performance of "April Showers," the Sinatraesque chicken's microphone stand itself screams "Frankie" and faints.

Though Warner had the most Sinatra cartoons, MGM had (at least arguably) the best in "Little Tinker."[11] Lonely and loveless, B. O. Skunk finds a book called "Advice to the Love-Worn" and applies rule 3, "Swoon 'Em." He puts on a "Frankie Suit" and croons "Rhapsody in Pew." Two intercut series of gags follow: One exaggerates his thinness—he hides behind the mike pole, falls through a knothole in the stage, is outweighed by a feather, takes oxygen and plasma, lies in an iron lung, and is measured by an undertaker. The other shows the reactions of the female rabbits—they scream, pass out, squeeze barren trees until they sprout, hit themselves in the head, hit each other in the head, and hit themselves in the head with each

other. An old rabbit falls into a grave with a tombstone marked, "Oh Frankie." Ultimately, the rabbits rush the stage, discover that B. O. is a skunk, and flee.[12]

The final Sinatra cartoon was a Paramount Noveltoon called "Goofy Goofy
Gander"[13] in which Little Audrey gets a tour of a jazzy nursery rhyme land by a hip
Mother Goose. They see "Little Tommy Tucker" and call on him to sing for his
supper. Tommy (Sinatra's head and bow tie on a body thinner than a broomstick)
obliges and both ladies moan and faint.[14]

Although these animated cartoons went a step beyond the comics of the day in that
they actually *showed* Sinatra, they were still quite innocent in their jibes. Four of them
drew Sinatra as a cute animal. Many of the gags were at the expense of his female
fans and the jokes at his expense were based on his physique and his feud with Bing
Crosby (which Sinatra made fun of himself).[15] The one exception to these generally
flattering portrayals is a moment in "Catch as Cats Can" when the Sinatra canary escapes from a trap, screams "Hit the road, stupid!" and blacks the cat's eye. Although
this could just be typical cartoon violence, its timing is noteworthy. The cartoon was
in production at the time of Sinatra's well-publicized altercation with journalist Lee
Mortimer. This joke might be the very first "Sinatra as tough guy" gag—a reoccur-
ring hook that would taunt Sinatra for the next fifty years.

Although animated cartoons continued strong into the sixties, Sinatra appearances stopped in the early fifties. At that time, with his career and personal life at
their low points, Sinatra was not especially funny. Jokes based on his looks or his
effect on women were old (the bobby-sox days were over). Pundits of today might
have exploited his sexual antics[16] or his receding hairline but no one back then
would dare. Cartoonists presumed their audiences would find such jokes unsa-
vory. Other media were not quick to pick up the mantle. Filmmakers, who avoid
topical parody because it gets stale fast, never really took aim at Sinatra anyway.[17]
Television was still maturing as a satirical medium.[18] Stand-up comedians, notorious for "pushing the envelope" of good taste, did not touch Sinatra[19] because of his
connections (real or not) with the people who ran the nightclubs where they
worked.[20] Comedy or novelty recordings similarly avoided him because of his obvious reach in that business.

For this portion of Sinatra's career, the only forum with an audience sophisticated enough to understand Sinatra's peccadilloes and writers willing to make fun
of them was the humor magazine. Unlike Britain's *Punch,* American magazines
that print humor usually specialize in another venue like literature (the *New
Yorker*) or adult content (*Playboy*) and those that do not either have an extremely
low circulation (the *Harvard Lampoon*) or short life spans (*Laugh-In Magazine*).
The two exceptions in Sinatra's lifetime were *National Lampoon* and *MAD.*

National Lampoon had its heyday in the seventies (spawning successful films
like *Animal House* and launching the careers of an army of print, television, and
film writers) by emphasizing a style of humor that was raw and relentless—what
was often called "edgy." During this period, Frank Sinatra himself was considered
edgy by few and *National Lampoon* left him almost completely alone. The few
jabs it did take at him were mostly mild (teaming him up in 1977 with Paul
McCartney for a prophetic album of *Duets*) and not particularly daring (a March

1982 "Match the Toupee" contest used a joke that was by then twenty years old).[21] The most edgy *National Lampoon* piece involving Sinatra was one which never ran. In the late seventies, the magazine planned a parody of a then-current luggage ad with a joke based on the plane crash that took the life of Sinatra's mother. The ad was stopped when good sense prevailed.[22]

Alternatively, *MAD* has been going strong since 1953. Often more sophisticated than its typically teenage reader was, it was a model of editorial and artistic consistency for over 400 issues before its format had changed (including the addition of once-forbidden paid advertisements at the turn of the twenty-first century). A search of *Totally MAD,* a seven volume CD-ROM containing every *MAD* issue through 1998, reveals over ninety-three separate appearances by Frank Sinatra and Sinatra-inspired characters over a forty-year period.

Sinatra's first *MAD* appearance was in June 1954 in a movie parody called "From Eternity Back to Here."[23] In the first of three panels, the Sinatra-based Majjio (surrounded by adoring women) breaks a chair over Fatso (the Ernest Borgnine-esque stockade sergeant) and protests, "These engagements at the Paramount are rough!" Later, at a club filled with buxom women, he implores his Montgomery Clift–like buddy Prewitt to "Look at them beauties! . . . Yessir! . . . Them ping-pong tables are sure beauties! Now if we can only get past these dopey girls . . ." Finally, when Prewitt avenges Majjio's death at Fatso's hands, the fat guard pulls a knife and announces, "He shoulda given me his autograph."

This was one of only a few of Sinatra's appearances in the magazine in the fifties and it points out the problems with Sinatra satire in that decade. The two Sinatra hooks were his name and his effect on women and they only worked as punch lines in 1954 if you accept that the movie was set in 1940 (when Sinatra still played the Paramount). Further, the ping-pong table joke seems un-Sinatra-like and the chair broken over Fatso's oblivious head is not a truly telling Sinatra-is-violent joke because it is actually a comment on the volatile Maggio-Fatso relationship in the movie.

Overcoming these early problems, *MAD* released a bounty of Sinatra satire in the sixties and seventies. One elaborate piece (from June 1962) is a virtual encyclopedia of Sinatra hooks. Titled "Celebrities' Wallets,"[24] it mocks the Rat Pack (and a particularly fawning Sammy Davis, Jr.), Sinatra's organized crime connections, his real estate holdings, his assistance in President John F. Kennedy's election, his violent propensity against reporters, his jargon, his desire for privacy, his drinking, and even his ongoing difficulty in proving that he did not dodge the draft in World War II. It is unclear exactly how many of these hooks were common knowledge in 1962 (especially to *MAD* readers), but this piece is hard evidence of how many were available to satirists who were willing to *make* them common knowledge.

Sinatra made dozens of other appearances in *MAD* in the sixties. Among the highlights: "Celebrities' Home Movies" (December 1962) depicts Sinatra narrating a "ring-a-ding home movie" in which he instinctively punches his friend the cameraman.[25] "Celebrities' Nightmares" (January 1964) shows a sleeping Sinatra dreaming about his toupee blowing off during a concert.[26] "Mad's Academy Awards for World Celebrities" (December 1968) presents a doctored photo of Sinatra and Mia Farrow (just divorced) holding Oscars for "Best Performance in a Romantic Farce."[27] There was even a "cameo" in the January 1969 movie take-off "Rosemia's Booboo,"[28] which contains a parody of the notorious satanic orgy sequence from the film and depicts a naked Sinatra—referred to only as "that skinny guy . . . singing, 'Scoobie Doobie Doo'!"

Sinatra appears in two panels of "A Mad Look at Celebrities in Real-Life Situations" from March 1970.[29] In the first, "Sammy Davis, Jr. Tells It Like It Is," Davis revels in the advances made by several African Americans only to answer a phone call from Sinatra with, "Yes, Master . . . ?" The other, "A Busy Day at the Home of Frank Sinatra" includes three visitors: A doctor who offers Sinatra a follow-up to his hair transplant (namely a muscle transplant), a plumber who asks for an autograph and gets punched (says the butler, "That's how he gives autographs!"), and a girl scout to whom Sinatra proposes.

MAD continued to produce Sinatra satire in the seventies and eighties but struck only familiar chords. "Whatever Became of . . . ?" (September 1976) predicts that, in 1996, Sinatra would be living in isolation in the Mojave Desert after having been kicked out of the "Old Singers Home" in Palm Springs "for slugging a night nurse."[30] The "Daily Rhyme" (October 1977) features three small animals punched by a touring Sinatra (in the South . . . "a possum in the mouth," in Duluth . . . "a hamster in the tooth," and while overseas . . . "a Pekingese").[31] *The MAD Nasty Book* (October 1979) lives up to its name with five nasty (and not particularly funny) Sinatra entries.[32] An April 1988, piece called "Celebrity Reading Lists" shows Sinatra perusing "The Big Book of Colorful Invective" as well as "Who's Who at the Bottom of the East River" and "Profiles in Arrogance."[33] Sinatra's final *MAD* appearance in his lifetime was in a May 1994 parody ad for the "Integrity Record Club," which offers an album called "Shut Up and Listen."[34]

In 1954, *MAD* portrayed Frank Sinatra as an ill-tempered brawler more interested in his celebrity than a fan's adoration. In 1994, he was portrayed almost identically (though heavier, balder, and wearing a tuxedo). In fact, except for his hairline and Mia Farrow, every Sinatra reference *MAD* ever used can be found in the 1962 "Celebrities' Wallets." A "model of editorial consistency," *MAD* proved to be just that—telling the same exact Sinatra jokes again and again for forty years.

Before 1980, Frank Sinatra was rarely impersonated professionally[35] and hardly ever appeared in editorial cartoons. That all changed when his friendship with President Ronald Reagan brought him into the dual headlights of political and show business satire. Both types of satire overlapped in two arenas, NBC's *Saturday Night Live* and Garry Trudeau's *Doonesbury*.

Since 1975, *Saturday Night Live* has followed *National Lampoon* (where many of its writers once worked) in producing hard-edged comedy, a break from television's nonsatirical comedic tradition. Situation comedies have rarely been a satirical medium[36] and variety shows took a long time before they personally parodied celebrities. In the fifties, Milton Berle or Jackie Gleason might joke with a personality such as Sinatra if he was a guest, but they would never do a skit at his expense behind his back.[37] In the sixties and seventies, variety was handed to performers like Rowan and Martin, Sonny and Cher, and Dean Martin who, if not personal friends of Sinatra, at least traveled in his circles and were not about to air his dirty laundry for a laugh.[38]

By the eighties, variety was nearly unknown in primetime network television, left to the exclusive domain of late night talk or sketch shows. Traditionally, talk show comedy takes the form of one-liners (Johnny Carson's monologue) or "reading pieces" (David Letterman's "Top Ten List"). Although Sinatra was undoubtedly mentioned on these shows hundreds of times since the days of Steve Allen, the material was neither collected nor indexed, and a review of his treatment by these satirists would be anecdotal at best.[39] As for late-night sketch shows, three have had some Sinatra content. *Fridays*[40] and *SCTV*[41] sketches were limited to mentions of his name, but *Saturday Night Live* has had two cast members, Joe Piscopo and Phil Hartman, who each "performed" Sinatra regularly.

Joe Piscopo's Sinatra impression involved minimal makeup, thin white hair brushed forward, black tie, and a hand-held microphone. The voice Piscopo used was not a perfect duplication of Sinatra's, but being a fellow New Jersey native, he did a faithful regional dialect peppered with "Sinatra-ese" ("I'm thinkin' in my skull about this Bush cat").

Piscopo played Sinatra a dozen times between 1981 and 1984. Many of the sketches involved then–President Reagan. In one that aired days before Reagan's inauguration, Piscopo's Sinatra "summoned" the president-elect (Charles Rocket) to convince him to oust George Bush in favor of Nancy Reagan ("your broad, your old lady, your chick").[42] A month later, Reagan and Sinatra addressed the nation regarding a question of national importance, "Is Frank Sinatra a hoodlum?"[43] In an October 1981 news interview, Sinatra explained that vacillating congressmen were persuaded to support Saudi Airborne Warning and Control (AWAC) sales with one word, "Muscle."[44] In honor of Reagan's seventy-first birthday in February 1982, Sinatra serenaded the president and his family with songs like "My Kind of Chief Executive," "The First Lady is a Champ," "Bad, Bad, Bad Al Haig," and (for Ron Reagan, Jr.) "Fairy tales can come true. . . ."[45] A year later, Sinatra and Bob Hope (Dave Thomas) convinced Woody Allen (Rick Moranis) to direct commercials for Reagan's reelection campaign.[46]

Several appearances involved Sinatra and other musical personalities. On a Mick Jagger variety special, he announced, "I've always had this theory: Rock singers make me puke."[47] Capitalizing on the success of *Ebony and Ivory,* Sinatra enlisted Stevie Wonder (Eddie Murphy) to join him in a duet which began, "You are black and I am white / Life's an Eskimo Pie / Let's take a bite/ That was groovy thinkin' / Lincoln, when you set them freeeeee. . . ."[48] On a Gumby (Eddie Murphy) Christmas special, Sinatra reworked *Silent Night* to include the lyrics, "Round that virgin chick, she had a kid / Who grew up to be famous, you all know what he did."[49]

The other appearances included a game show called "What Would Frank Do?,"[50] a visit with unemployed auto workers,[51] helping then–New York City mayor Ed Koch talk down a jumper,[52] and a "High Hopes" takeoff with Billy Crystal's Sammy Davis, Jr. ("Once there was a cat with one eye / Wanted to host on *Saturday Night* / They wouldn't let this black, Jack- / So I gave 'em a smack").[53]

Phil Hartman picked up the Sinatra banner in 1990. The makeup was similar to Piscopo's and the voice was equally irrelevant (unlike Piscopo, he never did parody songs). However, Hartman's Sinatra was harsher, with more thuggish attitude. He also brought more sexuality to the sketches. The only sketch to involve Reagan was a reenactment of the Sinatra–Nancy Reagan White House trysts alleged in Kitty Kelley's *Nancy Reagan: The Unauthorized Biography*.[54] A 1996 talk show called *Leg Up* was a graphic discussion of many of Sinatra's sexual dalliances.[55] A "restored clip" from *Ocean's 11* (taking a cue from a similar scene in *Spartacus*) put Sinatra in a bubble bath with Sammy Davis, Jr., promising, " . . . put on a dress and I'd take you out for the biggest steak you've ever seen."[56] Dana Carvey's Woody Allen was the unwilling recipient of Sinatra sexual advice ("You gotta keep your mitts off the *kinder*. Believe me, I thought about it myself a few times, but I took my business to the *john*").[57] Rapper Luther Campbell (Chris Rock) met with rare admiration when Campbell admitted he would rather discuss Sinead O'Connor's butt than her bald head ("I hear you, baby. Forget the head. Put a bag over it and do your business").[58] On the other hand, father-to-be Michael Jackson (Tim Meadows) got only sexual scorn ("Pull out that splotchy trouser mouse and we'll check it for kitty prints").[59]

The Hartman Sinatra did not limit his distaste for modern musicians to sexual matters. He mocked George Michael's love of his own backside;[60] berated "Sine-aid" O'Connor's politics ("You're lucky you're a chick, or you'd be nothin' but a stain on the road and a crewcut");[61] warned Paul McCartney to "Stay off the funny stuff, Ringo!";[62] and even showed contempt for Billy Idol's contempt ("What's with the sneering crap? . . . That's what killed Dennis Day").[63] In an orgy of derision during the recording of the *Duets* album, Hartman laid into Barbra Streisand ("Stay out of the cradle, Nose"); U2's Bono ("Go back to Dublin and find yourself a bottle to crawl into"); Liza Minnelli ("Your money's on the dresser, baby, I'm done wit' ya"); Kenny G ("They ain't payin' to hear *your* half"); k. d. lang and Wynonna Judd ("Never heard of 'em. Next!"); and even his own children ("This ain't no charity case. I gave you the name, now get out!").[64] In a curiously mild final appearance as a regular cast member, Hartman was introduced to finish Sinatra's curtailed Grammy speech. Contrary to what might be expected (and is that not the essence of comedy?) he said, "Here's the rest of my speech: 'Thanks for the award. Drive home safely. Good night.' "[65]

As biting and provocative as these impressions were, the Sinatra satire that came closest to libel was the work of Pulitzer Prize–winning cartoonist Garry Trudeau in his popular but often controversial strip, *Doonesbury*. Since its creation in 1970, *Doonesbury* has taken a handful of shots at Sinatra, mocking his relationship with former Vice President Spiro Agnew ("He's probably spending his days at the Palm Springs hideaway of an aging but curiously unretired crooner . . .");[66] his several comebacks;[67] his refusal to retire;[68] and even the "truly legendary . . . '67 Sinatra tan."[69] The jibes heated up during the Reagan inauguration when three strips dealt with the president's friendship with Sinatra (and his alleged criminal ties). "Someone like that should at least have the decency to stay away from the

Reagans. It could **ruin** them socially," lamented one oblivious character, "He seemed like such a sweet boy back when he sang with that nice Mr. Dorsey."[70]

The most notorious *Doonesbury* appearances followed Sinatra's receipt of the Medal of Freedom from President Reagan and an honorary doctorate from the Stevens Institute. Six consecutive strips (June 10 through June 15, 1985) counterposed these honors with his underworld ties and an ugly incident at an Atlantic City casino in 1983. The first two strips quote from the Reagan honor and the Stevens citation and then reprint actual photos of Sinatra with reputed gangland figures including Jimmy "The Weasel" Fratiano, Joseph Gambino,[71] and "alleged human" Aniello Dellacroce.[72] The remaining four strips depict an off-screen Sinatra bullying a blackjack dealer ("That's **Dr.** Sinatra, you little bimbo!"),[73] cursing at her when she insists on applying the house rules (he issues an "obscene gerund" and an "anatomically explicit epithet"),[74] and then, after consulting with some "made guys" at another table,[75] he orders the casino boss (based on Golden Nugget owner Steve Wynn) to "slap her around."[76] The strips provoked editorials and disclaimers, several newspapers refused to run them, and Trudeau was denounced in Congress.[77] It was also a rare occasion where Sinatra himself made a public comment about a parody saying, "I am happy to have the President and the people of the United States judge us by our respective track records."[78] Noted satirist Paul Krassner even did a satire *of* the satire, publishing a parody of *Doonesbury* in his magazine the *Realist*. The fake cartoon showed Trudeau and his wife, NBC *Today Show* host Jane Pauley, lying in bed, discussing possible reprisals from Sinatra, culminating in the discovery of the head of the NBC peacock under the covers with them.[79]

Although there was talk of litigation,[80] an unrepentant Trudeau continued to taunt Sinatra, naming his next compilation book *That's Doctor Sinatra, You Little Bimbo* and including an anti-Trudeau quote from Sinatra on the dust jacket, "He's about as funny as a tumor."[81] Over the next eight years, *Doonesbury* parodied Sinatra five more times including a full color "condensation" of Kitty Kelley's *His Way*,[82] a George Bush fund-raiser appearance,[83] two Gulf War references to his affair with Nancy Reagan,[84] and a *Duets* session with Jimmy Thudpucker (unlike *Saturday Night Live*, Sinatra does not abuse Jimmy—in fact, he does not even show up).[85]

Both *Doonesbury* and *Saturday Night Live* point out the distance that American comedy has traversed in Sinatra's lifetime. It is inconceivable that even the rawest night club comic of the sixties would utter the words, "I got chunks of guys like you in my stool!," but by 1991, that was one of the tamer insults leveled by the Hartman Sinatra.[86] It is even more unlikely to think that a cartoonist of 1947 would dream of publishing a drawing of Sinatra pummeling Lee Mortimer and yelling, "(Obscenity) homosexual!" That would have to wait forty years for Garry Trudeau.[87]

As recently as the 1960s, American comedy could be soft and unthreatening, but with the advent of shows like *Saturday Night Live* and cartoons like *Doonesbury*, humor has gotten more and more daring. This has meant targeting subjects and individuals previously thought to be taboo. Because it is such a "snowballing" process, it has often gotten out of control. Where "pushing the comedy envelope" was once the goal, it is now merely the means. Satirists no longer go for laughter based on recognition but rather on surprise and even shock. Though there must still be some basic level of recognition (or else there is no hook) it gets fainter the more often the joke is told and the more exaggerated the punch line becomes. With Frank Sinatra, the basic references were in place in the sixties but willing satirists (and an accepting audience) were not ready for them until the eighties. In that time, as the tenor of the comedy has become crueler, so has the public perception of Sinatra, and the two trends have fed on each other symbiotically.

In the years immediately before his death, Sinatra satire was sporadic. Phil Hartman was no longer a regular on *Saturday Night Live*[88] and other satirists ran the risk of overt distastefulness if Sinatra had passed away during the parody's shelf life. Among the few appearances were a quick gag on *The Simpsons,*[89] a Claymation Sinatra in an iced tea commercial,[90] and numerous gentle song parodies on the radio.[91] Following Sinatra's death in May 1998, there was naturally a period of mourning during which there were virtually no public jokes at his expense.[92] Tragically, Phil Hartman was murdered exactly two weeks later. As the reigning dean of Sinatra satire, Hartman left open the question of who would be the first to dare to do Frank Sinatra parodies postmortem. Nearly ten years after his death, no one has stepped forward.[93]

In *Sinatra! The Song is You,* Will Friedwald divides Frank Sinatra's career into "The Skinny Years," "The Hat Years," and "The Tux Years."[94] Sinatra satire breaks down similarly. During "The Skinny Years," Sinatra was the object of innocent fun in print and animated cartoons based on his looks and fan behavior. During "The Hat Years," Sinatra's public and private antics presented a variety of comedy hooks but, with the exception of *MAD,* there were no formidable satirists willing to use them. During "The Tux Years," Sinatra was almost continuously subject to comedic ridicule thanks to *Saturday Night Live* and *Doonesbury.* For an individual to have an extended period of multiple satires is a sign of prolonged celebrity. To have two periods shows personal evolution and multiple-generational appeal. To have three is the stuff of legends. While the hooks stayed substantially the same, the depths to which satirists went to bury them increased tenfold. One thing is certain—as an icon of both 1940s cartoons and 1990s late night sketch comedy, Frank Sinatra was a substantial presence in twentieth century American comedy.

Notes

1. This cartoon is reprinted in Nancy Sinatra, *Frank Sinatra: An American Legend,* 59. The origin and author of the cartoon are unknown as the only credit in the book is, "Comic photographed by Alan Berliner." This also applies to the next two cites.

2. Sinatra, *Frank Sinatra: An American Legend,* 63.

3. Sinatra, *Frank Sinatra: An American Legend,* 72.

4. Curiously, Disney never put Sinatra's image in a cartoon short, though his voice appears in "Pluto's Blue Note" (directed by Charles Nichols and released in 1947). However, their 1988 theatrical feature film, *Who Framed Roger Rabbit,* included a quick appearance by a singing sword with a young Sinatra head singing "Witchcraft" (with his actual voice). It is notable that a movie that was famous for the historic meeting of characters from multiple studios chose a Sinatra characterization as its way of depicting the great animation tradition of celebrity caricatures. It seems to imply that, if you wanted a celebrity cartoon

character instantly recognizable to a 1988 audience and yet appropriate to the 1947 setting of the film, Frank Sinatra was the obvious choice.

5. Directed by Frank Tashlin, released May 6, 1944. It was nominated for an Academy Award (the year before Sinatra himself won a special award for *The House I Live In*). For credits and synopses of Warner Brothers cartoons, see Jerry Beck and Will Friedwald, *Looney Tunes and Merrie Melodies* (New York: Henry Holt and Company, 1989), 150.

6. Directed by Robert Clampett, released January 5, 1946. Beck and Friedwald, *Looney Tunes and Merrie Melodies,* 164.

7. Directed by Robert McKimson, released April 20, 1946. Beck and Friedwald, *Looney Tunes,* 166.

8. Directed by I. Freleng, released November 1, 1947. Beck and Friedwald, *Looney Tunes,* 179.

9. Directed by Arthur Davis, released December 6, 1947. Beck and Friedwald, *Looney Tunes,* 180.

10. Directed by I. Freleng, released May 21, 1949. Beck and Friedwald, *Looney Tunes,* 198.

11. Directed by Tex Avery, released May 15, 1948. See Jeff Lenburg, *The Encyclopedia of Animated Cartoons* (New York: Facts on File, 1991), 129. Tex Avery was famous for presenting a gag, topping it several times, and then, when he had already gone as far as possible, taking it a step further. This technique is certainly in full force in this cartoon. Joe Adamson, *Tex Avery, King of Cartoons* (New York: Da Capo Press, 1975), 102.

12. He later finds true love disguised as a fox when he falls for a female fox who also happens to be a skunk in disguise.

13. Directed by Bill Tytla, released August 18, 1950. Lenburg, *Encyclopedia of Animated Cartoons,* 89.

14. Curiously, they moan, "Oh Brother!" Is it possible the creators were afraid to identify Sinatra any more clearly by having them say, "Oh Frankie?"

15. "You could stroll through an olive without disturbing the pimento," claimed Crosby in a USO appearance with Bob Hope from 1945. "Sticks and stones may break my bones and so can soft boiled eggs," was Sinatra's retort. *Frank Sinatra, An American Legend,* the CD that accompanies the book of the same name includes a radio broadcast of this appearance.

16. In fact, pundits of today have retroactively latched onto these hooks. For example, in the January 1991 *Saturday Night Live* sketch, "The Sinatra Group," Phil Hartman (as Sinatra) charges, "Next issue: Rita Hayworth or Ava Gardner. Who would you rather nail? I disqualify myself since I've done them both." Michael Cader, ed., *Saturday Night Live: The First Twenty Years* (Boston: Houghton Mifflin, 1994), 239.

17. Two exceptions: First, when Sinatra himself made the jokes. For example, his cameos in the Hope-Crosby road pictures like *Road to Utopia* (1945) or *Road to Hong Kong* (1962) or his simultaneously self-mocking and self-aggrandizing appearance in *Cannonball Run II* (1984). Second, nostalgic references in period films like the singing sword in *Who Framed Roger Rabbit* or the "Sinatra or Mathis" discussion in *Diner* (1982).

18. See notes 35–40 below.

19. Even years later, Sinatra has remained taboo among comics. Paul Provenza, in a provocative anti-Jesus routine of the mid-nineties quipped, "Why worship the Son of God? Who buys Frank Sinatra *Junior* records?" To which talk show host Jon Stewart warned, "It's one thing to mess with God, it's another thing to mess with Frank Sinatra." *The Jon Stewart Show* (MTV, 1994).

20. The exceptions to this rule were Don Rickles who, with Sinatra's blessing, made jokes about Sinatra's tough-guy persona and mob ties (see *Sinatra at 80* [ABC, 1995]), and Jackie Mason whose material about Sinatra and Mia Farrow allegedly earned him threats and physical harm. Kitty Kelley, *His Way* (New York: Bantam Books, 1986), 364–65.

21. *National Lampoon,* "Food Issue," March 1982, 96.

22. The recollection of *National Lampoon* editor Michael Reiss was that the author was warned by his peers, "If this runs, Frank Sinatra will have you killed."

23. *MAD,* no. 12, 11–13. Written and illustrated by B. Krigstein.

24. *MAD,* no. 71, 30–31. Written by Arnie Kogen. Illustrated by Jack Rickard.

25. *MAD,* no. 75, 22. Written by Larry Siegel and Arnie Kogen. Illustrated by Wally Wood.

26. *MAD,* no. 84, 8. Written by Don Reilly. Illustrated by Mort Drucker. Another panel was both ill-timed and oddly prophetic. It featured a sleeping President Kennedy (assassinated after the issue went to press but before its release) dreaming about a *London Daily Express* headline which reads, "Christine Keeler Emigrates to the U.S.—Plans to Settle in Washington, D.C."

27. *MAD,* no. 123, 26. Written by Frank Jacobs. Photos by Max Brandel.

28. *MAD,* no. 124, 7. Written by Arnie Kogen. Illustrated by Mort Drucker.

29. *MAD,* no. 133, 38–40. Written by Larry Siegel. Illustrated by John Johns.

30. *MAD,* no. 185, 13. Written by Frank Jacobs. Aging by Bob Clarke.

31. *MAD,* no. 194, 14. Written by Frank Jacobs. Illustrated by Bob Clarke.

32. *MAD,* no. 210, 11. Written by Tom Koch. Illustrated by Harry North, Esq.

33. *MAD,* no. 278, 32. Written by Tom Koch. Illustrated by Sam Viviano.

34. *MAD,* no. 93, special issue, back cover. Written by Charlie Kadau and Joe Raiola. Photo by Irving Schild.

35. John Byner apparently did an impression of Sinatra in August 1972 on his summer variety show, *The John Byner Comedy Hour.*

36. The totality of Sinatra satire in sitcoms is limited to several appearances on shows starring Danny Thomas and Tony Danza (whose comedic treatment bordered on idolatry).

37. Sinatra even had two unsuccessful variety shows of his own (on CBS from 1950 to 52 and ABC from 1957 to 1958) where he would make mildly self-effacing jokes like "The door was open a crack so I thought I'd slip in." *The Frank Sinatra Show* (CBS, 1951).

38. Johnny Carson, in a privately videotaped charity performance for the Dismas Halfway House in 1965 (available from the Museum of Television and Radio in Beverly Hills) made numerous jokes dealing with relevant hooks of the day such as Sinatra's power ("Joey Bishop couldn't be here—he slipped a disc backing out of Frank's presence"); his drinking ("I've never drunk on a stage before and fifteen minutes with you and I've already got a drink in my hand"); and his alleged criminal connections ("Ladies and gentlemen, our hoodlum singer . . ."). Nevertheless, this material would never have been appropriate for airing on Carson's *Tonight Show* for consumption by a national audience.

39. One such anecdote: Carson did not like to do jokes about Sinatra's (or anyone's) alleged gangland ties because of a threatening phone call he personally received in the sixties after he did a monologue joke about a dog who had gone missing from his owner, reputed gangster Mickey Cohen (and, the joke continued, was found with his four paws in cement). That type of joke, therefore, tended not to make it into the monologue.

40. During its February 13, 1981 episode, the ABC show *Fridays* produced a black and white film short called "The Frank Sinatra Story." Designed as a parody of cheap and unauthorized television biographies, it features real Sinatra songs performed by "Tony Marco" (who looked more like a cross between Humphrey Bogart and Garry Shandling than Sinatra) and vaguely traces Sinatra's true life story but makes no real jokes at Sinatra's expense (in fact, few real jokes are made at all in this puzzlingly unfunny sketch).

41. In a 1981 Christmas episode aired on NBC, *SCTV* did a parody commercial for a room deodorizer that looked like Sinatra (in hat and raincoat over his shoulder) called "Frank-Incense." Early in 1982, the show did an extended sketch called "Maudlin's Eleven," which deftly parodied the stylishness (and self-indulgence) of Rat Pack–caper films like *Ocean's 11* but did not mention Sinatra or any Rat Pack member by name.

42. *Saturday Night Live,* aired January 17, 1981. Cader, *Saturday Night Live: The First Twenty Years,* 130.

43. *Saturday Night Live,* aired February 14, 1981. Cader, *Saturday Night Live: The First Twenty Years,* 130.

44. *Saturday Night Live,* aired October 31, 1981. Cader, *Saturday Night Live: The First Twenty Years,* 131.

45. *Saturday Night Live,* aired February 6, 1982. Cader, *Saturday Night Live: The First Twenty Years,* 131.

46. *Saturday Night Live,* aired January 29, 1983. Cader, *Saturday Night Live: The First Twenty Years,* 131.

47. Cader, *Saturday Night Live: The First Twenty Years,* 131.

48. *Saturday Night Live,* aired May 22, 1982. Cader, *Saturday Night Live: The First Twenty Years,* 131.

49. *Saturday Night Live,* aired December 11, 1982. Cader, *Saturday Night Live: The First Twenty Years,* 131.

50. *Saturday Night Live,* aired October 15, 1983. Cader, *Saturday Night Live: The First Twenty Years,* 132.

51. Cader, *Saturday Night Live: The First Twenty Years,* 131.

52. *Saturday Night Live,* aired May 14, 1983.

53. *Saturday Night Live,* aired May 12, 1984. Cader, *Saturday Night Live: The First Twenty Years,* 132 and 151.

54. Cader, *Saturday Night Live: The First Twenty Years,* 240. Hartman also played a Reagan (taped before the live sketch) explaining the plaster that falls on his head in the Oval Office as "That's just Frank and Nancy going at it."

55. *Saturday Night Live,* aired March 23, 1996.

56. *Saturday Night Live,* aired May 11, 1991. Cader, *Saturday Night Live: The First Twenty Years,* 240.

57. Cader, *Saturday Night Live: The First Twenty Years,* 240.

58. *Saturday Night Live,* aired January 19, 1991. The sketch, a satire of "The McLaughlin Group" pitting Sinatra against an itinerant Sinead O'Connor (Jan Hooks), a cranky Billy Idol (Sting), Campbell, and the sycophantic Steve Lawrence (Mike Myers) and Edie Gorme (Victoria Jackson), was a tour de force for all involved and is reprinted in its entirety in Cader, *Saturday Night Live: The First Twenty Years,* 238–39.

59. *Saturday Night Live,* aired November 23, 1996.

60. *Saturday Night Live,* aired September 29, 1990. Cader, *Saturday Night Live: The First Twenty Years,* 238.

61. Cader, *Saturday Night Live: The First Twenty Years,* 239.

62. *Saturday Night Live,* aired February 23, 1991. Cader, *Saturday Night Live: The First Twenty Years,* 240.

63. Cader, *Saturday Night Live: The First Twenty Years,* 239.

64. *Saturday Night Live,* aired November 13, 1993. Cader, *Saturday Night Live: The First Twenty Years,* 240.

65. *Saturday Night Live,* aired March 12, 1994. Cader, *Saturday Night Live: The First Twenty Years,* 240.

66. *Doonesbury* Sunday strip of December 9, 1973. Every *Doonesbury* strip discussed herein can be accessed online at www.Doonesbury.com.

67. *Doonesbury,* December 25, 1976.

68. *Doonesbury,* March 22, 1979.

69. *Doonesbury,* May 20, 1980.

70. *Doonesbury,* January 18, 1981. Two other strips followed on January 22 and 23, 1981, the latter involving an associate of a miffed Sinatra threatening to break Attorney General Edwin Meese's legs because of "the brush-off I've been getting." A character also invokes Sinatra's name in a June 12, 1982 strip regarding Labor Secretary Ray Donovan's troubles, saying, " . . . (E)ither Mr. Donovan consorts with underworld types or he's the victim of the most extraordinary string of coincidences since Frank Sinatra."

71. *Doonesbury,* June 10, 1985.

72. *Doonesbury,* June 11, 1985.

73. *Doonesbury,* June 12, 1985.

74. *Doonesbury,* June 13, 1985.

75. *Doonesbury,* June 14, 1985.

76. *Doonesbury,* June 15, 1985. The strips were based on an appearance by Sinatra in the Golden Nugget where he supposedly intimidated employees to "bend the rules" causing a chain of events culminating in Atlantic City Casino Control Commission Joel R. Jacobson calling Sinatra an "obnoxious bully" and Sinatra promising never to perform in New Jersey again. Curiously, the *Doonesbury* strips so perturbed Jacobson that he extended an olive branch of peace to have Sinatra return to his home state. Daniel Heneghan, "Jacobson Says 'Doonesbury' Strip Was Unfair," *Atlantic City Press,* June 30, 1985.

77. Garry B. Trudeau, *Flashbacks, Twenty-Five Years of Doonesbury* (Norwalk, CT: Easton Press, 1995), 185.

78. Karen Heller, "Cartoon Clash: Sinatra vs. 'Doonesbury,'" *USA Today,* June 11, 1985.

79. *Realist,* no. 99, September-October, 1985, 1.

80. Andrew Radolf, "Don't Shrink the Comics," *Editor and Publisher,* April 30, 1988. In this article, covering a speech given by Trudeau at an American Newspaper Publishers Association Convention, he stated that he received a letter from Sinatra's lawyers protesting that the facts in the strip were wrong, to which Trudeau replied, "Well of course I misrepresented the facts . . . I made them up. It would have been a very short trial." See also Trudeau, *Flashbacks,* 186.

81. Garry B. Trudeau, *That's Doctor Sinatra, You Little Bimbo* (New York: Henry Holt and Company, 1986). The dust jacket also included Sinatra defenses from Angie Dickinson ("Absolutely dreadful") and Joe Piscopo ("Way off base").

82. *Doonesbury,* March 22, 1987. Interestingly, this was the only time Trudeau chose to draw a caricature of Sinatra.

83. *Doonesbury,* September 13, 1988.

84. *Doonesbury,* April 24 and 25, 1991.

85. *Doonesbury,* October 23, 1994.

86. Cader, *Saturday Night Live: The First Twenty Years,* 239.

87. *Doonesbury,* Sunday strip of March 22, 1987.

88. When he returned as a guest host on November 23, 1996, Hartman did appear as Sinatra on "The Joe Pesci Show" and, in spite of his bathrobe and intravenous tube, he managed to clobber Pesci, Michael Jackson, and the television camera (either personally or with help from "his boys").

89. In "Lady Bouvier's Lover" (written by Bill Oakley and Josh Weinstein) Bart Simpson, who must pretend to be his father Homer in order to intercept an expensive mail order item he paid for with his father's credit card, opens his front door to reveal a thug with a thick New Jersey accent announcing, "I got a special delivery for Homer Simpson." Bart replies, "That's me!" The goon punches Bart in the face and demands, "Don't write no more letters to Mr. Sinatra." Aired May 12, 1994.

90. Commercial for Lipton Brisk Iced Tea, 1996.

91. Television writer Monty Aidem, who does an uncanny impression of Sinatra's singing voice, frequently appeared on Rick Dees's syndicated radio programs doing topical song parodies. He continued to do the impression long after Sinatra's death, but exclusively in "tribute shows" and never in satirical contexts.

92. In what was the final published example of Sinatra satire in the twentieth century, the *Realist* ran a front page cartoon soon after Sinatra's death, showing numerous gangsters sitting around a table with a picture of the late crooner and a floral wreath bearing the insignia, "RIP: HE DID IT OUR WAY." *Realist,* no. 140, Autumn, 1998, 1.

93. Though not satirical, HBO's television film *The Rat Pack* (broadcast August 22, 1998) was the first depiction of Sinatra after his death. Played by Ray Liotta, and dealing with many of the subjects previously discussed (womanizing, Kennedy-cronyism, violent temperament, etc.), the performance could have signaled the end of a quiet period of Sinatra satire. As it happened, the film's critical lambasting, mediocre ratings, and vocal disavowal by the Sinatra family contributed to the opposite result. *The Simpsons,* arguably the most satirical show in the history of the television medium, has let Sinatra rest in peace, limiting his appearances to tender jibes like depicting him in the episode "I'm going to Praiseland" beside a *Saturday Night Fever*–era John Travolta in "disco heaven" where the unhappy Sinatra remarks, "For me this is hell. Ya dig, pally?" Aired May 6, 2001.

94. Friedwald, *Sinatra! The Song is You: A Singer's Art,* 7.

Selected Discography

The Concert Sinatra. Reprise, R/R9–1009. © 1963. Reissued on CD, Reprise/WEA, CN 47244. May 11, 1999.

Frank Sinatra with the Red Norvo Quintet Live in Australia, April 1, 1959. Blue Note, CD 37513.

It Might As Well Be Swing. Reprise, DC FS 1012-2. © 1963.

"Night and Day." Bluebird, January 19, 1942. RCA CD 2269-2.

"Night and Day." Columbia, October 22, 1947. Columbia CD C2K65244.

Ring-A-Ding-Ding. Reprise, CD 27017-2. © 1960. Reissued on CD, Reprise CN 46933, May 26, 1998.

Sinatra and Strings, November 22, 1961. Reprise, CD 9-27020.

Sinatra-Basie at the Sands. Reprise, CD FS1019-2. © 1966.

Sinatra in Paris, June 5, 1962. Reprise, CD 9-4587-2.

Songs for Young Lovers and Swing Easy. Capitol, CD CDP748470-2. © 1954.

Swing and Dance with Frank Sinatra. Columbia, CD CK64852. © 1950.

A Swingin' Affair. November 26, 1956. Capitol, CD 7-94518. Reissued on Capitol CD, CN96099, September 8, 1998.

The Voice. Columbia LP CL743 (78s recorded 1945).

Selected Bibliography

Academy of Motion Picture Arts and Sciences. Clipping files on Dick Haymes. Los Angeles, CA.

Adamson, Joe. *Tex Avery, King of Cartoons.* New York: Da Capo Press, 1975.

Allan, Blaine. "The Making (and Unmaking) of *Pull My Daisy.*" *Film History* 2 (1988).

Anon. [and Mort Drucker]. "My Fair Ad-Man," *MAD* 54 (April 1960). Reprinted in *William M. Gaines's Three Ring MAD.* Edited by Albert B. Feldstein. New York: New American Library, 1964.

Baker, Rob. "Tharp's Delightful Sinatra Songs." *New York Daily News,* January 27, 1984.

Barnes, Clive. "Tharp Dances to Sinatra's Beat." *New York Post,* January 26, 1984.

———. "Twyla Tharp and Modern Classicism." *Dance and Dancers,* September 1987.

Baryshnikov Dances Sinatra and More with American Ballet Theatre. Directed by Don Mischer and Twyla Tharp. West Long Branch, NJ: KULTUR International Films, 1984.

Beck, Jerry, and Will Friedwald. *Looney Tunes and Merrie Melodies.* New York: Henry Holt and Company, 1989.

Belgrad, Daniel. *The Culture of Spontaneity: Improvisation and the Arts in Postwar America.* Chicago: University of Chicago Press, 1998.

Bliven, Bruce. "The Voice and the Kids." *The New Republic,* November 6, 1944, 592–93.

Bloom, Harold. *The Anxiety of Influence.* New York: Oxford University Press, 1973.

Braudy, Leo. "'No Body's Perfect': Method Acting in 50s Culture." *Michigan Quarterly Review* 35 (Winter 1996).

Cader, Michael, ed. *Saturday Night Live: The First Twenty Years.* Boston: Houghton Mifflin, 1994.

"Can Sinatra Make Good on TV?" *TV Guide,* April 4, 1954.

Carr, Roy, et al. *The Hip, Hipster, Jazz and the Beat Generation.* London: Faber and Faber, 1986.

Clarke, Donald. *All or Nothing at All.* New York: Fromm International, 1997.

Coleman, Ray. *Sinatra: A Portrait of the Artist.* Atlanta: Turner Publishing, 1995.

Connick, Harry, Jr. "A Perfect Singer, Ever Since He began the Beguine." *New York Times,* December 9, 1990. In *The Frank Sinatra Reader.* Edited by Steven Petkov and Leonard Mustazza. New York: Oxford University Press, 1995.

Delamater, Jerome. *Dance in the Hollywood Musical.* Ann Arbor: UMI Research Press, 1981.

Dellar, Fred, and M. Peachy. *Sinatra: Night and Day: The Man and The Music.* London: Chameleon, 2000.

Dexter, Dave. *Billboard,* April 12, 1980.

Dick Haymes Society Newsletter, nos. 32–42.

DuBrow, Rick. "500,000 Await Elvis Today," *UPI Report,* March 5, 1960.

Dyer, Richard. *Heavenly Bodies: Film Stars and Society.* British Film Institute Cinema Series. London: Macmillan, 1986.

Editors of *Rolling Stone Press. Rolling Stone Rock Almanac: The Chronicles of Rock & Roll.* New York: Collier Books, 1983.

Falcone, Vincent, and Bob Popyk. *Frankly, Just between Us: My Life Conducting Frank Sinatra's Music.* Milwaukee, WI: Hal Leonard Corp., 2005.

Feuer, Jane. *The Hollywood Musical.* 2nd ed. Bloomington and Indianapolis: Indiana University Press, 1993.

Fiedler, Leslie. *Love and Death in the American Novel.* New York: Criterion Books, 1960.

Fitzgerald, F. Scott. *The Notebooks of F. Scott Fitzgerald.* Edited by Matthew J. Bruccoli. New York: Harcourt Brace Janovich/Bruccoli Clark, 1978.

Floyd, John. *All Music Guide.* San Francisco: Miller Freeman, 1972.

"Frankie Says: 'TV Racket's Too Tough!' " *TV Guide,* September 17, 1955.

Friedwald, Will. *Jazz Singing.* New York: Da Capo Press, 1996.

———. *Sinatra! The Song Is You: A Singer's Art.* New York: Scribner's, 1995.

———. *Sinatra! The Song Is You: A Singer's Art.* Reprint. New York: Da Capo Press, 1997.

Frew, Tim. *Sinatra.* New York: MetroBooks, 2002.

Giddins, Gary. *Visions of Jazz.* New York: Oxford University Press, 1998.

Gigliotti, Gilbert L. *A Storied Singer: Frank Sinatra as Literary Conceit.* Westport, Conn. and London: Greenwood, 2002.

Gilbert, Roger. "The Swinger and the Loser: Sinatra, Masculinity and Fifties Culture." In *Frank Sinatra and Popular Culture: Essay on an American Icon.* Edited by Leonard Mustazza. Westport, CT: Praeger, 1998.

Ginsberg, Allen. *Collected Poems 1947–1980.* New York: Harper and Row, 1984.

Gitlin, Todd. *The Sixties: Years of Hope, Days of Rage.* New York: Bantam, 1987.

Goldner, Nancy. "An All-Around Triumph for Twyla Tharp." *Christian Science Monitor,* February 6, 1984.

Granata, Charles, L. *Sessions with Sinatra: Frank Sinatra and the Art of Recordings.* Chicago: A Capella/Chicago Review Press, 1999.

Greenberg, Clement. "Avant-garde and Kitsch." *Partisan Reader: Ten Years of Partisan Review, 1934–1944.* New York: Dial Press, 1946, 378–89. Reprinted in Bernard Rosenberg and David Manning White, eds. *Mass Culture: The Popular Arts in America.* Glencoe, Ill., Free Press, 1957.

Grevalt, Ron. "Elvis Projection Needs Face-Lift." *Billboard,* May 16, 1960.

Grudens, Richard. *The Music Men.* Stony Brook, NY: Celebrity Profiles Publishing, 1998.

Guralnick, Peter. *Careless Love: The Unmaking of Elvis Presley.* Boston: Little, Brown and Company, 1999.

———. "Elvis Presley." Liner notes for *Elvis From Nashville to Memphis: The Essential 60's Masters I.* RCA, 1993.

———. *Last Train to Memphis: The Rise of Elvis Presley.* New York: Little, Brown and Company, 1994.

Hamill, Pete. *Why Sinatra Matters.* New York: Little, Brown and Company, 1998.

Hanna, David. *Sinatra: Ol' Blue Eyes Remembered.* New York: Random House Publishing, 1998. (Original copyright, Starlog Communications International, 1990.)

Harrison, Barbara Grizzanti. "Oh How We Worshipped the Gods of the Fifties." In *Legend: Frank Sinatra and the American Dream.* Edited by Ethlie Ann Vare. New York: Boulevard Books, 1995.

Hart, Dorothy, ed. *Thou Swell, Thou Witty.* New York: Harper and Row, 1979.

Havers, Richard. *Sinatra.* New York: Dorling Kindersley, 2004.

Hemming, Roy, and David Hajdu. *Discovering the Great Singers of Classic Pop.* New York: Newmarket Press, 1991.

Hirsch, Foster. *The Dark Side of the Screen.* New York: Da Capo, 1981.

Hughes, Robert. *Shock of the New.* Rev. ed. New York: Alfred A. Knopf, 1995.

Humphrey, Hal. "Sinatra Is Calling Own Signals Now." *New York World Telegram,* August 13, 1957.

"Is This a New Presley?" *Newsweek.* May 30, 1960.

Jacobs, George, and William Stadiem. *My Life with Frank Sinatra.* New York: HarperEntertainment, 2003.

————. *Mr. S: The Last Word on Frank Sinatra.* London: Pan, 2004.

Jewell, Derek. *Frank Sinatra: A Celebration.* Boston: Little, Brown and Company, 1986.

Jones, Landon. *Great Expectations: America and the Baby Boom Generation.* New York: Ballantine Books, 1980.

Kelley, Kitty. *His Way: The Unauthorized Biography of Frank Sinatra.* New York: Bantam Books, 1986.

Kerouac, Jack. *Desolation Angels.* New York: G. P. Putnam's, 1980.

————. *The Dharma Bums.* New York: New American Library, 1959.

Kisselgoff, Anna. "American Ballet Theatre Performs Twyla Tharp's Sinatra." *New York Times,* December 15, 1983.

Lahr, John. *Sinatra: The Artist and the Man.* New York: Random House, 1997.

Lawrence, D. H. *Studies in Classic American Literature.* New York: T. Seltzer, 1923.

Leaming, Barbara. *If This Was Happiness: A Biography of Rita Hayworth.* New York: Ballantine, 1989.

Lees, Gene. *Gene Lees Jazzletter,* August 1984.

————. *Singers and the Song.* New York: Oxford University Press, 1987.

————. *Singers and the Song II.* New York: Oxford University Press, 1998.

Lenburg, Jeff. *The Encyclopedia of Animated Cartoons.* New York: Facts on File, Inc., 1991.

Levin, Harry. *The Power of Blackness.* New York: Alfred A. Knopf, 1970.

Lipton, Lawrence. *The Holy Barbarians.* New York: Julian Messner, 1959.

Lowell, Robert. *Selected Poems.* New York: Farrar, Straus, and Giroux, 1997.

Macauley, Alastair. "Twyla Tharp Dance." *Dancing Times,* February 11, 1984.

McClure, Michael. "Jack's *Old Angel Midnight.*" In *Old Angel Midnight* by Jack Kerouac. Edited by Donald Allen. San Francisco: Grey Fox Press, 1993.

McDonough, John. "The Music," *Downbeat* (August 1998): 16–19.

Murphy, Karen, and Ronald Gross. "All You Need is Love." In *Pop Culture in America.* Edited by David Manning White. Chicago: Quadrangle Books, 1970.

Mustazza, Leonard. *Sinatra: An Annotated Bibliography, 1939–1998.* Westport, CT: Greenwood Press, 1999.

————. *Ol' Blue Eyes: A Frank Sinatra Encyclopedia.* Westport, CT: Greenwood Press, 1998.

Nicosia, Gerald. "Off the Road: A Portfolio of Kerouac Photos." In *Beat Angels.* Edited by Arthur Knight and Kit Knight. California, PA: Unspeakable Visions of the Individual, 1982.

————. *Memory Babe: A Critical Biography of Jack Kerouac.* New York: Grove Press, 1983.

O'Brian, Jack. "To Be Frank—A Long Show." *New York Journal-American,* October 19, 1957.

O'Brien, Ed, and Robert Wilson. *Sinatra 101: The 101 Best Recordings and the Stories Behind Them.* New York: Boulevard Books, 1996.

Perry, David. Booklet article, "The Jack Kerouac Collection," 7. In *The Jack Kerouac Collection,* Rhino CD R 70939, 1990.

Petkov, Steven, and Leonard Mustazza, eds. *The Frank Sinatra Reader.* New York: Oxford University Press, 1995.

Pignone, Charles, Frank Sinatra, and Quincy Jones. *The Sinatra Treasures: Intimate Photos, Mementos, and Music from the Sinatra Family Collection.* London: Virgin Books, 2004.

Pleasants, Henry. *The Great American Popular Singers.* New York: Simon and Schuster, 1974.

Pugliese, Stanislao G. *Frank Sinatra: History, Identity, and Italian American Culture.* New York: Palgrave Macmillan, 2004.

Quirk, Lawrence J. *The Rat Pack: Neon Nights with the Kings of Cool.* New York: HarperEntertainment, 2003.

Reich, Howard. "The Virtuoso," *Downbeat* (August 1998): 28–30.

Reid, Cornelius L. *A Dictionary of Vocal Terminology.* New York: Joseph Patelson Music House, 1983.

Reilly, Peter. "Dick Haymes: As Time Goes By," *Stereo Review* (May 1979). Reprinted in *Dick Haymes Society Newsletter* 39 (1996), 62–64.

Rigney, Francis J., and L. Douglas Smith. *The Real Bohemians: A Sociological and Psychological Study of the "Beats."* New York: Basic Books, 1961.

Ringold, Gene, and Clifford McCarty. *The Films of Frank Sinatra.* New York: Carol, 1993.

Rockwell, John. *Sinatra: An American Classic.* New York: Rolling Stone Press, 1984.

Rojek, Chris. *Frank Sinatra.* Malden, MA: Polity, 2004.

Schwarz, Ted, and Nick Sevano. *Sinatra: You Only Thought You Knew Him.* New York: SPI, 2004.

Scott, Bobby. "The Dick Haymes Enigma." *Gene Lees Jazzletter,* August 1984. Reprinted in *Friends of Dick Haymes Newsletter* no. 22 (1985).

Shakespeare, William. *A Midsummer's Night Dream.* New Haven: Yale University Press, 1965.

Shaw, Arnold. *Sinatra: Retreat of the Romantic.* London: W. H. Allen, 1968.

Siepmann, Charles A. *Radio, Television and Society.* New York: Oxford University Press, 1950.

Silva, Luiz Carlos do Nascimento. *Put Your Dreams Away: A Frank Sinatra Discography.* Westport, CT: Greenwood Press, 2000.

Silverman, Stephen M. *Dancing on the Ceiling: Stanley Donen and His Movies.* New York: Alfred A. Knopf, 1996.

Sinatra, Nancy. *Frank Sinatra: An American Legend.* Santa Monica, CA: General Publishing Group, 1995.

"Sinatra: Singer or Salesman?" *Variety,* November 6, 1957.

Sinatra, Tina, and Jeff Coplon. *My Father's Daughter: A Memoir.* New York: Simon and Schuster, 2000.

Sinatra, Tina. "Introduction." *A Man and His Music.* New York: Random House, 1991.

———. "My Father, Frank Sinatra." *McCall's,* December 1973.

Solomons, Gus, Jr. "Twyla Tharp and Dancers." *Dance Magazine,* May 1992.

Summers, Anthony. *Frank: The Flawed Genius of Sinatra.* London: Doubleday, 2005.

Summers, Anthony, and Robbyn Swan. *Sinatra: The Life.* New York: Knopf, 2005.

Talese, Gay. *The Gay Talese Reader: Portraits & Encounters.* New York: Walker and Co., 2003.

———. *The Greatest Story Ever Told: Frank Sinatra Has a Cold.* New York: Esquire, Inc., 2003.

Tarkanian, Jerry, and Dan Wetzel. *Runnin' Rebel: Shark Tales of "Extra Benefits," Frank Sinatra, and Winning It All.* Champaign, IL: Sports Publishing, 2005.

Tharp, Twyla. *Push Comes to Shove.* New York: Bantam Books, 1992.

———. Interview by John Gruen. December 8, 1983. The New York Public Library of the Performing Arts, Manuscript Collection, Dance Research Collection.

"The A-B-C-D's Of Comedy." *Variety* December 13, 1950.

Thompson, Thomas. "Sinatra's Swan Song." *Life,* June 25, 1971.

Tonelli, Bill. *The Italian American Reader: A Collection of Outstanding Fiction, Memoirs, Journalism, Essays, and Poetry.* New York: W. Morrow, 2003.

Trudeau, Garry B. *Flashbacks, Twenty Five Years of Doonesbury.* Norwalk, CT: Easton Press, 1995.

———. *That's Doctor Sinatra, You Little Bimbo.* New York: Henry Holt and Company, 1986.

Turner, John Frayn. *Frank Sinatra.* Lanham, MD: Taylor Trade, 2004.

Variety, June 5, 1950.

Variety, October 11, 1950.

Variety, January 17, 1951.

Variety, April 27, 1955.

Variety, September 21, 1955.

Variety, December 23, 1957.

Welding, Peter. Liner notes to *Where Are You?* Hollywood: Capitol Records, 1957.

"What's Happening to Sinatra?" *TV Guide,* February 8, 1958.

Wilder, Alec. *American Popular Song: 1900–1950.* New York: Oxford University Press, 1972.

Willoughby, Bob. *Sinatra: An Intimate Collection.* London: Vision On, 2002.

Wilson, Earl. *Sinatra: An Unauthorized Biography.* New York: Macmillan, 1976.

Woog, Adam. *Frank Sinatra.* San Diego, CA: Lucent Books, 2001.

Zehme, Bill. *The Way You Wear Your Hat: Frank Sinatra and the Lost Art of Livin'.* New York: Harper Collins, 1997.

List of Contributors

BLAINE ALLAN is associate professor in the Department of Film Studies, at Queen's University, Ontario, Canada. He wrote *Nicholas Ray: A Guide to References and Resources,* and he has published articles and chapters on subjects including the Beat generation, Canadian film and television, and music television in *Film History, Film Quarterly,* the *Journal of Canadian Studies,* the *Historical Journal of Film, Radio, and Television,* and the *Canadian Journal of Film Studies,* among other publications.

SAMUEL L. CHELL teaches English and film studies at Carthage College in Kenosha, Wisconsin, where he hosts a weekly jazz show on public radio and performs as a professional pianist. He has published articles and reviews on Victorian literature as well as a book on the poetry of Robert Browning. His articles on film and jazz have appeared in journals such as *Film Criticism* and *Journal of Popular Music and Society* as well as in several book-length anthologies. He also contributes music reviews regularly to Allaboutjazz.com and Billevanswebpages.com.

DAVID FINCK is a bassist who has played and recorded with diverse artists including Dizzy Gillespie, Aretha Franklin, Sinead O'Connor, Natalie Cole, Rod Stewart, Herbie Hancock, Ivan Lins, Al Jarreau, Tony Bennett, Rosemary Clooney, and Andre Previn. He has a discography that lists more than one hundred recordings including platinum and gold selling records with Rod Stewart, Natalie Cole, and Elton John. In 1991, the *Village Voice* invited him to write about Frank Sinatra as a jazz musician in a special issue celebrating Sinatra's eightieth birthday. He has also written liner notes for several recordings, including a CD of Gershwin music that he recorded in a duo with Andre Previn.

JOSEPH FIORAVANTI, professor emeritus at SUNY College of Technology at Delhi, has devoted the past twenty years to researching and writing commentaries on the great American songbook, focusing on singers, songwriters, and music makers. Articles and interviews have appeared in print in the *Daily Star* (Oneonta), the *Freeman's Journal* (Cooperstown), *Italian Americana, VIA,* and *The Italian American Experience: An Encyclopedia* (Garland Publishing, 2000) offering commentary and evaluation on three generations of pop singers (from Perry Como to Madonna), including personal interviews with jazz headliners, pianist Hank Jones and saxophone virtuoso, Al Gallodoro. From 1995 to 2003, he was a frequent guest commentator on Joe Campbell's *Sentimental Journey,* a weekly Saturday morning broadcast on WDOS-AM in Oneonta.

JEANNE FUCHS is professor emerita in the Department of Comparative Literature and Languages at Hofstra University. On two separate occasions, she has served as associate dean in Hofstra College of Liberal Arts and Sciences for periods of four and five years (associate dean for Academic Affairs and associate dean for Budget and Planning, respectively). She has a monograph on Jean-Jacques Rousseau, *The Pursuit of Virtue: A Study of Order in La Nouvelle Héloïse* (Peter Lang, 1993) and is coeditor of *The World of George Sand* (Greenwood Press, 1991). She has articles on Molière, Marivaux, Musset, Rousseau, André Chamson, and F. Scott Fitzgerald. A former Balanchine dancer, she conducted research for Lincoln Kirsten and Martha Swope for *The New York City Ballet* (Alfred A. Knopf, 1973), assisted Tanaquil LeClercq with all aspects of preparation for *The Ballet Cook Book* (Stein and Day, 1966), and translated substantial segments of an eighteenth century dance manual, *Le Maître à danser,* by Pierre Rameau for Jerome Robbins. Present projects include a study of Racine's plays and a memoir. She dedicates her work on this volume to her sons, Lee and Kyle.

PHILIP FURIA is the author of *Pound's "Cantos" Declassified* (Penn State, 1984); *The Poets of Tin Pan Alley: A History of America's Great Lyricists* (Oxford, 1990); *Ira Gershwin: The Art of the Lyricist* (Oxford, 1996); *Irving Berlin: A Life in Song* (Schirmer Books/Simon and Schuster, 1998); and *Skylark: The Life and Times of Johnny Mercer* (St. Martin's, 2003), the first biography of the Savannah songwriter. He has also written about modern American poetry in such journals as *PMLA, American Literature,* and *boundary 2* and about American popular song in the *American Scholar, In Theater, Style, Italian Americana,* and other journals and magazines. A native of Pittsburgh, he studied at Oberlin College (bachelor of arts, 1965), the University of Chicago (master of arts, 1966), and the Iowa Writers Workshop (master of fine arts, 1970). He received his doctorate in English in 1970 from the University of Iowa and taught for twenty-five years (and twenty-five *winters*) at the University of Minnesota, where he was also chair of the department of English and associate dean for Faculty of the College of Liberal Arts. He is currently chair of the department of Creative Writing at the University of North Carolina at Wilmington.

ROGER GILBERT teaches American poetry at Cornell University. He is the author of *Walks in the World: Representation and Experience in Modern American Poetry* (Princeton, 1991). He has published essays on topics ranging from contemporary poetry to the Chicago Bulls, film on video, and the meaning of applause. He recently edited a special issue of *EPOCH* devoted to the life and work of A. R. Ammons and coedited *Considering the Radiance: Essays on the Poetry of A. R. Ammons* (Norton, 2005). He is presently working on a critical biography of Ammons, for which he was awarded a Guggenheim Fellowship.

RUTH PRIGOZY is professor of English and Film Studies at Hofstra University. She is executive director and co-founder of the F. Scott Fitzgerald Society. She has published widely on F. Scott Fitzgerald as well as on Ernest Hemingway, J. D. Salinger, the Hollywood Ten, Columbia Pictures, film directors Billy Wilder and D. W. Griffith, and director Vittorio de Sica. She has edited Fitzgerald's *This Side of Paradise, The Great Gatsby,* and *The Cambridge Companion to F. Scott Fitzgerald* and coedited two volumes on detective fiction and film, one on the short story, and two collections of essays on Fitzgerald. She is the author of *F. Scott Fitzgerald: An Illustrated Life.* Her biography of singer-actor Dick Haymes, *The Life of Dick Haymes: No More Little White Lies,* was published by the University Press of Mississippi in 2006.

WALTER RAUBICHECK is professor of English at Pace University in New York. He is currently coediting a book on Bing Crosby with Ruth Prigozy that originated from Hofstra's Crosby and American Culture Conference in 2002. He has published essays on Dashiell Hammett and other writers of detective fiction, the directors Alfred Hitchcock and Orson Welles, and American authors such as F. Scott Fitzgerald, T. S. Eliot, and Walt Whitman.

LISA JO SAGOLLA is the author of *The Girl Who Fell Down: A Biography of Joan McCracken* (Northeastern University Press, 2003), a finalist for the Theatre Library Association's George Freedley Memorial Award for outstanding book in the area of theater and live performance. She is the Dance and Movement columnist and a theater and dance critic for *Back Stage* and has written extensively on dance, theater, and film for scholarly journals, encyclopedias, and trade publications. The choreographer of more than seventy-five Off Broadway, regional, summer stock, and university productions, Sagolla teaches dance at Columbia University, Marymount Manhattan College, and Dance Theatre of Harlem. She holds an educational doctorate in Art and Art Education from Columbia University.

RON SIMON presented an earlier version of this paper at Hofstra Univerity's Frank Sinatra conference in November 1998. Simon is television and radio curator at The Museum of Television and Radio as well as an adjunct associate professor at Columbia University and New York University. He worked with the Sinatra family in presenting the 1965 Rat Pack special and international concerts taped for television at the Museum.

ARNOLD JAY SMITH has been adjunct professor of Jazz History at New Jersey City University since 2000. He was the founder and host of *Jazz Insights* at the New School from 1979 to 2005 and is the treasurer of the Jazz Journalists Association and a member of the advisory board of American Jazz Venues. He has lectured at New York University, Michigan State University, Long Island University, Borough of Manhattan Community College, The Duke Ellington Society, and the Smithsonian's Duke Ellington Centenary Celebration exhibit. A former east coast editor of *Downbeat* magazine, he has also been on the music staff of *Variety,* as well as being a freelance journalist for the *New York Times, JazzTimes, Billboard, Newsday,* and *the Village Voice.*

JAMES F. SMITH is professor of English and American Studies and serves as head of the division of Social Sciences at Penn State Abington. His research has centered on American literature and culture. He has published articles on subjects as diverse as popular literature (Tom Wolfe, Stephen King); popular places (Bugsy Siegel's Flamingo Hotel in Las Vegas, Atlantic City casinos); and popular music (Frank Sinatra and Elvis Presley). He is coauthor (with his colleague Vicki Abt) of *The Business of Risk: Commercial Gambling in Mainstream America* (University of Kansas Press, 1985), one of the first studies of gambling in America to take an objective view of this important social, economic, and political force during the last half of the twentieth century.

PATRIC M. VERRONE is an attorney and television writer. He graduated magna cum laude from Harvard College where he was an officer of the *Harvard Lampoon* and he has a juris doctorate from Boston College Law School where he edited the *Boston College Law Review.* His television writing credits include *The Tonight Show* starring Johnny Carson, *The Larry Sanders Show, The Critic, The Simpsons, Pinky and the Brain, Rugrats, Muppets Tonight!,* and *Futurama.* He has been nominated for eight Emmy Awards in four different categories and won two. He was elected president of the Writers Guild of America west in September 2005.

DAVID WILD is an Emmy-nominated television writer, a contributing editor to *Rolling Stone* and served as the host of the Bravo series *Musicians.* Wild grew up in New Jersey, only a few miles from where Frank Sinatra's career began. Raised on Sinatra music by his father, Wild was honored to write the liner notes for the *Duets* album. He now lives in Los Angeles with his wife, Fran, and his sons, Andrew and Alec.

Index

Note: Page numbers in italics refer to illustrations.